Starting Small
and
Making It Big

Hands-on Lessons in Entrepreneurship and Philanthropy

Bill Cummings

Published by Cummings Foundation, Inc.

Sixth Edition

Copyright © Bill Cummings, 2020, all rights reserved
Registration Number TX8-548-605

Cummings, Bill.
Starting Small and Making It Big:
   Hands-on Lessons in Entrepreneurship and Philanthropy/Bill Cummings
Library of Congress Control Number: 2018941733
ISBN: 978-0-9998951-4-6 (trade pbk.)
ISBN: 978-0-9998951-5-3 (digital)

100% of all proceeds are used for charitable purposes.
Enjoy FREE domestic shipping on all orders.

Order direct via **Cummings.com/book** or **Amazon.com**
Individual: $16.95 paperback / $24.95 hardcover
Three-pack: $40.00 paperback / $60.00 hardcover
Case: $265.00 for 26 paperbacks / $210.00 for 14 hardcovers

For larger bulk purchases contact:
Book Marketing Manager, Cummings Foundation
200 West Cummings Park
Woburn, MA 01801, 781-935-8000

Set in Adobe Caslon Pro / Printed in USA by King Printing Company, Inc., Lowell, MA.
Cover design by Abby Johnson and Michael Lamothe
Cover photo by Jim Trudeau

Except for brief excerpts, the scanning, uploading, and distribution of this book via the internet or via any other means without the permission of the publisher is illegal and punishable by law. Please purchase only authorized electronic editions, and do not participate in or encourage electronic piracy of copyrighted materials. Your support of authors' rights is appreciated.

Dedication

Joyce Cummings

To my wife, Joyce, with my everlasting love—

You have quietly made me look good for more than half a century. Supporting me and our wonderful family, you have always been there and have always done whatever was needed, and so much more.

Thank you eternally for being my only true love, and for so carefully tempering and moderating our now fifty-three years together. You and our family are my life's greatest blessing.

Contents

Prologue — i

1. Early Lessons of Cost and Value — 1
2. A Marvelous Pathway — 15
3. On the Road with Vicks — 25
4. Still on the Road — 36
5. Finally on my Own — 45
6. The Perfect Partner — 56
7. Cummings Properties Emerges — 66
8. So Many Lessons Learned — 80
9. Branching Out, But Still Only in Woburn — 92
10. A New Generation Takes Over — 102
11. A Wholely Different League — 119
12. Lowering the Flags — 140
13. Carrying On — 152
14. Relocating the County Seat — 166
15. Cummings Foundation Matures — 183
16. The Giving Pledge — 189
17. Real-Life Monopoly — 201
18. Back to Africa — 211
19. Building the Future — 220
20. Setting a Better Pace — 230
21. New Directions — 238
22. Afterword — 247

A Special Remembrance — 256
Acknowledgments — 257
Index — 258
About the Author — 264

Prologue

JOYCE hesitated in May 2011 as she packed her suitcase for our early summer trip to the great Southwest. The event's registration materials stated that attire would be "casual," but what did that mean when we would be meeting with a group sometimes described as the top one percent among the world's wealthiest people? We had just joined the Giving Pledge, the philanthropic organization founded by Melinda and Bill Gates and Warren Buffett to encourage the world's most affluent people to donate at least half of their assets to charitable causes, either during their lifetime or upon their deaths.

Giving Pledge members submit written pledges to this effect. The complete, updated versions of our and other Giving Pledge members' letters are maintained within a philanthropy exhibit at the Smithsonian Institution. They can also be found on the Smithsonian's website and the Giving Pledge website.

For us, the donating part of the decision was easy. The issue with which we wrestled was revealing publicly, for the first time, that we met the prescribed billion-dollar net worth. The fact is, we never had a goal to attain any certain level of affluence, and over time we accumulated much more than we ever paid any attention to. As appears to be the case with many of the early Giving Pledge members, the decision to begin using our earnings philanthropically *during our lifetimes* came well before this association's formation.

The past few weeks had been a whirlwind in our otherwise relatively ordinary lives. Shortly after Joyce and I submitted our written pledge, a front-page, above-the-fold story in *The Boston Globe* "outed" us as billionaires, much to the surprise of many who knew us. Close friends and acquaintances were aware that we were well-off financially, but none had any idea that our assets placed us in this league. After all, I still delighted in finding golf balls in the rough, and Joyce still regularly used coupons at the supermarket. We had much the same lifestyle, habits, and friends as we'd had for decades, since well before we had the means to establish Cummings Foundation in 1986.

For the most part, our foundation's giving had been focused in northeastern Massachusetts—extremely local. We took it slowly, gradually increasing our gifts over a good many years until we decided to join the Giving Pledge. During that first year, the new group grew to a total of about seventy individuals and couples, all of whom acknowledge being billionaires—including at least one other member who, like Joyce and me, would still be a billionaire if he hadn't already given away the large majority of his assets for philanthropic purposes. Member Chuck Feeney, founder of the huge Duty Free Shops chain, went so far as to write in his autobiography with Conor O'Clery, "I am giving it all away right now, and I want my last check to bounce."

Then came the *Boston Globe* article, highlighting this major turning point in our lives—the switch in our primary focus from making money to giving it away. This change did not mean that I had stopped building. During a long and highly successful career in commercial real estate development, I built the Boston area company known as Cummings Properties and, together with a truly phenomenal team, we grew its portfolio to more than 10 million debt-free square feet. Now my new job, after four decades, was to help others build the foundation's capacity to feed the hungry, assist immigrants, support solid educational programs for young people, create homes for the elderly, and later, a strong interest in Holocaust and genocide education.

> After many successful years building and leasing commercial real estate in Greater Boston, Joyce and I came to recognize and believe that no one can truly "own" anything. With our ever-so-brief stays upon this earth, how can we possibly think of ourselves as *owning* land? How can we ever be anything more than caretakers of the ground that lies beneath whatever we might develop on a site? It was easy thereafter to start giving away much more.

At about the time we established Cummings Foundation, we first pledged to donate 10 percent of all our income each year to it. Gradually, as it became clear that our four children and any future grandchildren were well provided for, we also began donating many of our commercial properties to the foundation. We donated about 60 percent of the total family assets, giving Cummings Foundation sufficient resources to become a meaningful philanthropic factor.

When we publicly signed the Giving Pledge in 2011 it was with the hope that, with every new member, the association would gain momentum and provide encouragement to others who have the capacity to give more. We gave most of our assets first to Cummings Foundation. Now, with an enormous amount of volunteer assistance from an extremely diverse group of community leaders throughout northeastern Massachusetts, we have disbursed well more than $260 million of the foundation's earnings to deserving nonprofits.

Notwithstanding many references to the Giving Pledge within these pages, including some details from members' own biographies, this book is not *about* the Giving Pledge. *Starting Small...* is a feel-good book about business, entrepreneurship and philanthropy, but *disguised as* an autobiography.

BY ANY STANDARD, this story of a once-young couple from working- and middle-class American homes giving away so much to Boston-area charities is unusual. Noteworthy, too, is the story of what took place during the sixty-plus years spent building up to this level of philanthropic ability. Beyond the narrative, this autobiography is packed with great ideas about both entrepreneurship and philanthropy.

Although some people may be predisposed to an entrepreneurial lifestyle, highly effective entrepreneurship is something that can absolutely be taught and learned, if one has the right role models and teachers, and most important, a strong desire. Then, once success has been achieved, an entrepreneur must assume the mantle of mentor, passing on key business philosophies to others who will carry on and build upon his or her success.

Given the right environment, entrepreneurship can begin at a young age, as it did for me. From the classic lemonade stand to my days and months spent washing store windows, or buying, rehabbing, and reselling small boats, there are myriad ways that ambitious youth can gain basic business experience while earning their first dollars. Most children today may be missing out on these valuable pursuits simply because they lack discretionary time. American society seems to be denying young people the opportunity to develop the skills to enrich themselves, which they likely would do if given the time and freedom to explore and take risks.

Another significant difference from the time I started my career, of course, is technology. So many entrepreneurs today are focused on creating a smarter phone, a smaller electronic device, or the next great app. These are all worthy goals, but also be aware that the more mundane opportunities are still there, perhaps now even more than ever before. In fact, today's obsession with technology might have created greater opportunity for young adults, especially those willing to invest sweat equity in buying, improving, and reselling things like fixer-up real estate, for instance. This career that I effectively began fifty years ago still offers great promise today.

Regardless of the type of business one selects, many of the philosophies captured in this book can be readily applied. Being an opportunist, planning for succession, buying "right," and many of the other principles I discuss, can contribute so much to one's personal and professional growth, and increase the chances of success and profitability. Anyone trying to open, build, or grow any kind of new business may be either encouraged or discouraged by the contents of this book. Business people seeking guidance who are not geared for and ready to take on the workload should absolutely consider going in another direction. After all is said and done, anyone who wants to be a business success will likely never make it if the workload itself is not fun or fulfilling in some meaningful way.

Some of these entrepreneurial ideas and philosophies are reflected in the early stories I relate about selling things as a preteen and about a collection of self-initiated part-time moneymaking activities that closely parallel some of the early part-time work described in the 1995 Warren Buffett biography I read decades ago. My accomplishments thereafter pale by any and every comparison with Buffett—one of my few personal heroes.

One key concept of this book concerns the necessity of monitoring costs and buying things "right." How foolish is it to talk about buying substantial quantities of products or services based only on the perfectly silly notion of getting three bids first? How lazy is the buyer who does not work with prospective sellers to at least try to get them to give up their lowest effective price? Getting three quotes is fine, but start first with *one* quote, and then learn whatever you can learn from the first bidder to let each subsequent bidder know where he or she needs to be in order to stay in the game.

People who repeatedly purchase the same or similar things or services need to occasionally disappoint their low bidders by sometimes awarding a contract to a second-lowest bidder, making it at least appear that the "regular" low bidder has some competition.

Entrepreneurs must first work at distinguishing their product from others, so that they can then tout these differences in such a way as to make their product better, or at least worth more. In real estate, think of this as assiduous estate management. For instance, people with whom I work have heard so much over the years about the importance of cleanliness and maintaining good housekeeping details such as keeping litter out of the parking lots, or pruning bushes or low-growing tree branches so that they are not even slightly blocking sidewalks or signage. Think how off-putting it is to enter a restaurant when the front glass entrance door looks like no one has even thought about cleaning it all day. How about frayed or soiled carpet just inside the same door or encountering an unpleasant odor upon entering a business place?

It's a question always of looking out for the details that might reflect negatively on how anyone's property looks and feels, though the principle certainly applies far beyond real estate.

Bill Cummings

[1]

Early Lessons of Cost and Value

MY DAD, Gus Cummings, was classified as too old for military service during World War II. He spent the war years working for Bethlehem Steel Company at Fore River Shipyard in Quincy, Massachusetts, and took great personal pride in his work: painting the interiors of destroyers and light cruisers.

Sometimes he would spend a week just painting the intricate interior of a major gun turret, and he always stressed to me how important it was that he did his job correctly—even when his work couldn't be seen. Dad abhorred the waste, theft, and inefficiency he saw daily at the shipyard, and I remember him frequently telling my mother how lax the company was about workers repeatedly stealing tools and supplies by carrying them out under their coats or in their lunch boxes at the end of the day.

Bill and his dad in the "family boat," 1942, in the Fore River, in Weymouth, Massachusetts

Although Dad was meagerly paid, he took full advantage of the many opportunities to work overtime, especially at a double-time rate on weekends, to help alleviate his Depression-era debt. His steady work afforded our family some relief, but by no means any sort of affluence.

As a young man, Dad had served as a seaman in the U.S. Merchant Marine,

| Bill and his mother, Dorothy Cummings, 1939

sailing mostly between East Coast ports and South America. Unlike with his experiences at "The Yard," I rarely heard him talk about his seagoing days, probably because I did not know enough to ask. He never talked much about pool halls either, but I knew there were a couple of them he especially liked, and the opportunity to gamble was a big part of the appeal. He made out pretty well, hustling bets on his own abilities with the expectation of supplementing his otherwise lean income.

Augustus William Cummings, Jr., was born in Somerville, Massachusetts, in January 1899, and he left school after ninth grade. He spent most of his younger years around Davis Square in Somerville, and, from the stories I occasionally heard, he worked on his conditioning at a local boxing club, where he sometimes fought for prize money.

Throughout the 1930s, long before the days of electric refrigerators, Dad drove one of several milk delivery wagons for his father's modest milk company. He did this seven days a week. Since his horse knew the route by heart, Dad could frequently doze between his early-morning stops. The only time he couldn't chance a nap, he told me, was after the last stop, when the horse, if not fully controlled, would take off dangerously fast on its return to the barn. Even at the end of World War II, with no new motor vehicles available, all sorts of home delivery retailers had daily horse-drawn deliveries in my Medford neighborhood, where we moved just prior to my entering first grade.

My mother, Dorothy Purington Cummings, was born in 1904 in Sunapee, New Hampshire, but she graduated from Somerville High School after moving there with her family as a child. Grandpa Purington once told me that driving to Boston from their home in Goffstown, New Hampshire, now little more than an hour's ride, used to be a real adventure. It was a half-day drive, and the trip often included repairing a flat tire or two along the way. There were so few cars on the road at the time that drivers were pretty much expected to wave to each other in passing.

My mother's parents, John and Mary (Clarke) Purington, came to Massachusetts from Ireland in 1898, as best I can determine. Grandfather Purington, who became a skilled auto mechanic from about as early on as automobiles were invented, died when I was quite young, as did both of my paternal grandparents. My grandmother Purington suffered greatly during much of her early life from the virulent anti-Irish sentiment she encountered as a recent immigrant.

Grandma adamantly refused to talk with me about Ireland. "I am an American, Billy," she would say, when I asked about her earlier circumstances. Sometimes she would say just a bit more: "I am an American, Billy, and that's all you need to know." She would never admit in any way, even to me, that she was Irish. Until the day she died, she was afraid someone would "find out" she was Irish. As her mind weakened near the end of her life, Grandma feared she would be thrown out of the nursing home in her final days if "they" learned about her Irish heritage. All of that was such a shame.

The first time I ever told that story was fifty years after her death, while speaking at the 2013 annual meeting of the Irish International Immigrant Center in Boston. The comments were met with ready and complete understanding from many of those present.

> We know infinitely more about my father's side. Dad's first-known North American ancestor, Isaac Cummings, landed in Salem in 1638, and lived briefly in Salem and in Watertown before somehow then settling in the part of Ipswich that is now Danvers, Massachusetts. One of my several times great grandparents, Richard Cummings, became the second resident of Union, Maine, in 1776. The memory of Isaac Cummings and his descendants is kept alive through the work of the Isaac Cummings Family Association.

COST AND VALUE were themes I heard repeatedly throughout my upbringing. Mom never wanted me to hear Depression tales, but my sister, Marian, nine years my senior, still told me her stories and those of her friends who formerly seemed to have everything and then suddenly had virtually nothing in the meanest of times.

During one winter, Marian's chores included picking up coal from the railroad tracks that ran along nearby Boston Avenue, to help heat our rented apartment. Those were the days when coal-fired steam locomotives pulled the trains, and each train had a "fireman" shoveling coal into the firebox to keep the steam pressure high. One particular train worker on his daily run into North Station became Marian's friend. They would exchange waves, and then he would "accidentally" spill a shovelful of coal that she would pick up from the tracks to fill her bucket.

Dorothy Cummings

| Bill and his father, Gus Cummings

Economy was a family theme. Developed during the Great Depression, my parents' passion for frugal living was then strongly reinforced by wartime shortages, when "making do with what we had" was an absolute necessity. "A penny saved is a penny earned" was a regular reminder. So many things were rationed during the war: fresh meat, canned meats, butter, sugar, chocolate, gasoline…

Automobiles were not rationed, but there were simply none available. Everything was directed toward the war effort. Yet I remember that the auto companies' radio commercials persisted. One jingle I especially recall: "There's a Ford in your future / but the Ford in your past / is the Ford you have now / so you'd better make it last."

As more and more resources were diverted to the war effort, the community came to know when local stores received fresh stock of scarce items, and it often meant long lines on those days. Sometimes, my mother would ask her five- or six-year-old "Billy" to get into the neighborhood A&P market early and set aside certain things. She would then take quiet delight in arriving at the cash register, much later in the day, with her mayonnaise, corned beef hash, and canned salmon, all of which I would have hidden for her behind the Scott toilet paper. That was Mom teaching me from my youngest years how to be an opportunist.

Mom earned "five stars" running the family finances, with great emphasis on the importance of always "putting something away." She also preached about the necessity of hard work and ambition, "like Daddy." Mom and Dad's passionate financial goal was to own their own home. Saving enough money to secure a mortgage and then purchase a two-family home was our whole family's dream during the war years.

> What constitutes success in life is as individual as our lifestyles. I have always believed that learning to honestly assess our shortcomings as well as our strengths is vitally important in helping us know when we are aspiring to more than we should expect to attain. If we are honest with ourselves in setting achievement goals, our individual work will be far more satisfying.

To me, financial success means reaching a certain stage in life when one can feel adequately assured of living out one's days in a reasonably comfortable and happy lifestyle. I find it quite sad when intelligent people with limited resources get close to retirement before they begin making practical adjustments in their living and spending habits. So often they fail to act in a timely manner because they have become trapped in "keeping up with the Joneses," or they are just too intent on enjoying today's pleasures with no thought of tomorrow.

I also find it extremely puzzling that so many of today's young people appear to have no money sense whatsoever. Frequently, they do nothing to set money aside and out of reach. They often pay outrageous prices for clothes, concerts, fancy food and wines, sporting events, cars, and so on, and they can never figure out why they run out of money so quickly.

Saving money, economizing, and investing must be essential elements for everyone, from their teenage years through retirement age. While still in elementary school, I started to make (and save) money in all sorts of ways. My allowance was twenty-five cents a week, which was the first thing I deposited in my savings account at Medford Savings Bank at six years old. I still routinely had more pocket-cash than my friends and classmates seemed to have, even though most of my money went quickly in the bank. Such a savings account today would be a terrible investment for anyone with real income, but there are so many investment opportunities available now. For those with access to a company IRA and/or a 401(k) plan, it is usually financially foolish not to take maximum advantage of such accounts, and certainly so when a company offers meaningful matches. Investing a set amount or percentage of every paycheck will do wonders for younger workers. This type of thinking seems not to come naturally, however, if parents do not set examples and actively teach their kids how important it is to develop early saving habits and prepare for the future.

For three years during the war, we lived at 456 Salem Street in Medford. Our Salem Street home was a one-bedroom apartment in an old three-story wooden tenement above a liquor store and a taxi stand. My sister and I shared the apartment's only bedroom, and our parents slept in the living room, often struggling to pay the $10 or $12 monthly rent.

For the warmer months during the last two years of World War II, my parents also owned a modest summer cottage near the Fore River, in North Weymouth. The cottage was close to my father's work at the shipyard, and in those immediate post-depression days, I think they may have paid about $800 to own it. This kept him from having to make the rush-hour commute from and to Medford (before there was any expressway from Boston to Quincy), saving him more

| *Joyce Cummings, in front of the modernized entrance to the Cummings home of 1942-1945*

than an hour each way. Because of his long commute during the rest of the year, however, Dad received rationing coupons for gasoline and tires year-round. As a result, the Cummings family entertainment frequently consisted of taking rides to interesting places in Dad's old Model A Ford.

By age seven or eight, my friends and I frequently hung off the back end of the streetcars in summer, when the pull-down windows were all open. During swimming season, we took "free" rides up Fellsway West to the end of the line, near Wright's Pond. We all much preferred spending the five-cent fare on a Hershey or Mars candy bar to dropping it into the streetcar fare box.

Medford's old streetcars were discontinued on the Fellsway while I was still in grammar school, and we young free-riders watched in dismay as crews removed the tracks from the middle of the tree-lined parkway. Then the immediate rebuilding of the roadway that summer presented me with the ideal opportunity to develop my first business venture.

With the road rebuilding practically in my backyard, I purchased bottles of cold Pepsi Cola, orangeade, and 7-Up for a nickel each, and then quickly sold as many bottles as I could carry on my red Radio Flyer wagon for a dime each. Joe Costa, the variety store owner who sold me the drinks at regular retail price, encouraged my nascent sales career by supplying me with a perfectly shaped laundry tub for my cart and lots of chopped ice each day for several weeks. I had a great time with this early enterprise while the construction was active nearby.

IMMEDIATELY following the war, Dad returned to his former work as a house painter. Through a referral network of satisfied customers, he gradually built up a steady residential painting business, often with one or two helpers. During the summers, he mostly worked seven days a week, usually until nearly dark.

When he did arrive home, he was more than ready for our late supper. He typically then took a thirty-minute nap before relating much to anyone.

| *Dot Cummings at 23 Cherry Street, Medford*

After that, and for years, Dad and I would play checkers, chess, or Monopoly until it was my bedtime, while Mom read or enjoyed her favorite records. A compulsive reader, Mom loved biographies and best-selling fiction, and she was a regular patron at the Medford Public Library. The library's East Branch was a particularly convenient little storefront on Salem Street. Holiday gifts for Mom were always easy. If we bought her any kind of a novel or biography, or an Al Jolson record, it was sure to be a big hit. She would certainly have gone to college if she had been born a generation later, but college for young women was not common in her day, at least not for those with limited financial resources. She had an impressive vocabulary from voracious reading, and she always kept a dictionary handy, along with her current book.

Although Dad was always his own guy, he was also a loving husband who gave in whenever Mom took a strong stand on anything. Accordingly, for the first five years we lived on Cherry Street, Mom and Dad slept in what would normally have been the dining room, not unlike the way they had slept in the living room of the Salem Street apartment. A man named Mr. Williams rented the front bedroom, in a private corner of our flat, for five or six dollars a week— sort of like an early B&B without the breakfast.

DAD WAS AN EXTREMELY GOOD candlepin bowler, especially during the Depression, when he rarely had work. I later learned that in those days almost all of the family's funds for groceries and rent consisted of the cash he picked up hustling bets, either from bowling or at a billiards table. Mom was also an excellent bowler, and that and an occasional movie are the only things I remember them regularly doing together for entertainment. On couples nights at the former Hobbs Bowling Alleys in Davis Square, the prize was always a one- or two-pound box of scarce Fannie Farmer chocolates. Mom and Dad's high average seemed to score them a win almost every Saturday night.

Dad particularly liked the bowling in Somerville because there was more liquor around Davis Square. Although he would never think of taking a drink himself when he was bowling, Dad knew that when his betting friends had been drinking, they became both more vulnerable and more liberal with their betting. He told me they were much more interested in "getting even" with him after they had enjoyed a few drinks. I knew when he told me—repeatedly—about the role other people's drinking played in his success that he was on a teaching mission to instill in me an early sense of the importance of liquor moderation.

Although he didn't really like to *gamble*, Dad said, he was pleased to earn money by betting on himself. To him, such betting wasn't gambling because he felt he was "working," and because he simply avoided bets that he was unlikely to win. He seemed to know immediately just how many pins he could spot the other men to entice them to bet with him.

Dad never glorified any of those "games of skill," and he did not want his son anywhere near them. Indeed, the only time Dad was really upset with me was during my junior high years, when he discovered me working as a pinsetter after school at the Medford Square Alleys on Salem Street. He was beside himself. It was as though I had broken his heart. He loved that I wanted to work, but he wanted me far away from what he believed was a seedy environment.

Setting pins—an essential job before machines were created to do that work—I quickly learned how to avoid being seriously injured, or worse. The danger was real, especially when bowlers were firing balls down my two lanes at the same time, as often happened. Eastern Massachusetts bowlers, particularly in those days, mostly used the slender, lighter-weight candlepins rather than tenpins, and the pins occasionally careened and ricocheted about violently, even between the alleys. Several of my classmates set pins there too, but that did not matter to Dad. He was extraordinarily smart about how things worked and how to get things done, and he was always conscious of wanting me to "make it," although he never did tell me what that meant to him.

Sunday afternoons were our family time. During the late 1940s, if Mom was not cooking her favorite pot roast or chicken Sunday dinner, we would frequently shunpike up the back roads to US Route 1 in Saugus and on to Chickland, which each day had 100 or more chickens roasting on spits on the other side of the large plate-glass windows. Dad made a point of explaining to me how smart the restaurant people were, blowing the enticing exhaust from the barbeque out into the parking lot. He also thought they were pretty clever for offering large portions from a limited menu at bargain prices. "The chicken dinners were about seventy cents," Dad would say, "but look at all the cocktails they're selling at fifty cents. That's where they make their real profit."

There were three Boston newspapers in those days, and the daily editions cost two or three cents each. Ice cream cones were five cents, or ten cents for a rare double dipper, while gasoline was about fifteen cents a gallon. When Dad would sometimes ask for "a buck's worth of regular, please," no one ever laughed at him. And any trips we took were in the family car, which was also Dad's "company car," as he joked. We always had the smell of fresh paint with us, and maybe even a ladder or two on the roof if we were not traveling too far.

Weekly family time aside, from his earliest married days Dad's primary role was as family provider, with never much time for things like Little League or Pop Warner football, if they even existed then. Maybe that is why I never got involved much with organized sports or even pick-up games, though I loved shooting basketballs incessantly in my backyard after we moved to Cherry Street.

Dad did turn out to be a lifetime role model in other ways, however, with his strong "can-do" attitude. So many times I heard, "You surely won't be able to do it"—whatever "it" might have been—"if you don't try."

Cub Scouts and then Boy Scouts became an important part of my Medford upbringing. My best Scouting experiences were overnight camping trips and two weeks each summer at Camp Fellsland, in Amesbury. One year, I won two extra free weeks at camp by selling the most tickets door to door of any kid in town for the annual Fellsland Council Jamboree.

AS A YOUNG BOY, without ever thinking that it might be nice to be a builder someday, I always stopped longer and more often than other passersby to look in at construction sites, and I continue to do so to this day. Going back even to my third-grade days, I frequently let myself in to explore the construction site for the new bank building in Haines Square. Later, during junior high, in about 1950, I found great entertainment off and on for almost a year in exploring the "New Medford Square," consisting of fifteen or twenty stores under construction on Riverside Avenue. On several occasions, I recruited friends to be accomplices as we wandered the ever-changing site, but never doing a bit of damage.

WHILE I WAS IN junior high school, I established and operated a new venture from May through August for three summers. I figured out how to arrange a study hall as my last class each day, and then cut out of that period during May and June. After purchasing a state peddler's license, I conducted a surprisingly profitable afternoon ice cream business from a large dry-ice-cooled box attached to the back of my bike, mostly at the former Ford Motors auto assembly plant in Somerville, where Assembly Row shopping mall is now.

That early business experience gave me lots of great training in talking myself into and out of all sorts of situations, many of them literally on the street. Some of those acquired "street smarts" have surely been invaluable throughout my adult life. I also discovered at an early age how easy it was and still is to earn cash, for anyone who was willing to devote the necessary time to an activity.

After three seasons, it was time to enter high school, and my own imagined peer pressure convinced me that, at fourteen, I was too old to be riding my bike. Instead, I tried out several more-conventional after-school jobs for kids of that era. The first was at a store called Homier Music, on Boylston Street in Boston, where they had me doing all sorts of odd jobs for forty cents an hour. I learned to find my way around downtown Boston while making deliveries on foot. I also helped pack lots of orders of sheet music and books for postal delivery, and was everyone's first option to call for sweeping floors, straightening out display shelves, and running around the corner to pick up someone's sandwich.

I was happy to do whatever anyone wanted me to do to earn my keep, even if I often felt capable of doing a lot more. While working for others, I found it fun to do the best job possible, regardless of the task. Even then, my thought process was that I was being paid for my time, and I would accomplish as much as possible in return. That was my mindset from my youngest years.

My next hourly job was after school each day for a few months at Ruderman's, a small furniture store on High Street in Medford. My job was mostly polishing tables, sweeping floors, and unpacking deliveries from the furniture factories. As it happened, there was a local Brigham's ice cream and candy shop directly across the street from Ruderman's. I often dropped in there to purchase an ice cream cone for my walk home, and came to know the manager. He didn't have a hard time convincing me how much nicer it would be working for Brigham's for sixty cents an hour rather than cleaning furniture for fifty cents an hour. The free ice cream was a great bonus.

Bill, about 18 years old, and an unidentified Brigham's colleague

I stayed with Brigham's through high school, and then off and on through all four college years. The most enjoyable and worthwhile time for me at Brigham's was working full-time during all three college summers as a "vacation manager," moving from store to store, covering vacation weeks for store managers all over the forty-store system.

Brigham's was a terrific student work experience, especially because it included managing staff, almost all of whom were anywhere from a few to fifty or more years older than I was. While there, I followed my dad's example as an hourly worker at the shipyard, routinely working as much overtime as possible, sometimes logging more than seventy hours a week. This was much to the (mostly feigned) dismay of one of the senior supervisors, who fussed that because of all my overtime pay, my take-home pay was more one week than his was.

ANOTHER GOOD MONEYMAKER, and a valuable learning tool, was helping Dad buy and sell used boats from our backyard on Cherry Street. In those days, long before eBay and similar online auction sites, of course, people advertised items for sale in the newspaper. *Boston Sunday Globe* was especially prominent, often featuring a hundred pages of classified ads that usually included a couple of hundred used boats for sale. One of us would purchase an early copy of the *Sunday Globe* on Saturday afternoon, always without the news section because it had not yet been printed. We would then call everyone in our area who advertised a small boat for sale that looked like it might be a bargain. Showing up early on Saturday afternoon was not unlike showing up at a neighbor's 8:00 AM yard sale an hour or two earlier than the posted start time. It worked well for us.

We looked exclusively for small boats in the range of twelve to eighteen feet long. Oftentimes, people who were moving up to something larger would be selling a boat, an outboard motor, and, ideally, a trailer, as a package. Dad taught me how to determine a boat's value and bargain or negotiate with the seller on the price. We paid cash on the spot and then immediately towed our find-of-the-day home to resell it from our yard. Dad had the buying and selling talk down to an art form.

More often than not, we already had one of our own ads running in the same Sunday paper from which we made our purchases on Saturday. Occasionally, we would end up selling our Saturday afternoon purchase the same weekend, especially if it didn't need any cleaning or polishing. If a new acquisition needed to be scrubbed or painted, it paid well to do that work before offering the boat for resale. Looking back, the best part of our boat business was the one-on-one time I spent with Dad, and the opportunity he had to teach me about negotiating and finishing the sale. He was a terrific closer.

> Dad taught me few business lessons in any formal way, but he always wanted me to understand that the truest value of any item is "whatever you can get for it." A more formal definition of value is what a willing buyer will pay a willing seller, when neither party is under any compulsion to buy or to sell in a hurry, and when both parties are aware of any hidden defects or circumstances affecting the value.

The fact that he or we persuaded someone to sell us a boat at a bargain price, for instance, should have nothing whatsoever to do with how much we should ask a subsequent buyer to pay for it. At that early stage in his life, Dad also had strong feelings about the value of a neat, clear business signature—all the time. I was probably in second grade when he pointed out John Hancock's distinctive signature on a reproduction of the Declaration of Independence, and I recall reminding him then that I did not even know how to write in cursive. Dad also had a thing about wanting me to get into the purchase or the sale conversations, especially when we were trying to close the transaction because "someday you will be so glad for this practice," he assured me.

Even the simplest negotiating experience begins in the home and can be taught from childhood. Children who might politely argue with their parents, cajoling for more freedom and privileges, are practicing negotiation. They are already honing their negotiation skills, which may foreshadow above-average ability, even in issues as simple as asking, "Why do I have to go to bed so early?"

For several years, Dad owned an older inboard motorboat, and he became a member at Cottage Park Yacht Club in Winthrop. He later joined a dozen or so other mostly blue-collar guys when they all became founders of Riverside Yacht Club off Ship Avenue in Medford. The boat club filled a void in Dad's life that opened as Davis Square gradually gentrified. His old haunts there gradually gave way to the boat club and the nearby Mystic River.

I WAS AN IMPATIENT student and the youngest member of my class at Medford High School. School for me was mostly just something to be endured. Sophomore English was my favorite high school class because we spent much time writing, and the teacher, Miss Bagley, gave us plenty of encouragement. She would have been so excited to know she played a meaningful part in my writing a book so many decades later. If she was sixty-five years old then, she would be about 130 years old today. Other high school details are more than a little sketchy now, sixty years later, probably because my high school years were simply not that memorable.

During my final summer vacation before college, I landed a fine work opportunity at what was then the upscale and iconic Blacksmith Shop Restaurant in Rockport, on Cape Ann. I had earlier worked a few weeks as a convention floor worker for the Massachusetts Restaurant Association during two of its annual restaurant shows in Boston, and the convention manager offered to help if I ever wanted a good summer restaurant job "on the Cape." I was thinking Cape Cod, which I knew would be great fun. But even though one of us had our "Capes" mixed up, I earned significantly more in tips on Cape Ann during that summer than ever anticipated, or than would have been possible at Brigham's.

Always one to broaden whatever experience I could get, I had a split shift at the Blacksmith Shop, with just enough time to drive a local taxi on weekday afternoons and meet the early commuter train at Rockport Depot. I had my driver's license for only a year, and at that age, the idea of getting paid to drive someone else's car was extra special. I never had a taxi driver's license or any training, but in 1954 that didn't bother anyone in Rockport.

Near the end of summer, a young woman I had never seen before hailed my cab just as I was crossing over the bumpy tracks and into the railroad station. She was disheveled and appeared to be in great distress from a visible pregnancy. She asked me to take her "to the hospital" and "right now." Unfortunately, neither of us knew where the hospital was (in the next town over, which was Gloucester). As she talked, I drove slowly back over the tracks, and her panic escalated.

She quickly became unable to communicate at all. It was, of course, decades before the advent of cell phones or GPS. Without asking, I turned immediately toward the Rockport Fire Station amid increasing clamor in the back. We made it to the station with my horn blaring, which quieted my passenger and brought an immediate response from the station, but the six- or seven-minute drive was quite an experience.

The firefighters gradually calmed her down and moved her into their ambulance. Meanwhile, it became increasingly clear to me that they assumed I had a personal vested interest in the woman at least, if not also in the pregnancy. And I became more and more anxious about extricating myself from this situation. When they told me I should follow the ambulance to the hospital, I did not ask about collecting my fare and quickly escaped in the opposite direction.

❈ *From an historical perspective, there never seemed to be any concern at all about gender discrimination until long after the urgency of World War II brought millions of women into the workplace. Credit "Rosie the Riveter" for opening millions of new opportunities for women and for then starting the "Rosie" conversations about equal pay for equal work. I clearly remember learning that male teachers were paid substantially more than female teachers because "the men had families to support."*

❈ *With unemployment in the United States at 25 percent, accompanied by a 50 percent drop in international trade, The Great Depression of the 1930s started in the United States, but became a worldwide economic catastrophe. Thereafter, it was most certainly an overriding lingering cloud over all of my formative years. Saving money, working hard, not wasting, and "making do" were ever present in my parental lessons.*

❈ *Certainly the setting of life goals must be the biggest decision most of us will ever make, because we will spend the rest of a lifetime in pursuit of them. To many of us, the next question may inevitably be "how hard are we willing to work to achieve our goals?" But a lifetime of hard work should never be cause for regret.*

❈ *What we are is God's gift to us. What we become, and what we do with our lives is our gift to God and to humanity.*

❈ *A person with a good watch may always know the time, but a person with two good watches can never be sure.*

❈ *With such a long road ahead, set your sights not on the summit but only on the climb, and then do it!*

❈ *We are so often measured by the quality of the people with whom we surround ourselves.*

❈ *For me, job creation is the greatest single factor in evaluating new businesses.*

[2]

A Marvelous Pathway

WHEN I matriculated in 1954, Tufts University presented itself, then, as it does now, as a small Greater Boston school of special quality, squarely located within one of the greatest educational centers of the world. Founded in 1852 and located primarily in Medford and Somerville, the university rises above Cambridge and Boston in the distance. Looking down as it does from the top of Walnut Hill, Tufts is clearly not in the shadow of Harvard University or Massachusetts Institute of Technology, although it is influenced in many ways by their proximity. It is also influenced by four or five dozen other degree-granting institutions, all clustered within a comfortable bicycle ride from one another in Eastern Massachusetts.

Tufts competes to some extent with its more prestigious Cambridge neighbors for students, teachers, and research money, and it tends to do so quite well, most of the time. It also understands what it is, as well as its place in the world. Tufts has been and continues to be comfortable with itself as an institution of excellent quality, fully capable of providing all the educational opportunities any student might need. I sent a well-prepared but late application to Tufts after I realized how many of my Medford High School friends were applying there.

Although my high school grades were not going to get me into Tufts, my SAT scores were good enough that the then admissions director, Grant Curtis, told me they made him curious to meet me. My on-campus interview on a Saturday morning lasted a full 90 minutes, and Mr. Curtis was most encouraging at the end of the long interview, and I was soon admitted.

JUST BEFORE MY FIRST COLLEGE YEAR, however, on August 31, 1954, to be exact—Hurricane Carol, one of the deadliest modern-day hurricanes ever to reach New England, hit eastern Massachusetts. There were sixty-five deaths reported in the six-state area.

Without knowing much about the danger of hurricanes, I drove to Memorial Drive in Cambridge to watch the effects of the vicious storm as it battered the Charles River basin, where Dad had kept our small powerboat the previous year. There, boats were breaking loose from their moorings, and one of the largest boats was splintering against the rugged granite wall before it sank. Several other people had come to the public boat club, apparently with the thought of somehow saving their boats, but the ferocious wind and waves prevented anyone from even trying. On the dock, one small cabin boat lay on its side, pushed right out of the water by a larger boat.

My attention focused on what I remembered as the fastest boat in the river, an old open-top Gar Wood speedboat, powered by a huge twelve-cylinder Scripps aircraft engine. Fortunately, because of the way the boat was dragging its mooring and was tangled with another boat, the waves were crashing into the Gar Wood sideways—enough to fill it quickly with water and prevent it from crashing against the rough-hewn granite wall. I watched it sink in about twelve feet of water. I not only knew just where it went down, but also that it went under softly and was likely not seriously damaged.

I reached the owner of the speedboat by phone that evening. He was thrilled to learn that his boat was salvageable, and we made a deal. He agreed to pay me $400 cash if I could save it, but otherwise nothing. Either way, he would be my helper, and he would pay to rent the small amount of equipment we would need to give it a try. I was back in the boat business again, just as my first classes at Tufts were about to begin. But this would take only a day, if all went well.

We picked up several large rubber flotation devices, plus a portable gasoline-powered air compressor to inflate the rugged rubber air bags, and some extra-long air hoses, all of which the owner rented from a friend of my dad who hauled boats for a living. How might this experience later benefit me?

Dad had a ten-foot-long aluminum boat in the garage and a block and tackle, with a good 200 feet of manila rope which I used to hook the speedboat to the guardrail. By then, the boat was only about forty feet from the wall, although no part of it was visible below the surface of the stirred-up river water. But because the upper part was only five or six feet below the surface, however, I was able to easily swim down, wearing a dive mask, and push the first uninflated flotation device under the bow deck.

Everything worked out perfectly, and the boat was floating by early afternoon, earning kudos from several onlookers. The Gar Wood's owner was excited and pleased to pay me, and $400 then was worth ten times more than it is today. And since the Charles River was mostly fresh water above the dam, the two mechanics the owner hired to work on the large engine were confident that the brief immersion would cause little or no long-term damage. This was the perfect example of finding a need and filling it.

FOR ME, the single most worthwhile classroom learning experience at Tufts was my year with Professor Newlin Smith in his Business Law classes. Those courses and a basic two-semester General Accounting course fit nicely into my major of Business Administration. Another two-semester course in Industrial Psychology had some especially practical and worthwhile coursework that conditioned my thinking for decades to come, particularly in regard to logistical issues, time and motion studies, and things like that.

Freshman Writing, Composition 101 and 102, and two semesters of Journalism in my second year were also invaluable. To this day, I often think how well they all served my lifetime needs. I remember using my hurricane-salvage story for one of my first Tufts writing assignments. The opportunity to retell the story here is special, too.

Notwithstanding a lackadaisical pathway to Tufts, everything there worked extremely well—not only because of the academic opportunities, but even more so because of the many extracurricular offerings. I never really bought into the allure of the party scene, which certainly had a presence, but I took great advantage of other social and organizational activities, often more actively than I did my studies.

I have spoken with many college graduates who strongly concur that the college years primarily serve to help many students grow out of their teenage awkwardness. I certainly know how much better prepared for life I was after four years of college. Students who are not planning a future in sciences, technology, or medicine will often learn more from their exposure to the other students and to the diversity of their college experience than they might ever learn in actual classrooms. For the most part, that was true in my case, because I always had so many other activities going on. I might have been thinking even then about someday writing this book.

BACK IN HIGH SCHOOL, after somehow knowing enough to take a Saturday-morning qualifying exam for appointment to the Naval Reserve Officers Training Corps, I was one of only three who qualified among twenty or so Medford High School boys who applied. Then, however, I learned that I did not have 20/20 vision, and that was the end of four years' free tuition somewhere, and a possible career in the U.S. Navy.

Instead, when I arrived at Tufts, I joined the Air Force ROTC during my first and second years, participating on its excellent competitive drill team and on the rifle team. While the Navy program included full tuition, room, and board for four years, AFROTC provided no financial benefits for the first two years.

By the end of my first year, I had made myself conspicuous enough to receive a national award as Tufts University's 1955 "Outstanding Air Force Cadet of the Year." It was the closest I ever came at Tufts to receiving an academic award, prior to receiving an honorary Tufts doctorate a half century later. The unit made a big deal about the award, and I felt quite honored to receive it.

In my second year, I participated in several special Air Force flights out of nearby Hanscom Field, including one entirely unauthorized flight with a visiting fighter pilot—a young Tufts graduate and Air Force Reserves captain whom I had met at ROTC headquarters in Sweet Hall. He invited me to come to nearby Hanscom Field in uniform and join him on his previously scheduled training flight early that following morning. It seemed he was behind on the number of training hours he was required to log, and he couldn't afford to miss this opportunity after his original partner dropped out.

Bill at Hanscom Field, February 1956

The invitation to join my new friend was on the condition that I would "never say a word to anyone." But now, sixty-five years later, it should be okay. We would meet outside the base, he said, to avoid my having to answer any questions at the base on my own. Before we drove through the security gate, I donned one of his flight jackets, thus effectively impersonating a military officer. We flew far out over the Atlantic, well beyond Halifax, Nova Scotia, and then back along the south coast. Although risky, this three- or four-hour joy ride provided me with my most exciting plane ride ever. I didn't have any idea what the rules might be about my flying as a passenger in his jet fighter, but this was clearly one of those times when it was better not to ask.

> BACK ON CAMPUS, the ROTC rifle range was inside the old Cousens Gym, on an upper floor. Sometimes the range would be active all day long. The housekeeping protocol required each user to sweep up the brass casings from the mostly .22 caliber shells as we left our positions, but no one had any concern about recycling then. I never thought much about the brass either, but I realized that the lead bullets themselves had been accumulating for many months at the far end of the range. Never one to pass up a good *opportunity*, I volunteered to clean up under the target area, several times shoveling hundreds of dollars' worth of spent lead into burlap bags for recycling, a half hour's drive away in Chelsea.

After two successful years in AFROTC, I made the exceedingly difficult decision not to go forward with the advanced program. I knew by then that my minor sight deficiency would have disqualified me from flight school, just as it had from Navy ROTC. I was also aware of a latent bias against non-flying officers. Although I have never regretted that decision, I have often reflected on how different my life would have been had I managed to get into the Navy program or stayed with the Air Force all those years ago.

I ALWAYS KNEW I would become proficient in the *art* of business—in part because of some of my previous money-making experiences. I determined early on that grades were not going to be important to me, and though none of my friends regarded me as a saint, I was dead set against cheating to achieve a better grade. I would not, and did not.

Knowing how focused my parents were on managing their financial affairs for their later years, I quickly convinced myself that I could pay all my own college expenses through four years. I managed to do that by working hard whenever I saw the opportunity to earn money. And with that approach, I learned so, so much.

Phi Sigma Kappa fraternity was another significant Tufts activity. I was delighted when David Jackson and Mark Anderson from my old neighborhood in Medford followed me to Tufts one and two years behind me, and then both became Phi Sig brothers too.

DAY IN AND DAY OUT, formally or informally, the most critical parts of an executive's day are likely to be the time spent negotiating. Skillful negotiation is the highest and most critical business art form, and people who do it well must be carefully encouraged and nurtured. Good negotiators will often relish a back-and-forth "rehearsal" and will often appreciate hearing suggestions from colleagues before beginning any major session. Successful negotiations so much depend upon learning early on what is important to the other side and then figuring out what the other side can easily do, in return for receiving something it wants or needs.

> The best negotiators are competitive and quick-thinking. With an air of fairness and confidence and strength, good negotiators become careful listeners and even better observers who usually know exactly where the other side is coming from. Empathy and understanding are so important, as is the ability to read and play off another's ego. This is often particularly true when dealing with insecure people who are in positions of power or influence. Knowing where the other side is coming from can often be even more helpful when we don't let on that we understand the hidden objectives.

STILL REMEMBERING my tiny but highly profitable business selling ice cream novelties in junior high school, I started my second seasonal business during my first semester at Tufts with Don Knox, a classmate and a fraternity brother. During that first Christmas season, Don and I paid $500 to rent a vacant one-acre paved lot in Medford Square, where we sold more than 2,000 Christmas trees—well beyond our wildest expectations. Don's dad and mine both helped us take in the cash on the busiest weekends.

This former used car lot had a small twenty-foot by twenty-foot building that served as our office for overnight security, and we filled the surrounding lot with Christmas trees. Don and I took turns getting in and out of our sleeping bags to guard our investment. We both spent most days and every night there for three weeks, and took only strategic visits back to campus, especially for important tests and an occasional shower.

We bought our trees from among the many huge lumber trucks that lined up each day outside various produce distributors in Boston's old Faneuil Hall Market. The trucks from Maine and New Brunswick backed into their loading spots in the crowded site in the center of historic downtown Boston. Some days Don scouted out the trucks lined up in the morning, and then when we returned at day's end to make a purchase we had a better idea of which drivers might be the most anxious to make a deal. The drivers were always excited to sell their loads and drive back north, rather than spend another overnight curled up in the front seats of their logging rigs. Everything was, of course, sold for cash.

After doing so well that first year, we each sold trees for three more years, but as totally separate businesses with no need to split the profits—though we both hired other fraternity brothers to assist us. During the subsequent years, in different towns, Don and I individually sold more trees, and we each made more money than we had made together in 1954. Notwithstanding the close and enduring friendship that developed during that first business partnership, neither of us ever entered another business partnership with anyone again. We both shared information about our tree businesses with the highly practical chairman of the Tufts Economics Department, the late Professor Lou Manley. We received his enthusiastic understanding, if not his full endorsement, of our seasonal absences, which were giant doses of great entrepreneurial experience.

ONE ACTIVITY OTHER than fraternity and ROTC that maintained my special interest at Tufts was the Tufts Mountain Club, with which I learned to ski. I also occasionally participated in intramural sports, worked several months as a paid referee, and as a volunteer I sold considerable advertising for the 1957 and 1958 *Jumbo* yearbooks.

I was also quite active in the Tufts chapter of the National Newman Club Federation, a loose association of campus clubs for Catholic students at mostly nonsectarian colleges and universities, as well as in the overarching National Newman Club Federation itself. Another good Tufts friend and classmate from Medford who had served as president of the club in his sophomore year nominated me and I was elected president in my junior year. I was also encouraged by the then-new Roman Catholic chaplain at Tufts, Father Walter Gouch, PhD, who became an influential person in my college years.

A member of the Paulist order, Father Gouch came to Tufts from Johns Hopkins University in 1956, I think, and was the first priest with whom I really related in a meaningful adult way. He strongly encouraged me to think beyond the Baltimore Catechism when making moral decisions in such an ever-changing world. Without his early teaching about the need for educated people to forsake a "one-size-fits-all" attitude toward the Church, I might have had much more difficulty considering myself an observant Catholic today.

Tufts was historically a Unitarian/Universalist school, but in the 1950s the undergraduate population seemed to include about 25 percent each of Catholic, Protestant, Jewish, and "other" students. The Newman Club was at the time the largest student organization on campus, and we offered well-attended programming on Tuesday afternoons. Our speakers mostly focused on contemporary issues with student appeal. During my time in the office, we changed the club's name to Catholic Club of Tufts University, so people would more readily understand who we were. Then, in part to prove that we were not moving away from the umbrella organization, we hosted a convention of Newman clubs from throughout the Northeast, for which I was pleased to serve as chairman in 1957.

Holding the convention at Tufts required me to communicate extensively with the Archdiocese of Boston, particularly to secure a greeting from then Archbishop Richard Cushing, and then to obtain his approval to then arrange the first public Catholic Mass ever held on campus, appropriately enough in Cohen Auditorium. Everything went extremely well, and the whole process was another valuable learning opportunity.

> I HAD ALWAYS wanted to own my own business and first started talking about it during my junior high school years. With likely no idea what the consequences of that ambition might be, I had a clear goal. Yet it would be several years later, at Tufts, before I first heard the word *entrepreneur*, during a sophomore French class, and I remember feeling empowered by it. The word fully defined my interests in business, and I knew I was already well on my way to satisfying the definition.

As my final semester of college wound down, it might have seemed inevitable that I would become an entrepreneur upon graduation—after all, I had played around with so many different self-directed business activities from grammar school on. But when the time came to go out into the real world of business, I determined to find out what was out there before deciding what I truly wanted to be "when I grew up."

During February and March of 1958, I interviewed with seven or eight firms that conducted in-depth visits at Tufts through the placement office. I remember how excited I was to receive invitations from five companies to visit

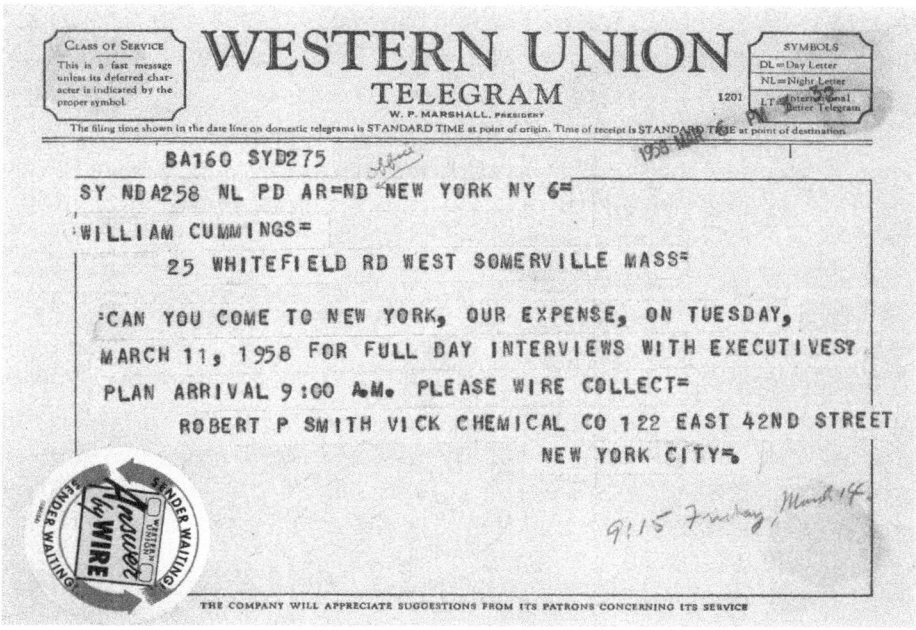

| *Telegram invitation to interview with Vick Chemical, 1958*

their corporate offices, and I subsequently received formal job offers from four of them. This job-search process felt a little like the college-application process four years before, except that now the travel and expenses were all generously reimbursed by the respective firms.

The spring of 1958, like 2018 and 2019, was a highly opportune year to be a new college graduate. In those days, Vick Chemical Company interviewed at the same dozen or so college campuses each year, with a goal of hiring one new sales trainee from each school. Vick sent a hand-delivered paper telegram to invite me to my interview, long before anyone began to imagine anything like the Internet. A short time after the interview I was delighted to accept the offer from Vick, feeling as though I had won the job lottery. Then located in Greensboro, North Carolina, Vick Chemical was the maker of Vicks VapoRub and numerous other proprietary cold remedies. Vick offered one of the best business training programs anywhere.

Tufts' placement director had urged me to sign up for the Vick interview, and I later learned that she was also instrumental in influencing the interviewer to offer the Tufts position to me, after three of us interviewed in New York. The starting rate was only $270 per month, as compared with other offers of up to about $500 a month for Tufts engineering graduates that year and maybe as much as $450 for liberal arts graduates like myself.

But I began the new job fully imbued with the Depression-era thinking of my parents. They had taught me from an early age to work a little harder than the next person and to always save whatever and whenever I could. This was the surest, if not the only, way for people of little means "to get ahead" in this world. They were great teachers, and I learned that lesson well. This mentality has followed me throughout my life.

COLLEGE TUITIONS had not really begun to skyrocket then, but Tufts' rates did seem like they were soaring when they increased from $600 per year in 1954 to more than $1,000 per year by graduation time. I was determined to pay all my tuition and my other college expenses myself, and was eventually able to do so. In what then seemed like fanciful exaggeration, Tufts trustees predicted in 1958 that by the time our kids attended college, tuition might be as much as $6,000 per year.

❀ *From retail to food service to internships, there are so many traditional ways for students to make money while gaining experience. Those who are entrepreneurs by nature, however, often find it more satisfying, exciting, and indeed, educational to launch their own ventures such as small one-time projects like salvaging a boat or harvesting spent lead, or longer-term repeatable undertakings like the annual Christmas tree sales.*

❀ *These types of early work experiences clearly demonstrate how creative thinking and extra effort can result in additional income. A student working for an hourly wage at a fast-food restaurant might earn raises over time, but would not typically be able to realize immediate returns on his or her investment of effort. He or she would always gain the commonsense background experience of learning what being an "employee" is all about. Extensive experience in dealing with co-workers and the general public can be extraordinarily helpful, too.*

❀ *In both business and personal relationships, it is incredibly important to ask questions and fully understand any problem before we start to correct any alleged shortcomings. Listen and project empathy. Empathy and patience are two of the most important but most overlooked aspects of deal making.*

❀ *Don't wish for your goals—work for them.*

[3]

On the Road with Vicks

Bill is shown (eighth from the left) with the well-outfitted Vick Chemical 1958 training class as they started a sales campaign in Detroit

MY WORK EXPERIENCE immediately after college showed me how naïve it is to assume that a person will be good at conducting business simply because he or she has studied business successfully in any school. Instead, I have found how many people seem happy to fill up their minds with facts and information to store, like a squirrel hoarding nuts, with little capacity for ideation. Oftentimes they can recite the information with scant ability to interpret it, or even fully understand it.

Education is working when it teaches us to internalize new information and effectively apply it. Increasingly, it seems to me, students of business learn disproportionately more about theories and theorems, and about computer models for maximizing profits, than they hear about how to "do business." They may learn about real estate syndications, limited partnerships, tax strategies, and how to make the numbers work, but what do they learn about how to build or create? They may also learn all sorts of ways to convert other people's money into their own. How much do they ever learn about the wonderful side of business; managing production, motivating people, creating jobs, and leadership? Job creation may be the single greatest factor in considering the true value of new businesses.

> Certainly, undergraduate and advanced degrees can be highly valuable, but businesses can make great mistakes when they persist in focusing so much on academic qualifications before considering what an applicant might really bring to the company. When making hiring decisions, examine a person's drive and determination. What about honesty, character, and personality? Steer conversations with a job applicant to determine whether he or she has the ability to size up situations and opportunities and achieve positive results. Obviously, there is no science in this subject, but often a personal interview will reveal vastly more about character than will any résumé.

Even in an age when it is becoming highly fashionable to be an entrepreneur, many people remain averse to risk-taking and innovation. Especially in large firms, which, perhaps only coincidentally, have more than their share of MBAs, there seems to be a great fear of doing something wrong. Many employees don't want, or care enough, to rock the boat. Similarly, many managers lack the confidence and maturity to encourage suggestions, or even involvement, from the employees they supervise; instead, they persist in treating them strictly as underlings. Events, staff, and entire companies will often just drift along.

While it is true that I studied economics at Tufts University, my professional interests have always been more directed toward "business," and I took enough practical business courses to receive my bachelor's degree in either economics or business administration. In the end, I selected the latter to the mild consternation of my department chairman, Professor Louis Manley, and was likely one of the last Tufts graduates to earn a Business Administration degree from Tufts' Department of Economics.

That Economics Department today is probably staffed entirely with academic economists, to the exclusion of any practical teachers of how to do business. They may not look down on the more plebeian side nearly as much as they did when I was a Tufts undergrad, but they are well aware that there is a difference. Ironically, however, my degree never once made an ounce of difference to me or to anyone else over the sixty-one years since I graduated. A degree in philosophy would have been almost as useful, as long as I had picked up the few practical business courses that I was fortunate enough to find.

JACK KEROUAC READERS will surely remember his timeless classic *On the Road*. Kerouac included in that book many of his own memorable experiences while he completed the same Vick Chemical Company sales training job I was about to begin. Indeed, it was perhaps his only real job before he attained great fame as the "voice of the Beat Generation." Kerouac's mass appeal was surely one of the reasons for Vick's special employment allure in my age group in the late fifties.

By some accounts, Vick may have played an inadvertent role in the actual writing of *On the Road*, which Kerouac, according to some reports, completed in just three weeks. Some historians have suggested that many writers of that day used stimulants made from wads of crushed up Vicks inhalers that contained the decongestant L-methamphetamine, the less potent component of the dangerous street drug known as "speed."

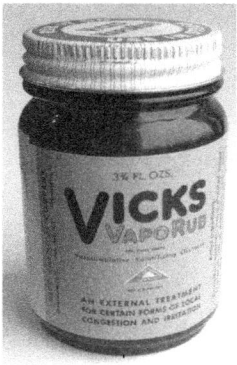

Although the Vick job paid less than any of the four other offers I received through the Tufts placement service, it held unique value and potential. A seven-day expense account covered 100 percent of my living expenses, with the exception of personal air travel and entertainment. Seven days a week, I spent every night between early June 1958 and Christmas week in a hotel or motel, and because of a generous expense account, I was able to bank my entire paycheck every month. There was also a significant salary increase after the first nine months of employment—just wait until March.

The Vick orientation team had a carefully arranged program and did a superb job of conditioning and exciting each year's new class of trainees. They emphasized the large number of candidates interviewed and how carefully we were selected. The majority, plus another dozen summer trainees who were hired for ten weeks only, were mostly from far more privileged backgrounds, and I found myself quietly learning from several whom I came to know fairly well. I particularly noticed their easy manner and smart attire, even though I was never the type to buy luxurious Hickey Freeman suits.

The formal training program began with several jam-packed days and nights at Vick's administrative headquarters in the Chanin Building, at 122 East 42nd Street in New York City, and at what was then the Commodore Hotel, directly across the street. A half century later, I learned from Roger Lowenstein's 1995 Warren Buffett biography that Buffett, whom I have long regarded with great admiration, was affiliated with the Graham-Newman mutual fund, and worked in the same Chanin Building shortly before I worked there.

Vick's program was well-known and respected in the proprietary drug industry, but after the first ten weeks, the wide range of sales and marketing challenges in which new staff participated was even better for building substantial general sales skills. The other trainees and more senior colleagues with whom I worked were an extremely talented and interesting group. Their drive, when aligned with their good training and high self-confidence, made them strong team members.

One of the first lessons business leaders must learn is the importance of identifying their own and their colleagues' strengths and weaknesses, and the Vick management team did that with great skill. For some managers, that may be difficult, especially if they equate evaluating other people's abilities with being "judgmental," but that task remains one of any manager's prime responsibilities. From an employer's perspective, the end goal must be to keep staff engaged by having them do the things at which they excel, whenever practical.

> Even though I did well on the graduate school aptitude tests, I never again considered returning to school after being "deferred for two years" by Harvard Business School (HBS), which I fully interpreted as being rejected. Rather than using standardized management styles learned in business school, most good entrepreneurs will develop individual management styles that are appropriate for their businesses. They generally have a strong bias toward acting ingeniously, discounting overwrought explanations, and totally discarding excuses. They make things happen. Yes, I was rejected by HBS, but we were thrilled in October 2019 when second-year students studied Harvard's newest case study, "Bill Cummings: The Cummings Way," and this book was used as required class reading.

For a not-so-poor-anymore Medford kid, always mindful of being from the less-affluent side of the tracks, my Vick training eventually served me extremely well. The Vick job, with a brand-new company car, expense account, and constant travel all over the country, was a dream job for almost any young single guy of my day, or at least it was for me.

Known around the world by its familiar blue glass jar, Vicks VapoRub was a mentholated chest-rub for relief from the symptoms of the common cold. It was widely promoted during the almost-worldwide influenza pandemic of

1918. John Barry, in his book *The Great Influenza*, chose, however, to liberally asperse Vick as an almost villainous predator of that day.

VICK MANDATED a rigid dress code of business suits with white or blue shirts and conservative ties. Probably every new hire in my twelve-member "class" also had to go shopping for his first straw hat before showing up "properly attired" on his first day. (There were most certainly no female colleagues in 1958.) We then needed to purchase our first felt hats immediately after Labor Day. Although business dress codes elsewhere were mostly much less stringent by 1958, we always respected our program. We were much in the minority regarding our clothing, but most of us felt a quiet pride in our roles as "the Vicks guys."

> Our clothing style may tell others a great deal about us, but clothing is only one small part of anyone's lifestyle. How do we act, talk, and think about things? How do we live, work, and treat others? What guidelines do we try to live by? Individually, where are we going? What are our objectives? What is our overall lifestyle? Where do all the pieces fit together? Do we have a separate business lifestyle, too? How do we meld the often-conflicting forces in our lives to achieve real fulfillment? What examples do we try to set?

Each of us has dozens of opportunities every day to demonstrate the style we have programmed for ourselves. We may often flounder and waver in this regard as young adults, but with age we gradually develop consistency and responsibility. Vick mandated the image that it wanted us to project at all times as representatives of the company.

Eager and ready to soak in each new experience, I worked to be the best first-year recruit Vick ever had. And according to the weekly recap summaries Vick shared with us, I typically made more sales calls, had higher average sales per call, and had much higher sales of new products than my peers did, and I just had so much fun doing it. This was especially true during the company's big campaign every summer to promote oversized orders of Vicks cold remedies before the start of cold season. I made it a game to attain the best results I could. We never saw any kind of interim cash incentives, but my sales record paid off well in terms of salary after early 1959.

The setting of realistic life goals is one of the biggest decisions most of us will ever make, because we may spend the rest of a lifetime pursuing them. To many of us, the next question may inevitably be, "How hard am I willing to work to achieve my goals?" Some people achieve their goals because of extraordinarily good luck, just as others may be destroyed by really bad luck. Sometimes good luck is as simple as positioning ourselves and conducting our lives in such a way that good things can happen. Positioning ourselves often involves taking chances on colleagues, including our superiors, and making determinations about *their* character, as well as their presumed good intentions, and reliability.

> One of the most important things to remember about good luck is that we must train ourselves and our colleagues to recognize it when it comes along. Although mudslingers love belittling people with whom they disagree as "opportunists," they are entirely missing the point. Indeed, taking advantage of opportunities is really the essence of how and why businesses exist. Businesses thrive by recognizing a need as an opportunity and then filling the need. My dad liked quoting Thomas Edison: "Most people miss opportunities," he said, "because they look too much like work."

Knowing that I probably worked harder, completed more sales calls, and had better results than anyone else of my rank, I felt comfortable taking off most of one weekday to explore Imperial Coal Mine in Clymer, Pennsylvania. I had serendipitously met the mine's maintenance director at a nearby restaurant, and when he invited me to venture underground with him the following morning, I nearly leapt off my chair to accept. The only way in and out of the mine, however, was through a narrow tunnel, lying face down on a rubber conveyor belt. One mistake could surely have ended my days, but at least my last one would have been the most exciting.

I also took time that summer to rendezvous with my parents along Lake Michigan where we all pulled up for a day at the beach. They were on their way home by car after visiting with friends in Chicago.

| *Dorothy Cummings*

| *Bill Cummings*

| *Gus Cummings*

AFTER LESS THAN A YEAR with Vick, my professional career was briefly interrupted when, in early 1959, I was called (not unexpectedly) to six months of active U.S. Army Reserve duty at Fort Dix, New Jersey. Many young men in that era elected to join military reserve units rather than perhaps being drafted for longer periods of active duty under the Selective Service process. I had assumed that my call to active duty would come eventually, and had alerted Vick of my status as a member of a U.S. Army field hospital reserve unit in Boston.

I reported to Fort Dix and after eight weeks of basic training was assigned as a recruit to Company D, Specialists Training Regiment, otherwise known as Cook School. Vick was liberal about almost all benefit issues, but I did have to give up my company car for the duration of my service and was without a vehicle for the first time in quite a while. Since hitchhiking was still common then, especially for men in uniform, there was never one bit of difficulty hitchhiking to Boston whenever there was enough time off to make the trip worthwhile. One time, I took a bus to New York City and had a fine time crashing the after-hours portion of a Vick sales meeting while still in uniform.

U.S. Army Cook School was an enjoyable two months, especially because I was selected as class leader for the twenty or so other privates who needed someone in charge. The job included a temporary promotion to acting sergeant, albeit with no change in pay status. The other interesting part of Cook School was working and living with the now illustrious Ralph Nader.

I first met Ralph earlier at the old Boston Army Base, now part of Boston's Innovation District, when we were both receiving our pre-active-duty physicals. Later, we also found each other on our induction day, and then sat together during our Greyhound bus trip from Boston Army Base to Fort Dix. And by the time we again ended up together at Cook School, we knew each other fairly well.

Ralph, my *de facto* assistant class leader, had recently graduated from Harvard Law School following his undergraduate years at Princeton. He made my job as class leader much easier because he was such a steady, no-nonsense type of guy, and he always tried to assist me in making our class look as good as possible. Two classmates, however, were constant troublemakers.

Being the class leader gave me the luxury of a private bedroom on the second floor of the barracks, whereas Ralph was on the main deck below. I had few responsibilities beyond keeping track of the other recruits. One night, when I was sound asleep, however, Ralph rushed upstairs to wake me up. Even then a take-action kind of guy, Ralph already had my camera in his hand. "Come quick," he said as he hurried out of the room. "We can get the goods on them." Sure enough, our two troublemakers were excitedly conducting a craps

Bill (center) is shown above with U.S. Army Cook School classmates Barry Rich of New York City and George Sexeny of Winchester, Massachusetts, in 1960 at Fort Dix, New Jersey

game on the ground floor of the barracks.

Ever the diplomat, at least in his Army days, Ralph decided that the photographic evidence of this "serious transgression" would be most useful in simply encouraging better behavior from the participants, and his logic did work, at least for our final two weeks together. My commitment to the U.S. Army included several years of service in the Reserves following six months of active duty between the years of the Korean conflict and Vietnam. At one point I was actually transferred to the U.S. Navy and the USS Loesser in Norfolk, Virginia, but then was honorably discharged by the Army after being transferred to California with Vicks.

Ralph quickly went on to much greater things, including publishing his 1965 blockbuster book *Unsafe at Any Speed*, much to the chagrin of General Motors and the rest of the American automobile industry, though probably in their long-term best interests. Ralph's national social activism led him to become a five-time candidate for the presidency of the United States, beginning as a write-in in the 1992 New Hampshire primary. It was no surprise to me that Ralph became so prominent. But where was he in November 2016?

It would be several decades until we reconnected, in early 1992, when Ralph called in advance of a trip to Boston. I was publishing our first weekly newspaper then, and it included Ralph's syndicated column. The two of us spent some enjoyable time catching up during that visit, and we have kept in touch ever since. In September 2015, Ralph opened this country's first tort law museum, the American Museum of Tort Law, in a former community bank building, in his life-long home town of Winsted, Connecticut. Located less than two hours' driving time from Boston or New York, this truly exceptional museum fully justifies an educational stopover.

RETURNING TO VICK CHEMICAL in late 1959, for my final assignment with the company, I covered a terrific sales territory within Vick's West Coast Division. That meant working out of Long Beach, California, and managing the company's sales business in Arizona, Utah, Colorado, Nevada, and part of New Mexico. And for some reason, I managed the accounts in San Diego County, California. What a fun region that was to work in at age twenty-four. Instead of my constant driving each week, there was an all new routine of flying off to a different region each Sunday afternoon or Monday morning. Once there, I would be off in my rental car until Friday afternoon, unless I chose to remain on the road over the weekend as was often the case.

By the start of that third year, Vick had me doing some interesting promotional work along with primarily calling on key accounts. This meant dealing with some of the largest accounts in the country, including a mammoth regional headquarters of Safeway Supermarkets, promoting wider displays and thus greater sales of Vicks on the shelves. There were also opportunities in representing the firm and its products at events such as the annual conventions of the American Dental Association and the American Medical Association.

One special project was helping to promote a major campaign in the fall of 1960 called the Vicks Care Crusade. The objective was to showcase numerous large display bins of assorted Vicks cold remedies on supermarket and other retailers' floors, with each display featuring advertising for the CARE organization, a prominent national charity that sent enormous numbers of food packages all over the world.

The campaign included a drawing for a grand prize: free passage on the first commercial flight into space. I have often wondered whatever happened to that grand prize. Was the prizewinner perhaps among those hundreds of high rollers who, in 2019, are reportedly on the wait list for the inaugural flight of something like Virgin Galactic?

In addition to doing guest interviews on a half-dozen regional radio stations, it was great fun doing live television appearances promoting Vicks and the whole campaign in Salt Lake City and Denver. The live TV interview in Denver was on a regional daytime show, where the host invited me to rehearse, the evening before the actual show. He was passionate about doing well by the Vicks Care Crusade, and I was grateful to have the opportunity to practice.

There was almost a full crew in the studio for the dry run, which included

Bill is pictured, in 1961, appearing on KSL TV, Salt Lake City. Bill did live interviews with two Rocky Mountains television stations. (He was not discovered to be a television star.)

everything except the makeup routine. The next day, the host seemed quite excited with the net results of the extra effort, and I was certainly impressed with his work. I then learned this was the first time either of us had done a live interview.

I CONTINUED what turned out to be my final year at Vick, still feeling that as long as I was on Vick's payroll, it was up to me to do my best possible work in return. But weekends were still all mine, especially when stationed out West, with fun stays in several great ski resorts or national parks, depending on the season. There were more carefree weekends then than I would have for the next thirty years. Weekend lodging was always readily approved as part of the give-and-take that Vick managers encouraged. Resort lodging, which frequently came with built-in opportunities for activities like snowshoeing, group horseback riding, and equestrian care, was especially enjoyable. One of my most adventurous weekends out West involved taking the famous mule ride down the trail that is cut into the south face of the Grand Canyon and is only three feet wide in some places. The mules were aging but fully experienced.

Vick Chemical filled a critical role in my life and was an ideal first real job. I learned so much about what one version of corporate America was all about, and was able to do the job my superiors wanted done more than adequately. It was a magnificent learning opportunity, specifically because it frequently put me in meetings with new friends, just a few years older, almost all of whom could help me to learn. We really enjoyed the associations, and as a group they helped me to greatly broaden my skill set. There was a real art form to learn about not taking "no" for an answer, and how to do it tactfully and gracefully. I learned to seek out colleagues who felt the same way and who would revel in finally closing a difficult account. When a prospect just would not say "yes," we all wanted to at least change that to "not yet." That little trick of the trade often led directly to breakthrough moments.

But there was also the restlessness factor. Sometimes, irrespective of anything a company does, excellent employees will simply get antsy because of factors that are entirely unrelated to their work. Employees may be ideally suited, well paid, respected, and secure, but when some almost insignificant thing pops up, they will chuck everything and go elsewhere, often resulting in a great waste of talent. On the other hand, quite frequently such valued employees will quietly pack up and move on because they have been working, frustrated, at the whim of underperforming or disgruntled supervisors. Careful exit interviews with departing employees can be extremely useful in uncovering situations that senior managers might easily modify or correct.

Today at Cummings Properties we sometimes hire young people for professional positions that will be their first jobs, but our longevity factor with that sector is always troublesome. We have a much higher retention rate among new recruits who have first worked for a few years elsewhere. The average seniority among our entire Cummings staff is slightly shy of eleven years (as of January 2018), with many employees now at or approaching forty years.

❊ *A college education has become more and more important over the years, especially given the rapid advances in technology. Entrepreneurs, however, should never underestimate the value of on-the-job learning and should not blindly follow a path to an MBA simply for the prestige that might come with it. Whereas a higher degree may be beneficial for some business owners, others will gain so much more practical knowledge—like I did—by launching their careers and actually experiencing the world of business. Key colleagues at Cummings Properties have worked their way into top leadership positions with only bachelor's degrees. Among them are the firm's first four presidents and most other officers over the last half-century.*

❊ *Certainly the setting of life goals must be one of the most important decisions most of us will ever make, because we will spend the rest of a lifetime in pursuit of them. To many of us, the next question may inevitably be "how hard are we willing to work to achieve our goals?" But a lifetime of hard work should never be cause for regret.*

[4]

Still on the Road

I WAS NOT at all thinking about leaving Vick, but in late 1960 Don Knox, of my Phi Sigma Kappa and Christmas tree selling days, unexpectedly called me in Long Beach, California. Don told me he was on a mission to recruit me to join Gorton's of Gloucester, Inc., in Gloucester, Massachusetts, where I soon accepted a great offer to manage the marketing of a new liquid fish fertilizer. At that time, Gorton's was pushing to help develop at least a regional local market for the sale of "fish solubles," a semi-viscous, nutrient-rich substance loaded with proteins and minerals that often produces extraordinary growth with many types of plants.

| *Bill in the early 1960s, during his time with Gorton's*

I was not in any way unhappy with Vick, but left for what seemed like a long-term career with Gorton's, a classic old Massachusetts firm. With Vick, I had worked in thirty-five states, after spending my first 180 consecutive nights in nothing but hotels and motels. Before eventually leaving Gorton's too, my assignments there brought me to all the remaining lower forty-eight states not previously worked in with Vick.

I was hired by Paul Jacobs, Gorton's late president, and by the late E. Robert (Bob) Kinney, its chairman. Bob later became chairman of General Mills, after it acquired Gorton's, following my years there. I once had the good fortune to have both of these men, whom I so greatly admired, quietly mentoring me at the same time, but independently of one another. I much appreciated and took advantage of their generous coaching at every opportunity.

> A good mentor helps, but most people who do well in business ultimately do so because at some point in their lives they decide what they want, they set goals, and they make up their mind to sacrifice in order to reach them. Having brains and friends who are willing to help you is great, and those things can surely make our lives a lot easier, but nothing is as important as hard work, desire, persistence, and dedication. What idle pleasure(s) are we willing to give up to achieve what we truly want?

I knew nothing about fertilizer products and not much more about things horticultural. And while it is not necessarily true that a good salesperson can sell anything, it was true for me when it came to non-technical products and services, which certainly include VapoRub, fertilizer, and fish. My new product was essentially the liquid byproduct that resulted from processing fish and fish oil. We chemically strengthened and stabilized the natural product, and added a coloring agent. And that was that.

First, Don and I dreamt up the name, Mer-made Fish Emulsion Plant Food. Then we created a family of both retail- and commercial-sized containers for marketing what we called "plant food" rather than "fertilizer," because market research showed that household users preferred the former term. We used translucent high-density plastic bottles and offered three retail sizes of this fine, natural product, starting with an eight-ounce flask. Each had a small plastic insert in the neck of the bottle, allowing users to neatly squeeze out just an ounce or so of liquid at a time. For use on houseplants, most people would mix an ounce of the highly concentrated product into a half-gallon of water and then either root-feed or foliar-feed.

The professional-sized containers came in one-gallon and five-gallon sizes, as well as fifty-five-gallon drums for use by commercial flower growers, several of whom I personally visited and sold to, including many in northeast Ohio.

It was this specialized commercial market we most wanted to crack. This was particularly so because a competitive "Atlas" product, from the West Coast, was not a major factor there.

One of the first things Don and I did on the retail side was to take a booth at the annual Boston Spring Flower Show, where we could easily talk with hundreds of retail shoppers, many of whom were fascinated with our new local product. Don was in his element there, especially because of his considerable experience with landscape work and design in graduate school. Our key reason to present at the Flower Show was to have firsthand access to the opinions and attitudes expressed by home gardeners toward our new product as we assessed the retail market. We wondered if we should try talking about East Coast fish being better for plants than West Coast fish, but we never tried that pitch. If we were to do the same thing today, however, I can readily imagine playing the "buy local" card for New England markets.

The most helpful thing we learned at the Flower Show was that many people who purchased a bottle or two of Mer-made first unscrewed the cap and took a sniff. Many shoppers were mistakenly, but naturally, concerned that Mer-made might smell up their homes. Unlike two other West Coast fish emulsion brands, which were a sort of yucky brown, Mer-made had enough inexpensive coloring in it to give even the diluted product a pleasant green color. But the product was not formulated with enough deodorant, or reodorant, to completely mask the mild fish odor. That first evening, Don and I returned to Gloucester to investigate possible solutions, opting to forgo the night out so often associated with trade shows.

> Someone suggested adding vanilla extract to the product, but instead of adding anything to the contents of our bottles, we took about 500 of the small plastic inserts that we typically pushed into the top opening of each bottle to restrict the outflow and soaked those inserts overnight in the vanilla extract. We effectively marinated the plastic inserts in real vanilla.

The next morning, before the Flower Show opened, Don and I opened the entire inventory we had there and substituted the newly sweet-scented plugs. Customers that day may have wondered why we appeared so pleased when they continued to open the bottles. "Mer-made just smells so great," they told us over and over. Some of them, who were users of other fish emulsion products, even mentioned those products by name. We knew from a few growers, who by then were starting to use large quantities of the product in their indoor greenhouses, that neither Mer-made *nor* our competitors' products caused any odor problem at all when diluted and used, but we certainly provided a much better first sniff. Don and I gave ourselves merit badges for innovation.

BEFORE MUCH OF anything was really accomplished with Mer-made, I was asked to transfer to the "real" Gorton's, but at its Blue Water Seafoods division in Cleveland, Ohio. This assignment came as Gorton's and the Mer-made developer accepted an offer to sell the partially developed Mer-made line, although Gorton's continued for some time to do the manufacturing. The Gorton's interest in the fish solubles really had much more to do with the company trying to help Gloucester's overall economy by building the market for this fishery byproduct than it did with actually making a market for itself.

When I moved to Cleveland, my sales area started in Toledo, in northwest Ohio, and extended all the way to Montana, Idaho, and beyond. I was tasked with creating a supply chain for our frozen institutional seafood products in my "frontier" market, especially the vast area between Minneapolis and Oregon where we had almost no distribution. Ironically, my most substantial problem also yielded my greatest opportunity, and, in my mind anyway, the net result was as much a logistical masterpiece as it was an impressive sales success.

In an effort to make this new sales territory work, I needed to plan carefully when assembling and shipping orders and was able to organize my sales calls so that full truckloads of frozen product could be dropped off in logical sequence to the many new distributors I established. Our fresh frozen cod portions were cut with high-speed band saws from forty-pound blocks of cod fillets that were often processed at sea and were promoted as "fresher than fresh." These blocks were cut into four-ounce sandwich-sized pieces, lightly breaded, and then used primarily by fast-food restaurant chains for their hot fish sandwiches. "Fishwich" was our trademarked name.

Blue Water had recently been designated as the exclusive national supplier of frozen breaded fish portions for all the McDonald's restaurants. There were not many McDonald's in New England in 1961, but the chain was strong in the West. In my territory, that contract was a huge tool whose power could be measured by much more than the amount of fish actually consumed in the McDonald's outlets there.

Each new distributor we signed up to serve the McDonald's outlets gave me many opportunities to sell other Blue Water brand products to these same new distributors, which would, of course, resell to their other customers, we hoped, as well as to McDonald's. The distributors benefited by reaching the minimum-size orders necessary for effective shipping costs.

If Gorton's brand was available, each McDonald's in the area was required by McDonald's national office to use our brand. That proved to be a marvelous selling tool. Whichever distributor was bringing in the frozen fish portions to its local McDonald's knew that it, too, would have an excellent opportunity to supply some of McDonald's other needs. I would then, of course, use the same logic with the distributors, motivating or enabling them to stock Gorton's or Blue Water branded shrimp, scallops, and lobster tails, as well as other sizes and shapes of frozen fish, in order to meet our shipping minimums. Everyone was delighted over my consideration for their needs. All of this ultimately made for a remarkably successful distribution and sales experience.

> It always helps to show people that you are on their side before trying to get them on yours. Consider other people's points of view when plans and procedures change. Work on decisions until they are as fair as possible to all concerned, to avoid building up sides and cliques. Respect the inevitable cultural or philosophical differences that will cause people to see some things differently from how you might see them. Always listen carefully to find things that might be thrown into a deal to sweeten it for the other side, often at little or no cost to you.

Unlike most salespeople in the company, I left my home base of Cleveland to start out on my sales itinerary almost every Sunday afternoon, often flying then to the far end of my territory. I then worked my way back from places like Billings or Helena to Fargo and Cheyenne, and then perhaps to accounts around Milwaukee. Other times, I would jaunt up to the Twin Cities area, then to Omaha, down to Davenport, and maybe Milwaukee again. I was always working to instill excitement in the distributors and their sales staffs about our Blue Water products, and I often attended regional restaurant shows. I pretended (to myself, at least) that the whole company was mine.

Working for Gorton's, I, surprisingly, found myself once again happy to travel almost every week. Although it would hardly be newsworthy today, my picture appeared one day in a Cleveland daily newspaper with those of a half-dozen other inaugural members of what must have been a predecessor to United Airlines' frequent flyer club. In those days, United Airlines awarded membership in its 100,000 Mile Club for accumulated lifetime mileage: "In Appreciation for your Outstanding Contributions to Air Transport Progress." While it was easy for a businessman to accumulate air miles, they had zero value. The miles were not redeemable for anything then, other than access to priority reservations and a fancy walnut plaque, which I still have. Women

| Bill at a booth for Blue Water Seafoods at the Minnesota Restaurant Association Show, 1963

were rarely seen on weekday flights then, except for flights heading to vacation destinations, and flights were almost never full or even close to full. We can all now readily see what wonders women have done for the airline industry.

JUST AFTER NEW YEAR'S 1963, following my two years of frequently praised and highly productive work at Blue Water, the senior vice president there started my day by calling me aside. "I have some news for you," he said. "We've thought about this a great deal, but the appointment as the company's new assistant sales manager is not going to you." Instead, the attractive new job would go to a much more senior salesman who, I was told, had a family and really needed the new job and a raise. "You might have been the better choice for this job, Bill, but surely you are not going to let this get in your way now, after all you've accomplished here."

I suggested that they give me the new management position and give the money to the other guy, whom I certainly liked and who supposedly really needed the money. "Tell me in a year if I deserve a raise," I argued, but I got nowhere. The SVP offered me a great raise and my choice of whatever territory I wanted, almost as a consolation prize instead of the promotion, but I was not interested. I had been thinking for some time that any kind of a bump in the road with Gorton's would be my signal that it was time to go off on my own.

So it did not take me long to decline the generous raise and give my notice.

Here, let's re-emphasize some of what I discussed earlier in this chapter. Managers, like mine in Cleveland, must be constantly aware of opportunities to improve and enhance relationships with their key employees, lest they later be required to train replacements. It is generally far less expensive and less stressful to salvage existing employee relationships than it is to create new ones. Some of the most critical ingredients in employee satisfaction are consistency, opportunity, and fairness on the part of the company.

Businesses that take the trouble to carefully think through and codify their employee policies provide a strong emotional bridge in times of individual employee stress. Access to easily understood information concerning company personnel policies seems to be of immense value in reducing employee frustration and turnover. If employees feel their employer is fair with them, they are far less likely to quit when some little thing goes wrong.

Job security, and letting staff members know that they are truly appreciated for what they contribute, can never be overemphasized. When managers are overworked or rushed, it is easy for them to take people for granted. Every one of us needs to know that what we do is worthwhile, and when employees don't hear this from their superiors, the employees will often prove how valuable they are by leaving.

There were bruise-colored clouds and a cold wind blowing in from the Cuyahoga River as I walked out of the office that day but my heart was really excited. I did not have any hint about how to start out on my own, except that I would take a few months' vacation first. Like my decision a few years earlier not to continue with advanced AFROTC, I have reflected many times on this pivotal decision to leave corporate America, but I have never regretted it.

I SOON BOARDED the RMS Queen Mary in New York with a low-cost windowless cabin akin to steerage class, and a Eurail Pass good for three months of unlimited deluxe and first-class rail passage throughout most of Europe. On the Queen Mary, however, I managed to insinuate myself easily into the first-class routine of the ship with the help of a couple of older female accomplices, whom I met the first night. I also had an underground booklet called *The Inside Route to First Class on Cunard*. These ladies changed their table assignment so there was always an empty seat for me at their table in the first-class dining room. I even coupled with one of my new best friends to win a three-day bridge tournament. The other essential tool I brought with me was an early edition of Arthur Frommer's *Europe on Five Dollars a Day*. The book provided two-thirds of my hotel rooms in Europe, and the comfortable high-speed trains provided most of the rest of my lodgings.

Though my passport was brand-new when I left the United States, I still needed to have extra accordion-style pages added to accommodate what I anticipated would be dozens of back-and-forth border crossings, plus Russian and eastern Mediterranean visas. By entering Russia via Finland, I found it no problem to get there. I will never forget watching Swan Lake at the Bolshoi Theatre, or enjoying a live hockey game in Moscow, and hearing the Star-Spangled Banner played to start the game, even though the score ended up at about nine to one, the wrong way.

I probably visited every nation in North Africa and Europe by rail, boat, or plane, and enjoyed a fabulous winter. Later in my trip, when I traveled to Egypt, Syria, and Kuwait, the added pages in my passport allowed me to snip off evidence that I had earlier visited Israel—otherwise, I would not have been allowed into those Middle Eastern countries. That would have been a great loss.

In Damascus, I once found myself surrounded by a dozen soldiers, all with drawn guns. I had rented a bike and was riding around and innocently taking pictures of the wrong things during a short revolution there, but after yanking the film from my camera, and certainly scaring me more than I had ever been scared before, they let me go.

Later, in nearby Lebanon, I met up with a friend from Vermont whose brother had given her, and seemingly everyone else she knew, the use of his chalet on a mountain at Cedars of Lebanon for a week-long ski blast.

My three days there turned out to be almost my only real "vacation" during my four months of constant travel. Just a week later, however, I booked myself into Athens' King George Hotel to top off the splendor of that beautiful city. Clearly not an Arthur Frommer choice, the King George, in a single night, gave me all the super luxury I needed for the entire trip.

RETURNING FROM EUROPE in May 1964, I was excited to begin looking for my new start in life. Having just enjoyed a four-month "adventure of a lifetime"—or so I thought then—it was time to get to work.

For me, business is enjoyable for its own sake—even more than it is for the financial rewards it may bring. The money we earn does serve as a score card, but successful entrepreneurs may otherwise pay only the scantest attention to their financial bottom lines. I have never once tried to add up my net worth, at least not in the last forty years, and to the best of my knowledge no one else has either. Neither have we ever failed to pay a debt, or to pay it on time.

Starting my formal business career with Vick Chemical Company and then Gorton's of Gloucester was especially beneficial to me, because those firms gave me an essential close-up view of how solid, established businesses operate. Those five-plus years of traditional business experience in two smart, highly principled national companies would be so valuable to me even decades later, and would have been for most others.

❃ *Management experience at two fine national companies showed me firsthand the importance of seizing opportunities to enhance relationships with employees through thoughtful communication and expressions of genuine appreciation for work well done. Many employees, in fact, crave fulfillment more than money alone. At Gorton's I would have happily taken greater responsibility and no raise in preference to the inverse, and I readily embarked on my own adventure when I felt the secure job no longer aligned with my goals.*

❃ *William Faulkner once wrote that Ernest Hemingway "has never been known to use a word that might send a reader to the dictionary." Hemingway shot right back: "Poor Faulkner. Does he really think big emotions come from big words?" Hopefully, we have somewhat of a middle ground in this book.*

❃ *A good mentor helps, but most people who do well in business ultimately do so because at some point in their lives they decide what they want, they set goals, and they make up their mind to sacrifice in order to reach them.*

❃ *What is so often mistaken as "luck" is being smart enough and prepared enough to recognize and take advantage of good opportunities when they happen to come along.*

❃ *The best way to have a friend is to be one.*

[5]

Finally on my Own

AS I SETTLED in following the grand trip, my Dad at first expressed no opinion about what business he thought I should get into. Little did I know—until later—that he was biding his time, and he waited just long enough before asking me to humor him by taking a look at the "funny old business" he had mentioned to me in passing months before. Funny indeed: It was a fruit-punch business. What would Dad know about which kind of business I should buy? I thought. But for that matter, what did I know?

| *Bill Cummings with a Starline refrigerated dispenser*

The business was Wilmot H. Simonson Company, and its owner, Llewellyn H. Farnsworth, was a well-to-do West Medford resident who had begun spending the warmer months in Jonesport, Maine, where he grew blueberries. He was about seventy years old, tall and lean, and favored blue jeans and red plaid shirts. Except for the large gray cowboy hat he wore most every time I ever saw him, he was a pure Down East Yankee.

Mr. Farnsworth met me in his lovely West Medford home on a Friday afternoon in June 1963 after Dad took me to the business location, five blocks from Cherry Street, that same morning. "My dad says I should buy your fruit-punch business," I said, "but I don't know why I would want to pay anything for a business that had almost no sales and no net income."

Mr. Farnsworth immediately began telling me about the vast potential of the business and about what he considered its valuable secret formula. Wilmot Horatio Simonson had supposedly acquired this formula in 1890 from the makers of Old Medford Rum. Mr. Farnsworth suggested that the price to purchase the business should be "at least a six-figure number," but he would let it go for $40,000 because he knew I "would not be able to finance much." The total gross sales for the business the entire previous year had amounted to a scant $10,000 or $11,000.

We had a friendly conversation, but eventually he came to realize that the business itself was not worth anything at all if the maximum earnings to be made from it, based on its then-current volume, might be about twenty cents an hour—a small fraction of the minimum wage even at that time. Eventually I offered him 10 percent of his asking price, with full payment that day, but "not a dime more." When he finally agreed on my offer of $4,000, he did so based on the value of the sugar and other ingredients, and the gallon-sized glass jugs he had in inventory, but he still wanted $2,000 more for "goodwill."

I told him again, "That was it." He could have my friendship and goodwill for free, but there wasn't any more money to give for his. He was not at all happy with the price, but we shook hands at $4,000 in 1950s dollars, say perhaps $40,000 today. At the end, he seemed satisfied and pleased, saying, "Old Medford will soon be out of my life."

Dad was visibly pleased with the Farnsworth purchase. He was excited that I had agreed with his assessment, and that we closed everything about this deal in that *one day* at what he thought was such a bargain price. He seemed especially proud that he had just played a significant role in his son's career path. "Mr. Farnsworth just wanted to get rid of the business," Dad said. "You bought it for a song."

> That evening, Dad gave me some advice that has remained extremely meaningful to me. "The most important thing about being lucky," he said, "is recognizing good luck when it comes along, and then taking advantage of it. Life is mostly what we make of the opportunities that come our way." Good genes or good luck may be the same thing, but wherever they lead us is highly dependent upon what we do with them.

Simonson Company, as it continued to be known during our first two years, was supposed to have been an aging descendant of the Old Medford Rum Company, but Simonson made only one product—Old Medford fruit-punch concentrate. The company received an award from an advertising association in the 1920s for holding the oldest brand name in continuous use in North America. It sold its product mostly to catering firms and fancy restaurants in and around Boston and the North Shore. But the customer list for this delicious product also included two university accounts, Harvard Law School and Massachusetts Institute of Technology—both in nearby Cambridge. Over the next few years, we (which I sometimes use as a pontifical "We") built the backbone of the company on what we soon did with these two tiny college accounts. Though their Old Medford orders initially were limited, these two prestigious schools became extremely important steppingstones for far greater business.

Wilmot H. Simonson Company at 54 Fulton Street with Whiting's Milk Company picking up Old Medford fruit-punch base, 1964

Another especially interesting new account my first summer was Whiting's Milk Company on Rutherford Avenue in Charlestown, directly next door to the area's milk giant, Hood Milk Company, and a few blocks from the old Charlestown State Prison. Coincidentally, Whiting's Milk was the company to which my grandfather, also named Augustus Cummings, sold his small milk-delivery company, including his three horses and their milk wagons, in 1936.

In late June, I telephoned Arnold Bullock, Whiting's president, hoping to convince him to have his drivers sell our Old Medford fruit-punch concentrate in retail-sized bottles for home use. As it turned out, he liked the product's taste so much that he decided to buy our concentrate just as it came, and we had our first real volume customer. Impracticable as it was, Whiting's chose to add water and sell a ready-to-drink fruit punch.

Someone at Whiting's could easily have concocted a comparable product from scratch. Alternatively, we could have delivered a far more concentrated product at a much lower cost, to which Whiting's could have added even twenty parts water instead of five parts water, and its own sugar. Instead, through early September Whiting's continued purchasing many truckloads of our completely standard fruit-punch concentrate. They added five parts water and then sold it as "Whiting's own original recipe" old-fashioned fruit punch.

The only thing we did differently for Whiting's was that we bottled our concentrate in Whiting's own gallon-sized reusable glass milk jugs and issued a credit for the savings on the cost of the jugs we would otherwise have used. We were surprised that it took someone at the milk company nearly the whole summer to realize that it did not need us for what it could do on its own for a dramatically lower cost.

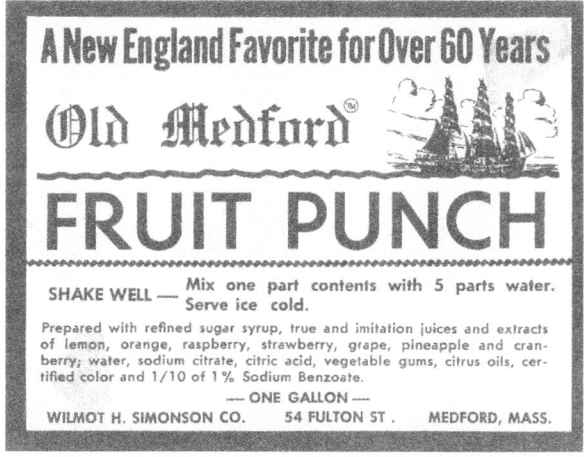

We operated out of Mr. Farnsworth's twenty-four-by-forty-eight-foot, two-story wood frame building at 54 Fulton Street, Medford, for more than a year. The facility was tucked behind two homes, but the regular visits of large delivery trucks began to pose a logistical challenge for our busy residential neighborhood. One memory from those early days was how much Mr. Farnsworth seemed to enjoy dropping by on the first or second of each month to see how we were doing, pick up the $50 rent check, and cheer us on. "It has been so long since I've made any money off this old place," he once told me.

THE MOST SUCCESSFUL entrepreneurs I have known almost always demonstrated great self-confidence, optimism, and often, personal magnetism, as well as a willingness to work prodigious hours to make things happen to their satisfaction. There is almost always a way to get the job done, and the true entrepreneur will persevere with some things to the point of obsession. Entrepreneurs hate to lose every bit as much as they love to win. Entrepreneurial mistakes, however, must be freely accepted because calculated risk is inherent to the concept of entrepreneurship. Oscar Wilde may have been the first person to write, "Experience is the name that we give to our mistakes."

Entrepreneurs must have an aggressive risk-taking nature, tempered by a reasonable understanding of how great any impending risk might be. Purchasing Simonson in one day, without any due diligence, was my risk-taking nature in command. I knew that this little business could be turned into a successful venture with a combination of creativity to improve the efficiency of production and hard work to dramatically cut costs and sell an even better product. I have always had a wealth of intellectual curiosity, along with extra ability to innovate in the face of adversity. And innovate we did.

Sales and production steadily increased during our first year, as our original two-person sales team and I were out on the street peddling our concentrated fruit punch. We went from ordering five hundred or one thousand pounds of sugar at a time to five thousand pounds per delivery, all in one hundred-pound bags. But one day, I personally unloaded and stacked twenty thousand pounds (two hundred large bags) of sugar by myself to stock up before an upcoming price increase. We soon thereafter switched to liquid sugar syrup, delivered by tanker trucks, which was a far more appropriate form of sweetener. The liquid cane sugar was pumped directly from the delivery truck into a two thousand-gallon stainless-steel storage tank we had set up in an adjacent garage.

| *Student worker Jack Kerins in the bottling room, 1965*

The meager bottling equipment from the original company was almost immediately inadequate to keep up with the production demands our sales results generated. We installed a pressurized water tank with a half-inch inlet, but with a two-inch-diameter discharge valve to accommodate the increased need for water in a hurry, and we configured the piping to allow the liquid sugar and water to pour into the mixing tank simultaneously. A new six-bottle siphon filler allowed one operator to fill six jugs much faster than two operators had previously filled two jugs. We also purchased a used electric conveyor belt to replace a rope-pulled dumbwaiter (in the office) that brought the finished products from the basement up to the loading-dock level. Our one-gallon glass jugs soon gave way to less-fragile plastic jugs that worked far better for our needs, cost less than the glass jugs, and were lighter to ship. Every penny per gallon we could save on the cost side created a substantial difference in the profits, and we were always looking to save those pennies.

Penny-saving principles of cost control are frighteningly simple, and they come into play so often, but they are sometimes maddeningly ignored by smart people. Saving money through efficiency and eliminating wasted motions and unnecessary repeating costs is easy, once one starts to look out for it, though even well-meaning staff will sometimes surely mislabel cost control as miserliness.

WHEN WE FIRST took over the tiny wood-frame building on Fulton Street, it contained considerable ancient-looking equipment from the days prior to World War I, when the company also made pie filling mix, which was packaged by hand in small retail-size boxes. Before we removed these large antique wooden mixing machines, I used them a little disingenuously to make the company sound busy when visitors were in the one-room front office. These loudly clunking machines had huge, old electric motors, and wide leather belts connected the machines to one another. The whole building seemed to rumble when we turned them on. It was impressive, even if, for decades, the antique equipment had done nothing more useful than make noise on command.

And judging by the buzz around the office on November 9, 1965, one might have thought that Simonson Company/Old Medford Foods was undertaking a massive office changeover of some sort. In reality, the "big occasion" was that we had transitioned that day from an ancient Underwood click clack typewriter to a new IBM "Selectric" model.

Before my mother joined us at Old Medford earlier that year, she had not worked outside her home for thirty years. She was always an excellent typist, however, and she loved her work at Old Medford. At the same time, she was completely spooked that she would now have to "learn to type all over again, after all these years." Mom wanted nothing to do with this "totally unnecessary" new contraption, but nevertheless we proudly made the momentous change to our new Selectric.

How ironic it was when that same afternoon brought the Great Northeast Blackout, supposedly the largest power outage in American history at the time, affecting more than 30 million people in the northeastern states. Mom, in her *post hoc* thinking about the monster outage, attributed this blackout, only half-jokingly, to her new electric typewriter. Late that afternoon, she was elated to put the old Underwood back into service one last time, to type out the final few bills of lading.

THE CHALLENGE OF developing new recipes that were efficient to manufacture and profitable to sell kept my mind churning while I worked. The first new formulas were for lemonade, Concord grape, and orange, because we were already utilizing all of the frozen juices for these flavors with the fruit punch. These three new varieties and the punch all had about the same ingredients cost. The last three new flavors we developed were lemon-lime, wild cherry, and black raspberry, none of which had any meaningful juice content at all. These were not as popular on their own, but most buyers who used any flavors other than fruit punch soon tended to rotate all seven flavors.

| *Dot Cummings at 54 Fulton Street, 1965*

> One important business question here was pricing. Should we vary the selling prices to reflect the 30-percent-lower contents cost for the three juiceless varieties? We quickly determined, however, to price all seven flavors the same, and the subject of price differential never came up again. Old Medford fruit punch was the fastest seller, with Concord grape and lemonade a close second. The other four flavors all about tied for third place. The uniform pricing was certainly also to our advantage, as it kept everything simple. We determined that reducing the selling price of the less expensive flavors would not have helped us sell any more product and would have only reduced our profits. The single most important factor in determining how much something is worth is finding out how much customers will pay for it.

The first important new growth for Old Medford started at Massachusetts Institute of Technology, one of the Company's thirty or so existing small customers (there were no large ones) when we purchased the firm. MIT had been loyally serving Old Medford fruit punch at conference sessions, parties, and other special events for decades, but while the purchases were steady, they had historically totaled about $500 per year. Perhaps we had that account because of an early "buy local" initiative at the school.

Although MIT's food service team loved Old Medford punch for its staff parties and special events, no one ever considered serving it to students—even though the person who ordered it for the administrative and faculty parties was the same person who supervised the school's broader food and beverage purchases and ran the Walker Memorial Dining Hall. But when we floated the idea, he cited the obvious problem of how impractical it would have been to set up punch bowls in the cafeteria service lines.

Two days later, we purchased our first two oversized refrigerated drink dispensers from the former Dripcut Starline Corp. in Santa Barbara, California, each equipped with a fourteen-gallon clear Lexan tank. We immediately received MIT approval to set them up, filled with Old Medford fruit punch, next to the milk dispensers, and the students loved it. Then a day and a half after the Walker dining hall installation, we were asked to install dispensers in the dining rooms at MIT's Burton House and Baker House dormitories, and soon thereafter for all other student dining halls and cafeterias on campus. Those first two oversized refrigerated dispensers started a whole new business for us, and were of monumental importance to the firm.

Moving forward, we eventually provided these refrigerated dispensers to several hundred large institutional users to display and dispense Old Medford drinks, but almost exclusively in college dining halls and large hospitals all up and down the east coast. That was in 1965, shortly after most college cafeterias had started moving their classic Norris milk dispensers off the serving lines and into the dining rooms. Rather than be limited to one or two glasses of milk per meal, as was previously typical, students could now drink all the milk they wanted, and of course, all the Old Medford fruit punch, too. Students loved having the choice and were often vocal in their support of the change. If only we had had Twitter in 1965 to spread the news faster and farther.

Aside from selling the quality and appeal of our delicious product, the most important factor in marketing Old Medford fruit punch drinks was the "free" Starline dispensers we installed. Many customers often needed four or even six machines in a single large dining hall. Old Medford drink concentrates had a uniform list price of $10.60 per four-gallon case, including a $3-per-case premium until we recovered our cost of whatever equipment was provided. Thereafter, we automatically reduced the invoice price to $7.60 per case, but we still owned all the dispensing equipment and maintained the machines at our expense.

If another supplier had come along trying to compete with us, there would have been little or no room for it to replace our dispensers and still make a profit on its juice sales. A strong point here, however: "Don't get greedy." Our customers were already benefiting from our substantial discounts for purchasing large volumes and paying promptly. Most of our college accounts used enough concentrate to fully pay off the surcharges for whatever equipment they needed during the first semester's use. And in some years we had absolutely no bad-debt expense—zero losses.

Large accounts paid about two cents, again in 1965 dollars, per serving for our concentrated fruit drinks, compared to their approximately five-cents-per-serving cost of milk. Food-service directors tended to feel that their thirsty students would drink every bit as much as they could hold. With that in mind, the more Old Medford they consumed, the more money the school would save on milk.

Sugar was not a bad word in those days, and even if it had been, we soon converted all the flavors to sugar-free products at an enormous savings to us in production cost, and even shipping cost after we switched to much lighter weight plastic gallon jugs, too.

With MIT using Old Medford at a marvelous pace, we quickly turned to the other school account we had inherited from the original business, Harvard Law School. Like MIT, the Law School at Harvard originally used Old Medford only for its special parties and for conferences. Along with hot beverages and a few trays of brownies or cookies, the school often served Old Medford along with coffee and tea during afternoon break periods for meetings and seminars.

| *Old Medford delivery case, circa 1920*

Pauline Harkovitz was the highly regarded food-service director and an American Dietetic Association dietitian for Harkness Commons at Harvard Law School. "Sure, we can try it," was her prompt response to my pitch for offering Old Medford in her main dining hall. Once again, Old Medford provided the extra-large capacity dispensers, and the account needed only to purchase the concentrated drinks. Before we knew it, America's top-ranked future lawyers were drinking Old Medford at a pace that I could never have imagined a year before.

Once we established ourselves with the Law School food service team, who were employed by Stouffer's Food Service Group, we thought we would, of course, soon at least be talking with the university's own dining staff who handled all the many remaining dining halls, but we made no such headway.

After several months, however, Fred McCauley, one of Old Medford's first two sales associates, and I were attending a food service seminar at University of Massachusetts in Amherst when he noticed a key food service director from Harvard walking into a men's room.

It happened to be Charlie McCarthy, who for many years ran Kresge Dining Hall at Harvard Business School, and Fred followed him into the UMass restroom. All of fifteen minutes later, they finally emerged from the restroom together, with Fred obviously happy. Fred recognized that opportunity when it came along, and Harvard Business School soon led all of the remaining Harvard dining halls into the Old Medford camp. Kresge Dining Hall proved every point we hoped to prove.

Tufts University was another early Old Medford client, for obvious reasons including the campus' location, which was just two miles from the Old Medford facility at 54 Fulton Street. Despite being an alumnus, I was not known there at that time. Yet, to my surprise, Tufts' food-services director, Richard Ballou, remembered that I had worked for a short time as a kitchen helper and food monitor at the school's Carmichael Hall during my student days. Tufts students in all Tufts' dining halls soon joined the ever-growing throng raving about our delicious fruit punch and by then six other tasty flavors.

At about $400 each, the Starline dispensers sometimes created a strain on cash flow, even as Old Medford sales grew rapidly (thanks to those exact machines). The results clearly justified the investment, but these high up-front costs did compel me, in mid-1966, to apply for a business loan at the local branch of what was then the Middlesex County National Bank. By that time, we had been doing all of our banking with Middlesex for a year. The bank didn't exactly say no. Instead, a snippy assistant branch manager told me, "Get your mother to co-sign it, or there will be no loan." I was sure he had never met my mother. Moreover, I was twenty-eight years old at the time (and looked my age) and stood more than six feet tall. As far as *he* knew, at that point, we were still friends.

How pleased I was when, just a few days later, an up-and-coming assistant manager from another bank came to our front door. Lawrence J. King from the old Malden Trust Company, in Malden, came to make a sales pitch, after he had somehow found out about us. I told Larry all about our history and our current cash need and why we needed a loan. He quickly said, "Sure."

"Take this, and open the account for us," I said, handing him the deposit envelope we had all ready to send to the old bank, "and let's get going." As he was leaving, instead of asking me to get my mother to co-sign, Larry said, "Are you sure you don't need board approval or something?" Larry's entrepreneurial attitude won him a new customer on his first surprise visit. If the old wooden mixing machines had still been there, I would have surely turned them on for effect. We banked with Larry for decades to come.

Eventually, some twenty years later, I was delighted to introduce Larry to the owners of Saugus Bank and Trust Company, who we knew had a highly attractive opening for a senior executive at their bank. Fred England of the Saugus bank quickly liked Larry enough to hire him as the bank's president. We then for many years maintained a substantial relationship with Saugus Bank and later with Eastern Bank, which absorbed Saugus Bank in 1994. I had earlier become acquainted with Fred, and his wife, Valerie, when Fred and I served for a number of years together on the board of his family's former Tanners National Bank in Woburn. Joyce and I enjoyed being around Fred and Val and came to know them quite well.

Saugus Bank grew dramatically under Larry's leadership, while Fred and his close colleague Don Lewis, whom I did not know then, were engineering the rise of Hastings-Tapley Insurance Agency. This was nevertheless the start of what is today still a significant relationship for Cummings Properties with the firm that is now USI Insurance, in our building at 12 Gill Street, Woburn. USI has for decades handled insurance for all of Cummings Properties' commercial real estate, and is also a key Cummings client.

> Watching a business develop momentum and establish a sustained pattern of growth is so satisfying in itself to the entrepreneurial people who make that growth happen. Seeing the month-to-month and year-over-year improvements in sales and profits will stimulate competitive urges that drive business leaders and give them the resources to engage more and more qualified colleagues and eager clients at every level.

❈ *It is highly important for business and institutional leaders to take active roles in their respective home or business communities. For me, one of the most meaningful roles was serving as an elected member and chairman of my town Planning Board, especially because, by that time, I was routinely appearing on the other side of the table in Woburn and elsewhere. Membership on the board of Woburn Boys & Girls Club also paid enormous personal satisfaction for many decades.*

❈ *The successful entrepreneur embraces risks with informed optimism—with Old Medford, I took a chance in acquiring the company while knowing virtually nothing about it, but knowing that the (bargain) price I paid justified this with a huge potential upside.*

[6]

The Perfect Partner

| Bill and Joyce Cummings at 23 Cherry Street, Medford, 1966

DESPITE THE FINANCIAL SUCCESS of Old Medford Foods, the best thing by far about that great venture was meeting my future wife in 1965. I was making a sales call at Massachusetts Eye and Ear Infirmary, where Joyce Jutkins was the hospital dietitian. She was not far removed from her days at the University of Alabama and her subsequent dietetic internship at Massachusetts General Hospital. I was smitten the first time we met.

    I had noticed and talked with Joyce in mid-1965, the same day I met with her boss, Mass. Eye and Ear's longtime food-service director, Herb Kirshnit, and driving away I could not get her out of my mind. After reaching my office I called Herb and when he told me that Joyce was not involved with anyone, I went back into Boston to ask her out that same evening, directly after work. She said, "yes."

I had never dated a southern woman before, and in those days, all of the Miss America winners seemed to come from Alabama and Mississippi. My days were so much sweeter after I got to know Joyce. And yes, the hospital did start ordering more Old Medford (although Joyce has vigorously denied any involvement).

Claiming that I "tricked her" into going out, Joyce still jokingly fusses at me occasionally for having taken her that night to a fancy grand-opening party at Boston's then brand-new Prudential Center. It seems that her white uniform was not at all what she would have imagined wearing to such an event. Suffice it to say, Joyce did not take off her coat, and we did not stay long, but things went exceedingly well from then on. Fifty years later, we still exchanged Christmas cards with Herb and Charlotte Kirshnit.

When Joyce first asked me, "How come you're not married?" I was slow to answer. For her part, she was ready, but perhaps other guys were scared off by her notion that she had always wanted to have six children—"all boys, please." I was not necessarily opposed to the idea of marriage or a large family, but I had been focusing much more on remaining single than on family size. Early on, we talked with some specificity about work-life balance regarding my career, setting the tone for a lifetime of open and frank discussion.

In time, we also had conversations exploring our respective attitudes about things like race and religion. The talks about race were in light of Joyce's strong southern background and all the racist turmoil right at that time especially in her hometown of Birmingham, Alabama. We tested each other's viewpoints on this issue a few times and found complete compatibility, and we always have since. Joyce's thoughts much more closely mirrored those of my Boston-area friends than those of some of her hometown acquaintances.

> UNLIKE THE MAJORITY OF MEN I knew, my identity gradually became closely intertwined with my newly launched entrepreneurial career, even if I did not yet have any idea what that career would eventually be or where it might take us. Serious entrepreneurs seldom feel satisfied working "normal" hours, and I was convinced that drive, determination, and sheer willpower will overcome almost any obstacle. Entrepreneurs thrive on challenges, problem solving, and new ideas, and they tend to love their work.

As success blossoms, there is tonic-like satisfaction that helps justify all the extra efforts of entrepreneurship. While many others may find the pressure stressful, serial entrepreneurs I know thrive on it, sometimes wondering why they enjoy their work so much.

Before Joyce and I married, my Old Medford salary was $25 per week. Living with my parents on Cherry Street did not suggest much of a career perhaps, but I was putting everything possible into this tiny fruit punch factory and enjoying considerable great sales gains each month. I did not believe that this particular new business was my lifetime career, but it had plenty of potential to keep me plugging.

With no demonstrated career certainty, we married in 1966, when Joyce was twenty-five and I was twenty-nine. Before then, I had agonized for years over choosing the right partner, but now I certainly knew she was the one. As I write this paragraph in August 2016, we have just returned from celebrating our fiftieth anniversary in Venice, Italy; and on the Dalmatian Coast of Croatia; and in Montenegro.

It is so important to have a partner's "buy-in" well before marriage. Choosing the right person to share both the highs and lows of a family business has to be one of life's greatest challenges for people with that career path. Joyce has always been that supportive partner for me. New and thinly financed companies will rarely be successful without extraordinary personal commitment, and Joyce understood that I would put much more energy than most people into my work, while also being fully committed to her.

Still, I was extremely lucky that she was so tolerant of her busy husband and that she readily took primary responsibility for the daily activities of raising our four (not six) children—two boys, two girls. The allegiance of our marriage grew stronger still through our mutual interest in community service and involvement, which would truly blossom much later.

Joyce had been a food and nutrition major at the University of Alabama, Tuscaloosa, during some of that school's early sports glory in the Bear Bryant and Joe Namath era. In college, she was active with Phi Mu, a national women's sorority, and she excelled academically. She was also heavily involved in Girl Scouts and served as head swimming instructor and waterfront director at an Alabama Girl Scout summer camp. In her senior year at University of Alabama, Joyce completed a student internship at Walter Reed Army Hospital in Washington, D.C., and, after graduating from Alabama in 1962, went on to her American Dietetic Association internship at MGH in Boston.

Joyce eventually gave up her daily train commute to Boston in order to raise our family, and we soon had three of our four children. Daniel, Kevin, and Marilyn were born in 1967, 1968, and 1969, all at Winchester Hospital.

Looking back, Joyce still regards the "three under three" stage with considerable disdain. Nevertheless, she showed uncommon patience with our children and my work life, despite the full house.

We have not had a storybook marriage every single week throughout the last half-century, nor should anyone expect that. By constantly learning and understanding more about each other, however, we have developed our own deep, enduring romance built on ever-growing love and respect. We have somehow survived all the pressures I probably still bring to our life together, and even when I turned eighty we still had every hope for a couple of perhaps even better decades yet to come. But just in case, we rarely go to bed or wake up in the morning without telling each other, "I love you."

> After noting how important Joyce has been to me and how critical her ongoing attitude toward the company and Cummings Foundation is, I would be greatly remiss to not recognize how extraordinarily important every management spouse can be within any organization.

AFTER WE SOLIDIFIED the Harvard account, our team's most common sales pitches usually sounded something like: "We would not begin to suggest that you should like our program just because someone else is using it, Mr. Jones. At the same time, I can tell you that this is exactly the same product and the same dispensing system now installed in every dining room at Harvard, MIT, and Tufts." The implied endorsement resonated well with other colleges, and we used it to great advantage, especially because so many of the local-area school food-service managers shared ideas with one another. Mentioning our highly successful programs in other prestigious local universities was extremely influential with prospective clients.

Leapfrogging personal referrals from existing accounts to other prospects was Old Medford's principal means of growth. We never purchased any media advertising, relying instead solely on personal contact and word of mouth. After we received an unsolicited endorsement from the home office of Saga Food Service of Menlo Park, California, then one of the top college and university food-service management firms in the country, we were really off and running.

FOR DECADES, I have regularly delegated many of the most difficult decisions to trusted colleagues. If we have carefully considered the reasons to resolve an issue one way or the other and have not seen a compelling reason to decide either way, I will almost always invite a colleague to make the final call.

If the colleague is going to bear responsibility for carrying out such a decision, then let it be his or hers from the start. The key thought is that decisions can often be called in either direction with no net difference. In those situations, delaying or waffling about a decision will often be the worst thing.

> Most companies have clear personalities, just as people do, but the personalities of true entrepreneurial companies are often indistinguishable from the personalities and styles of the individuals who founded them. Several things have characterized the essence of my business style from well before the start of Old Medford Foods: precise writing, strong negotiating, and ever-present frugality. None of these are specific to any one firm or industry, but they should be thought of as indispensable for any entrepreneurial business.

The personality, motivation, and reputation of the founder or founders are crucial to the success of a business. Their personal skills and dedication will often outweigh all else. It is also essential that an entrepreneur have a broad understanding of all the key positions in the firm, so that incompetence masking as sound professional advice is easily spotted.

I am more than a little bothered when information offered by a staff lawyer or accountant contains errors so obvious that they jump out even at me. Thereafter, I may pay particular attention to that person's work and find myself often more than a little disappointed if the shoddy thinking or careless work reappears. Usually then there will be serious consequences for that professional person's future with the firm. Résumé credentials can never be assumed to mean what we might like to think they should mean. Always hire the person, not the résumé.

I have repeatedly learned how important it is to recognize that few business owners know all the answers and that fewer still can run their businesses alone. At the same time, the business owner must know and understand the needs of the business enough to fully recognize which key staff members are competent enough at their respective roles to be implicitly relied upon. I have often thought of my business interests as being like a baseball team's. I must be able to accurately assess the ability of every position player on the team, and be able to either personally jump into, or at least fully understand, every position.

AS A RESULT of Old Medford's exponential sales growth within the first two years or so, the company soon needed larger manufacturing space and more office quarters, even if we had to give up paying our $50-per-month rent for 54 Fulton Street. Additionally, the "funny little business" located behind two old houses that had been there since well before many of its older neighbors were even born was increasingly perceived as a neighborhood nuisance. Our rapidly growing truck traffic on Fulton Street was also problematic.

In February 1966, we began searching for a new home for Old Medford. Ironically, considering my profession today, it never occurred to me to explore leasing rather than buying. We eventually purchased a beat-up six thousand-square-foot concrete-block building on one acre of land at 10 Henshaw Street in Woburn, for which we paid $60,000. Five miles north of Fulton Street, the new location was also just off Interstate Route 93 but still inside Route 128, metropolitan Boston's well-known circumferential highway.

Old Medford's new concrete home was only forty years old. After clearing everything out, we engaged Telfer Construction Company of Salem Street, Medford, to expand and remake it to suit our needs. The price for the needed construction was about $80,000. Many years earlier, Elmer Telfer had been one of my regular Salem Street window-washing customers, and his daughter Nancy was a classmate at Medford High School. Not by coincidence, from the earliest beginnings of my career as an entrepreneur I have always tried to patronize businesses owned and run by qualified people we know and with whom we have had other interactions. I have a strong sense of give-and-take, and mutual loyalty has been a significant factor in our success.

After substantial planning and a little waiting for the right time, Doug Stephens, another Phi Sigma Kappa fraternity brother, joined Old Medford as treasurer, in August 1966, just before we moved the business to Woburn. Also, a retired U.S. Navy chief petty officer joined us as a full-time warehouse shipper. As he learned the production side of the business, this shipper soon transitioned and completely took over the day-to-day product manufacturing as volume steadily grew. By then, Steve Collins, Fred McCauley, and Don MacEachern were the sales force, and all three of them, plus Doug, remained for as long as I owned the firm. Fred and Doug later worked with me at Cummings Properties for many years, as well, and Fred's son, Paul, still does.

> Few things are more vital in business than employee satisfaction and continuity. Well-trained, experienced employees don't appear anywhere on the balance sheet, but their value in a properly run organization is often far greater than managers realize. Not everyone will be a superstar or future leader, but the core strength of a firm is the high-quality workers who get the job done, day in and day out, year after year. Failure to properly recognize the value of the firm's staff at all levels can be extremely damaging.

Jobs that can be tailor-made for certain workers often pay big dividends. Businesses are far more productive when they can find and feature people's strengths. It is the job of managers to carefully observe new workers and form opinions about where they will best function. Assigning work to people who enjoy doing it well

Fred McCauley, the company's first sales associate, sampling Old Medford at a Restaurant Association event, 1967

will exponentially improve the quality of the work. If managers keep employees busy enough working with their strengths, many weaknesses can be overlooked. This is one more area where flexibility and accommodation in the workplace can be to everyone's advantage.

An important corollary to knowing others' strengths is for managers to know their own strengths and weaknesses, and then capitalize on their strong points. For example, my mind works quite nimbly. I am extremely comfortable bouncing among multiple issues simultaneously. I also tend to assess the issues and make generally good decisions quickly. I am equally as fast to change direction when new information is introduced. On the down side, Joyce hates it when she catches me tinkering with our family plans or other social plans as they progress. She tends to be extremely thorough and beautifully organized and never appreciates my last-minute "interfering."

In addition to the stainless steel liquid-sugar storage tank we moved from Fulton Street, we now had a new five thousand-gallon heated tank to store much more viscous high-fructose corn syrup. We mixed this sweetener at a 50–50 ratio with liquid cane sugar from Domino, a recommended blend to achieve our best drink taste and "mouth feel," while still yielding significant cost savings.

With the new plant open and two liquid-sweetener systems up and running, Old Medford's production capacity immediately quintupled over our former forty thousand-cases-per-year capacity at Fulton Street. The new facility could comfortably yield about 210,000 cases per year. Though the new plant was by no means a modern marvel, it was no longer a quaint backyard cottage industry, either. Without serious changes, we could easily have increased our volume to about $5 million in today's dollars, or $15 million with automated equipment, if there had been that much demand.

With ongoing changes, we achieved great savings with no detectable difference in product flavor or mouth feel, according to our unsophisticated taste testers. There was nothing scientific or democratic about the way I handled product development, but it worked at Old Medford. We carefully adjusted all our ingredient labels to reflect any product changes and prepared staff members on how to best handle anticipated questions about revised recipes and processes. We heard so few comments and no complaints or concerns whatsoever from customers.

New accounts soon started coming in unsolicited, and our sales group was both delighted and excited. Much of this business resulted from colleges served by one of our several large food-services management companies referring us to other colleges within the same management group or geographic area. It was highly satisfying to challenge the production team to keep up, especially with all the fast-paced process changes being pushed through as we learned more and more about the business. We fell into the college food-service field at a propitious time and rode beautifully with the trend.

ONE DILEMMA WE faced at Old Medford, with our growing geographic spread, was how to accommodate the fast-rising shipping costs. We considered increasing our price for the more distant clients, or making the product more concentrated, perhaps, say a ten-to-one rather than five-to-one concentration.

Instead, within a year of relocating to Woburn, we developed a completely new sugar-free product, which we first used exclusively for all of our new clients outside New England. We followed all required labeling requirements, of course, including the mandatory message that the product was "sugar-free" and contained non-nutritive artificial sweeteners. We did not, however, otherwise differentiate between the two versions. Our profit margin was noteworthy before, but with the entirely sugar-free product, the cost savings were extraordinary.

> The contents cost for some flavors with all non-nutritive artificial sweeteners was less than half the contents cost than the all-sugar variety, but once again there was simply no reason to reduce the price. Any possible competitors continued to use all sugar.

We, on the other hand, however, soon converted all of our production to the sugar-free variety, and because of its significantly reduced product cost it was now practical to travel even farther for business—even to the Caribbean. Although we necessarily had less direct contact with our three large Puerto Rican colleges, it took no arm-twisting to convince Fred and Don to make occasional winter visits there. Joyce and I even managed to work in a long weekend around some customer calls there in 1970, for some rare vacation days alone. It did seem counterintuitive, however, for us to be shipping fruit punch from Boston to tropical Puerto Rico, though we were of course delighted with Old Medford's expanding reach.

We liberally referenced our "delicious sugar-free fruit beverage bases," but never spoke of the recipes as being "new and improved" or anything like that. We didn't hide anything, but neither did we call attention to what we had changed. We also referenced the "empty calories" of other fruit drinks and were as matter-of-fact as possible. As with the situation a year or so earlier when we blended the cane and high-fructose corn syrups, we never heard any complaints at all. This move to a sugar-free product proved successful beyond our wildest dreams, and the sugar-free version was soon well received across all accounts. Our later good friend, famed Harvard nutritionist Jean Mayer, who eventually became the tenth president of Tufts University, was unknowingly helpful to us at that time as one of the early and most vocal advocates for reducing consumption of sugar-sweetened beverages. Today there seems to be near-unanimous condemnation of sugar-sweetened colas and other carbonated drinks, but non-carbonated drinks like the sugar-sweetened Old Medford would deserve almost as much bad press.

When I sold the drink business in 1970 to Green Textile Associates, Inc., it signed a five-year market-rate lease for the building at 10 Henshaw Street to go along with the sale. The firm that Llewellyn Farnsworth handed over to me in 1964 for $4,000 yielded more than $2 million in today's dollars, and that was at a time when having cash to bankroll a real estate business really meant something. These sale proceeds from Old Medford made an enormous difference as I started in the next—and quite different—chapter of my early business career.

While it was not always customary for business owners to personally guarantee debts, I always did so and still would, although no one asks anymore. That is just the way we have always managed our finances. I always wanted every creditor or lender to be comfortable giving us the lowest selling price or interest rate because of the certainty of payment. Having a personal relationship with a bank and its manager can also be highly valuable, and any relationship based on personal trust must be treated as different from all others.

Good business people will be innovators, but even more importantly, they should be opportunists. First, they will see the opportunity to make something better or to make it less expensively, and then they will innovate the best way to accomplish this goal. They will continue to always think about what something costs before they make decisions to buy. They will think about how to get large potential purchases at a better price, and they will hate getting "taken."

I soon arranged our first bank mortgage on the then fully leased Old Medford plant at 10 Henshaw Street. The mortgage proceeds, plus the payout from Old Medford, provided us with extremely valuable working capital at a time when market interest rates were going sky high. That increased capital-in-hand enabled us to always avoid the hassle and time-consuming process of finding construction financing for our typically all-speculative construction. Doug Stephens initially stayed with Old Medford, but eventually, he returned to work closely with me for another quarter century in my soon-to-emerge commercial real estate development firm.

- *Inherently risky, serious entrepreneurship is not for the cautious or faint-hearted. To be successful in business, it may be necessary to gamble a bit, as we did so many times while bidding for building the courthouse, buying Choate Hospital, opening a three hundred-seat restaurant, and flipping a $300,000 coin. Dozens and dozens of times, we have purchased existing commercial buildings, or we have constructed brand-new buildings, with not even a hint of who their clients might be. Bear in mind, however, that none of these were reckless gambles made without thought. Rather they were calculated risks that we could afford to lose if things did not go our way.*

- *Creative people will move quickly in capitalizing on the unexpected. They recognize that "getting lucky" is, most importantly, recognizing when they have been, and then taking advantage of it. Creative people in management make things happen.*

- *A huge advantage to small private companies without outside investors is the ability to avoid a focus on short-term profitability in favor of long-term equity.*

- *Many people, maybe most, don't want a career… they just want a good job, a fair paycheck, and a responsible family life. The best companies will find ways for most employees to achieve these goals.*

- *Managers' jobs begin in adversity. They handle the exceptions.*

[7]

Cummings Properties Emerges

THE REAL FOUNDING date of what, in time, became Cummings Properties is 1969. The first property I built then for rental purposes was the well-located concrete-block structure directly north of Old Medford on the same one-acre lot. We engaged a Woburn general contractor to build this two-story addition at 12–14 Henshaw Street. At the time, I thought of it simply as an opportunity to invest in a one-off building to lease to others, and it never occurred to me that I was laying plans for a new career that would quickly supplant our fruit-juice syrup business. Our first client leased the lower 7,500-square-foot warehouse at a lease rate of a $1.90 per square foot/per year. We leased the unfinished upper floor with no office space for $1.50 per square foot/per year.

We already owned the needed land for this additional fifteen thousand square feet, for which there would likely never have been any use in connection with Old Medford. Additionally, the existing utilities were either readily available or already of sufficient size. The necessary site work also had been almost all completed in connection with our original cleanup of the property. The economics of this kind of investment, then, were extraordinarily good. We were taking advantage of what for the next fifty years I would continue to call free extra "buildability" that came with the deed. Identifying such additional construction potential from newly acquired properties became a regular occurrence in the new commercial real estate business that was about to take shape.

After promptly and profitably leasing this newly constructed addition, we purchased an adjacent two-and-a-half-acre vacant parcel on the south side of the Old Medford building for $90,000 in cash. If this vacant field next to Old Medford had not become available when it did, our foray into property development would likely have started and ended with that single addition at 12–14 Henshaw Street. Instead, we built out 2–8 Henshaw Street, in three phases, as our first from-the-ground-up building.

Opportunistic in every sense of the word, top businesses, like athletic teams, must be aggressive enough to make things happen. Only then are they capable of converting opportunities into success. Overall awareness and the ability to react quickly to opportunities are often characteristics of the best teams in business as well as in sports. Disappointingly, many athletes in their later working years appear to have no idea how to carry over the same competitive principles to a business setting.

Sometimes good business people will try to take advantage of opportunities that are not at all in their best interest, as I did in late 1969 by purchasing the Gift Boutique card shop, now a Starbucks, at 542 Main Street in Winchester. That was the first real business "mistake" I recall making. We bought and then finally sold it all within three months, but the purchase price was low enough that we escaped without any damage. There was a large lesson there, however, about business owners not diluting their attention with extraneous enterprises, like a gift shop. There is a lot to be said for "minding one's own knitting."

After deciding that we wanted no part of retailing, and that we really enjoyed building and leasing commercial real estate, we then purchased twenty prime acres on Washington Street in Woburn, and we started building what is now Cummings Park. During those first years, each of the buildings was laid out and designed on Joyce's dining

| *Joyce with Patricia, Daniel, Kevin, and Marilyn, 1976*

room table at 23 Ash Hill Road, Reading, where our growing family lived from mid-1967 through November 1970. Drawn with not much more than a $10 drawing board, a couple of plastic triangles, and a yardstick, my designs were simple but functional enough to get by. The Cummings Park land cost was $26,000 per acre.

At about this same time, notwithstanding Joyce's reluctance to leave Reading, we made an offer on a house we both really liked at 2 Mayflower Road, Winchester, but it was a low, low offer. It was low enough that the seller's broker, who later became a good friend, was more than a little annoyed. The home had everything we wanted, plus a sizable swimming pool that we had yet to appreciate. On the other hand, the lot was unkempt and overgrown, the pool water was a murky brown, and the shrubbery looked as though it had suffered for many years. It became a standoff with the seller for several months, and Joyce would not let me raise the offer. When the broker eventually called to tell Joyce, "You have won," she cried for having to leave Reading.

Sandy Thompson, Joyce Cummings, and Joyce's Co-chair of the Fair, Dennis Clarke's mother, Nancy Clarke

We already had a few roots in Winchester, including three Winchester Hospital births by then, and several friends in town, and Joyce soon accepted that Winchester would be delightful. One of Winchester's major community events there is the En Ka Street Fair, operated by a women's service organization called the En Ka Society, founded in 1902. We had taken our kids to this fair twice before we moved to town, and we all already liked it. *Aha*, I thought. Joyce might become involved in the En Ka Society, because she is such a well-organized, type-A person. While she never really became active in my business, this venerable service organization could be a great way for her to meet interesting people. Joyce initially laughed at me for what she clearly took as an almost outrageous suggestion.

By the time our children were at Winchester High School, however, Joyce was co-chair of the En Ka Fair. And after serving in many other roles with En Ka, she was elected president of the several-hundred-member organization in 1990 and later served for six years as the society's historian. Joyce's En Ka work turned out to be one of her most cherished activities, and she has so many excellent memories from her almost forty years of service. We have had and continue to have a marvelous life together in Winchester and are still heavily involved, both individually and together, in many aspects of the community.

IN THOSE EARLY days of what grew to become Cummings Properties, the company avoided any construction that required municipal zoning variances or special permits. That was true of the Henshaw Street buildings and also of our two much larger Cummings Park developments on either side of Washington Street. There, we purchased the twenty-one-acre commercial lot from Kenneth Anderson in April 1971 at what even then was a remarkably low price of a half-million dollars. By way of comparison, a twelve-acre parcel on South Boston's undeveloped waterfront reportedly sold in 2019 for $300 million, or about $25 *million* per acre, versus our $26,000 per acre.

Aerial view of Cummings Properties' first significant development, Cummings Park, a 340,000-square-foot mixed-use development in Woburn at the junction of Interstates 93 and 95

With its great highway location and well-suited zoning, our large and mostly level Cummings Park lot could not have been much better or easier to develop. And over the next two years, we improved that parcel with three highly similar single-story, multiple-occupancy buildings designed for office, research and development (R&D), and distribution space.

It was really quite remarkable how quickly Cummings Properties emerged as a significant factor in the north suburban Boston real estate market. Although I never specifically planned it that way, the business fed upon itself. We routinely took almost no cash out of the business, preferring to reinvest all that we could. Our equity was always 100 percent, and we could always borrow easily against a recently completed building as needed, with minimal red tape at local banks.

Most important of all, there was never a time when we even talked with anyone about construction lending. Such borrowing is probably the most common method by which local construction projects are funded, but I would not even know how to go about it. Financial independence has always been central to all Cummings construction. By never having a need for any kind of private financing, we saved huge amounts of time, as well as cash, on every building we built. We have the added benefit of not having to prepare the *ad nauseam* cost documentation normally required to satisfy lenders. Never having to deal with things such as lenders' inspections and architects' documentation in order to obtain funds to pay our bills allowed us to focus solely on building. With no outside investors or unwarranted city interference, we were able to move and change plans and strategies with barely a nod to anyone, as long as whatever we did met all codes.

We also process tasks on an accelerated basis from a design perspective. Our colleagues, working together, need to be free to make frequent changes as we go along with any project. Avoiding redundant layers of regulatory oversight from financial partners is a true blessing in any building or construction activity. We have also been exceedingly fortunate in that city inspectors came to know we would never take shortcuts with building code issues. In most towns, they have been relaxed and helpful in expediting our plans. In Woburn, they also have been acutely aware of our strong local hiring policy, and that we have generated huge increases in the city's tax base.

While we obviously know the cost of all the components as we carefully negotiate them, we never even bother to estimate the total cost of a prospective new building for decision-making needs. Partly, this is because our buildings have never involved anyone else's fractional ownership. But also, it has always been my philosophy that the right answer about whether or not to build was never determined by the project cost. Our costs were extraordinarily low, especially because our "soft" pre-construction costs were always so low. Clearly, we are in a much different position than if we were doing construction work for a third-party payer, who would certainly need to have a clear understanding of what the exact project cost would be before making any commitments.

Instead, we will typically review any newly proposed project, considering the needs it will fill and how efficiently we can build it—if indeed we do want to build it. We carefully track all capital and maintenance expenses for tax purposes, but the construction costs are never featured or discussed, even among the company's senior management team. There is simply no need for us to know in advance how much new structures will cost to build or remodel, because we know we can always secure competitive pricing for components and labor, and the buildings are always profitable. Today, the only number we think about is how much after-tax income we can provide to Cummings Foundation.

FROM THE BEGINNING, ours has been an extremely vertical business model. Relying, for instance, on the extraordinary talent of our in-house engineering, design, and purchasing professionals, and a marvelous team of supporting contractors of all sorts, we will carefully shop every phase of the development to obtain the best prices as we go along, and then we just do it.

We have our own large staff of building tradespeople, along with our business professionals. With three hundred sixty or so full-time, year-round staff members at Cummings Properties, we have a fascinating array of mechanics and technicians, including, for instance, dozens each of electricians, plumbers, carpenters, and maintenance technicians, plus painters and roofers and at least sixty grounds workers. Our in-house legal team includes four attorneys, while about a dozen other lawyers fill other professional positions. For the company's first twenty years, and especially for active construction projects, I was personally at every building site almost every day. When there was site-work going on with excavators, trucks, and bulldozers, I was there—all day, every day, and always with my boots on.

> I was not one bit distressed when a *Boston Globe* reporter once described Cummings Park as "plain vanilla" buildings that were "very neat and very full." They were neat, and they *were* full, and so "plain vanilla" was okay with me. All those early structures were built in a solid but economical manner, at a cost averaging under $18 or $19 per square foot, at a time when space was leasing at a gross rate of $2 or so per square foot. The three single-story flex buildings at Cummings Park, totaling 340,000 square feet, were completed in 1972.

While fast project turnaround speed results in part from the use of a somewhat standard palette of materials, we also have the ability to fully customize build-outs to meet almost any client requirement. Cummings has designed and built dozens of specialized facilities, including Tempest rooms, clean rooms, TV studios, biotech labs, hospital operating rooms, and complete medical centers, as well as many thousands of office, retail, warehouse, and R&D spaces. Over more than forty-five years, we have accommodated multiple clients that have leased more than one hundred thousand square feet, as well as hundreds of office spaces as small as a few hundred square feet. Residential uses have never been a major factor, but altogether we presently operate some six hundred residential units.

By October 1973, all three Cummings Park buildings, plus the first of six major buildings in what later became West Cummings Park, were completed—a total of a half-million square feet of space. By the end of the year, all of it was leased.

THROUGH THE 1970s, I was constantly reading and borrowing from other firms' commercial lease forms. I never once even considered engaging any attorney about details of what our lease should look like. Since I was constantly talking and negotiating leases with attorneys of prospective clients, I used what I had learned from those conversations to develop a better and greatly streamlined printed lease document.

Long before I ever became aware of any other commercial lease that included a cost of living escalation, Cummings Properties added such a provision in our lease, near the top of every lease we executed. Again, this was ten or twelve years before we began to see them regularly in most other firms' leases. This clause alone has surely provided a net gain of many millions of dollars of direct cumulative benefits over a period of four decades now.

Other New England firms began inserting cost of living clauses especially after the prime rate of interest was reported at 21 percent after major banks across the country jumped the rate by a full one percent on December 16, 1980. Such escalation clauses can always be adjusted for tenant planning purposes so that there is a set maximum amount of rent increase in each year of a lease, or on a cumulative basis, but most of the time the clause remains unchanged or perhaps its use is delayed for a year or two. An automatic lease extension clause we developed in 1985 seemed to become common in everyone else's commercial leases after the mid 90s.

Another extremely important aspect in creating Cummings Properties' business model was our developing a keen understanding of the fundamental aspects of business law as they pertain to commercial real estate. We all fully knew and understood its importance. Having first cobbled together our own pre-printed Standard Form Lease document, we then became highly adept at preparing even complicated versions of that Standard Form Lease to eventually suit the needs of thousands upon thousands of client firms.

Then there was an equally important need to establish an in-house legal staff, which today consists of our senior vice president/general counsel plus three other top full-time attorneys. Although the firm has always tried to be non-litigious, there are so many issues, mostly involving client financial failures, that do require court action, and these are so much better and more efficiently handled by our own in-house lawyers.

Dealing as they do with our short and straightforward document, and the convenience of frequently repeating fact patterns, our attorneys tend to be highly adept at handling all cases that arise. They seldom seem to require outside legal assistance when dealing with the typical landlord/tenant issues that continue to arise, but we have three times shepherded lease issues through as precedent-setting cases in Massachusetts' Supreme Judicial Court.

TWO YEARS AFTER we completed Cummings Park and 200 West Cummings Park, it was time to get going again in what continued to be a wonderful market for our eminently flexible multiple-occupancy buildings. During 1977 and 1978, we teamed up with the Woburn Redevelopment Authority and purchased many separate newly developed North Woburn lots on which we busily constructed another half-million square feet of floor space. Doug Stephens ran all our financial affairs, allowing me to spend the large majority of my time on the construction sites.

During the early 1970s, between getting buildings built and then filled with happy clients, I gradually adapted a Standard Commercial Lease form from somewhere to create our much shorter *Cummings Commercial Lease*. We proudly printed this up as four pages in small font on a single 8.5-inch-by-22-inch sheet, and we used it effectively for more than forty years each time we prepared a lease for a prospective new client. It wasn't until April 2017 that we finally abandoned that process in favor of computer-generated leases. In all of our thousands upon thousands of lease transactions, except for leases with the federal government and the commonwealth of Massachusetts, every lease is prepared on our standard form, with whatever negotiated changes might be necessary. Our evolving standard form lease as such, however, was reprinted at least fifty times over forty years—a thousand or two at a time.

Back in 1974, we were the first firm we knew of to include a cost-of-living escalation as a standard clause in virtually all of our leases, to keep lease rates in current dollars. Later, we also became adept at including an automatic extension provision in the large majority of all leases. Both practices produced extraordinarily good results. Many long-term clients have operated for *decades* under their original lease agreements.

Cummings Properties has always offered only full-service leases with gross rental terms, in virtually all cases including the cost of real estate taxes, snow removal, landscaping, structural and interior maintenance, and building insurance. Especially because all our leased properties are relatively close together geographically, it became practical to keep an ever-growing maintenance and construction staff. The members of that team tend to become really exceptional at doing whatever needs to be done. Communication among our field crews, the design team, property managers, and client firms happens smoothly, because they all see one another so frequently and their interest in meeting the client's need is so strong.

Despite building only speculatively during our early years, we somehow managed to lease every building we constructed almost as soon as each building was ready for occupancy. Relations with the city of Woburn remained exceedingly strong under Woburn's enormously respected late Mayor Thomas Higgins and its equally esteemed late building commissioner John Brophy, especially regarding permitting. And because many city functions in Woburn were so much more customer-friendly than they seemed to be in other communities, the ease of permitting helped us to build a large portfolio of taxable property in a short time. Indeed, the continuum of real estate taxes paid and the thousands of excellent new jobs provided in Woburn, decade after decade, has had an enormous impact. By calendar year 2019, we were paying more than $8 million annually in real estate taxes to Woburn alone.

AS IT GREW STEADILY, the company gradually learned how to build better, more efficient, and steadily lower-cost buildings. We had our own niche, which often included buying underutilized land with grossly neglected buildings. Most of the existing structures were highly adaptable commercial buildings, and the lots often included future buildability for substantial additional space. The early properties we acquired and built were virtually all multiple-occupancy speculative properties; none was ever pre-leased. As soon as one building was completed and in the process of being leased, we would find a place to build the next one.

Working southward from 200 West Cummings Park, we purchased a row of eight mostly single-story Washington Street houses. A former longtime Woburn teacher and real estate broker, Joe Crowley, worked comfortably with us for two years as a member of the Leasing Department. "They just gave me a bag full of money to buy up the whole row of small homes in the light-industrial zone," he said. "That's where they built the rest of West Cummings Park, on Washington Street."

Those homes earned a unique and extremely favorable federal tax treatment. Rather than tear down the homes we purchased, we moved seven of the eight homes to new lots a half-mile south, on a street off Washington Street that we created just for these homes (and named Marilyn Court, after our first daughter). By moving and upgrading the houses, we were able to allocate 60 percent of the sales price as a credit against the purchase price of the homes from their original owners, thus almost fully eliminating the non-depreciable basis for the West Cummings Park land. If we had demolished those eight homes instead of salvaging them, the entire purchase price would (by law) have been imputed to the cost of the land and would never have been one bit depreciable. It was a major coup.

All of our early buildings until then were one or two stories high, but then we learned how to build our first mid-rise structure, a six-story office building we called Tower Office Park. At the time, it did seem like a tower to us. We subsequently built four more six-story structures in quick succession, directly across Washington Street at West Cummings Park where the row of homes had been. The four new buildings there were almost identical to one another, and each contained about 180,000 square feet.

In every business I have owned, my employment goal was to first seek capable colleagues from among people we knew or knew of. We were careful not to poach from other companies or to solicit people who already had jobs, but when I knew a friend or acquaintance was looking for a job, I was happy to match him or her to an open position at Old Medford or Cummings Properties or, later, at our *Woburn Advocate* newspaper. Relationships are so important.

Surrounding myself with trusted people has always allowed me to coach them and help to hone their skills to use over and over again. That approach so often greatly improved their confidence and initiative, and their value to the firm.

Today we have truly extraordinary corporate longevity. Our treasurer, Doug Stephens, who had been with me since starting at Simonson Company in August 1966, and Steve Frohn, who joined Cummings Properties in the late

The first management group of Cummings Properties: (shown left to right) Fred Wilbur, Doug Stephens, Dennis McClay, Dot Cummings, Bill Cummings, and bookkeeper Margaret Connor

1970s, allowed me to focus completely on land acquisition and construction, particularly the site work, which I have always enjoyed so much.

Real estate management combines elements of both art and science, and Cummings Properties excels at both. As an art form, property management is a people business, one of listening closely and responding definitively and promptly to client needs. Cummings Properties' real estate professionals at all levels use their experience and resources to fully address both elements. And no one is too important—or too junior—to be involved in any issue that may arise. All phones are still routinely answered with a live, personal presence, and I have a real fetish requiring that no one's phone calls, including mine, ever be screened.

The amenities offered at a major development are also extremely important. Good highway access and public transportation are vital, as are nearby food services, day care, fitness and exercise facilities, and well-kept, nicely managed open areas. Our experienced maintenance and construction staff are able to deliver highly efficient and prompt building services in part because of proximity—the relative closeness of our properties helps us greatly in delivering excellent client services. That is another way Cummings Properties differs from many of the huge national and international real estate giants, business cartels, and real estate investment trusts that dominate most big-city markets.

MOST START-UP FIRMS will commonly need an owner or owners to work seventy- or eighty-hour weeks, or even more; this certainly applied in my new venture into real estate, but at least it was mostly me putting in those hours. When partnerships are involved in start-ups, it is the uneven contributions and work commitments of the partners, more than anything else, that has the greatest potential to introduce serious discord. Other than working with Don

Knox for our first Christmas tree business together, I have never had a formal business partnership with anyone. Perhaps that is why I have always felt so close to so many of our extraordinarily loyal and supportive senior team members.

> At Cummings Properties, one of our major early goals is to find out what good employees do best and then try to keep them busy doing that. Our once most-senior carpenter, Richard Irwin, liked to teach new carpenters the tricks of the trade. With his agreement, as he aged and grew less agile, we successfully made him a full-time mentor and job coach, and he continued working as our most highly-paid carpenter well into his seventies.

By the mid 1970s, I was becoming involved in the Woburn community. Because of my long-term interest in the city, I was delighted to become a director of what was then still the Woburn Boys Club, where I served for forty years (and still serve as an honorary director). As it turned out, my early Boys Club involvement paid huge dividends in an unexpected way with employee referrals from the club's executive director. He thought I was doing him favors, but it was the other way around.

In November 1976, Charles Gardner introduced me to George Holland in the first of what would be three such referrals. Before George became our first heavy-equipment operator, he had been one of the club's earliest "Boys of the Year." At the time Charlie made the introduction, George was a newly minted Marine Corps veteran. I hired him on the spot.

With forty-three years now of continuous service, as of 2020, George is the dean of Cummings Properties' entire three hundred sixty-person roster of active staff. At his thirty-year milestone, George received a ceremonial captain's chair and told me he was looking to start a new tradition by receiving a company *rocking* chair upon reaching his fortieth anniversary—as he recently did. Now, he said, he is eager to see what the company will do for him when he reaches his fifty-year mark.

| *George Holland with a super snowblower*

The thirty-year captain's chair award is named the Stephens Chair, in honor of Doug Stephens, the first colleague to earn one. Therefore—the rocking chair will hereafter be named the Holland Chair in George Holland's honor. On the actual anniversary of his fortieth year with the firm, however, George seemed stunned to receive not only a suitably engraved rocking chair, but also the keys to the company's first-ever brand-new backhoe, which had his name painted prominently on the door. Building relationships is *so* important.

George married Sue Ellen Martin, who, in November 1982, opened Little Folks School in West Cummings Park, our first children's preschool. After forty years, Little Folks is still an important client firm, as are a dozen other privately operated daycare centers that now lease space in various Cummings buildings. All three of the Holland daughters worked during school vacations in the Cummings Properties home office, and George and Sue Ellen's now-grown daughter Emily opened a personal-training studio at our TradeCenter 128 campus. The Hollands' involvement with Cummings Properties is now truly a family affair.

Charlie Gardner made a second employment referral in 1979. This time he recommended James "Jamie" McKeown, a Woburn native and a more recent Boy of the Year from the Woburn Boys Club. Jamie was a 1977 graduate of Salem State University who had just also earned a master's degree in school administration at the University of Vermont. But fortunately, for me anyway, he had started looking for a full-time public school teaching position in one of those "off" years, when there just weren't many teaching jobs available. So, instead, Jamie joined us for what turned out to be his only post-college employment.

In 1983, Charlie introduced us to a third long-tenured colleague. This time it was Charlie's own son, Kevin Gardner, who by 2019 had more than thirty-six years of service at Cummings Properties. Kevin takes great pride in ably assisting the administrative support team in the company's main office. Company records show an extraordinary history of employees with long tenures at the company. This is partially owing to our early practice of offering paid vacations, paid health coverage, 401(k) plans, and many other benefits at a time when this was an unusual practice for small construction-related firms.

❧ *As we built up the nascent Cummings Properties, familiar themes of constructive opportunism and attentive risk-taking remained prevalent in business decisions as well as hiring. Quickly bringing on people we knew (or knew of) to support the company's growth embodied both themes. Taking a risk on capable employment referrals is often justifiable (they are effectively "known quantities" that a trusted individual is willing to speak for), and the unique opportunity such hires present for all parties can translate into unusually strong professional relationships.*

❈ And, as with Old Medford, we continuously reinvested Cummings Properties' earnings with the goal of sustained growth. Entrepreneurs who opt for more proximate payouts (perhaps to announce "I've made it!" with expensive cars or houses) will often fetter their venture's long-term potential. We have also always made a point of investing in colleagues through mentorship. In addition to enhancing an employee's immediate abilities, this fosters trust, which, in turn, invites further mentorship, creating a highly positive feedback loop.

❈ Management must constantly optimize combinations of quality and cost.

❈ During my first year in the real estate business, I purchased an old GMC dump truck with a plow for $600. In 1970, I sold the first truck for $1,000 and bought a much larger one for $3,000—a 1949 Autocar diesel dump truck. To replace it with a brand new equivalent would cost more than $100,000 today, but the 1949 truck still runs during every major snowstorm. Seventy years later, this Autocar is still the most powerful snow vehicle among the sixty we operate!

1949 Autocar diesel dump truck

❈ In the building trades, the best construction deals usually come from the simplest, most easy-to-understand bulk orders, after architects and others have carefully reviewed the plans to eliminate as many non-standard sizes, cuts, colors, etc. If there are a few small details, it often works to ignore them until after the price has been set, and then try to get the details thrown in by the supplier or subcontractor at no additional cost.

❈ When you are doing a poor job and no one comments, it is often because others have given up on you.

[8]

So Many Lessons Learned

| Patricia, Marilyn, Daniel, Kevin, and Bill skiing at Zermatt, Switzerland, August 1981

ALTHOUGH JOYCE AND I had previously managed to take several international trips with our children, accompanied by one of our especially reliable high school babysitters, we took our first three-week, family-only trip to Europe in August 1981, when the kids were thirteen, twelve, ten, and six. We started out in Paris and then traveled to eastern France, Germany, Austria, and Switzerland. In Switzerland, we skied through the spectacular scenery in the Matterhorn area, where the greatest dangers were falling into open crevasses and getting a sunburn. Before the kids started off on their own, we managed a half-dozen big family trips abroad.

While sports in general have never been a significant part of my life, golf did become important to me after we moved to Winchester and joined the town's long-established Winchester Country Club. Neither Joyce nor I had played golf before, other than when I played a little on Tufts University's former six-hole on-campus golf course. We had come to know Winchester Country Club mostly for its great dining room. Later, however, what we cherished most was its intense sense of community and camaraderie, especially as golf became an important, if limited, part of our summers.

Golf, I think, offers an interesting comparison to business. Golfers, like business people, will always need to make corrective shots, gradually closing the distance to the hole on the putting green. In business, our own errors will often obstruct our best-laid plans, or obstacles may come in the form of someone else's errors or bad luck, or from circumstances over which no one has any control. These trying moments are some of the crucial times in any business when managers must address the problem and hit that next shot correctly, no matter how far off track the first shot may have gone. People who just hate to deal with problems and/or conflicts should probably not aspire to becoming entrepreneurs.

Our business interests were still highly centered in nearby Woburn, and we had little reason, it seemed, to change this. We worked closely with city officials and were often consulted, at least under Mayor Thomas Higgins and much later under Mayor Scott Galvin. City officials today would routinely request advice on construction issues with which we often had helpful engineering or building experience.

> This was also a period when I served on several local boards, including those of the then Woburn Boys Club, Tanners National Bank, and, briefly, Choate Hospital in Woburn, including one period when I was simultaneously also on the board of Winchester Hospital. I also served several years as a justice of the peace, an elected member and then chairman of the Winchester Planning Board, and ten years as a charter trustee of Tufts University. Business leaders have a responsibility to serve in appropriate community positions. Other formal roles included licensed real estate broker, licensed construction superintendent, and licensed Massachusetts auctioneer.

One of the greatest challenges any business owner eventually faces is that of learning to let go. But gradually, as more and more qualified people become involved, tasks must be moved from the founder's purview. Business leaders should look carefully at their own firms and determine who solves the problems. Who always seems to say the right things at just the right time? Who always listens carefully and *then* comes up with the right negotiated solutions? Who makes things happen?

WHEN JAMIE MCKEOWN started at Cummings, he was twenty-four years old and still quite unsure of himself about business issues. "Just a kid," I thought, "but extremely street-smart." And he was the kind of person everyone immediately liked, because he had such a genuinely congenial and unaffected manner. This was one reason he was so successful at Cummings, and in life.

Jamie grew up in a solid middle-class Woburn neighborhood within easy earshot of Interstate 95, then called Route 128. He once told me his proudest day ever as a kid was when he graduated from the "Goldfish" program at the Woburn Boys Club and got to swim in the deep end of the pool, "like the big kids."

One of Woburn's late chiefs of police, Leo McElhinney, was a founder of the Woburn Boys Club. When I hired Jamie in 1979, Leo told me he had first come to know a seven-year-old Jamie in 1964, and had watched him grow up as a club member. "Jamie always did his own thing, but he absolutely got along with everyone; even the cutups in the Club liked him, though he never joined with them," said Leo. "I remember watching one day when Jamie, as a teenage lifeguard, cajoled three of the tough kids into the swimming pool, and he somehow made them learn to swim, right then and there. It was just remarkable. One of the three was even older than Jamie was."

Initially, into the summer of 1979, Jamie worked at Cummings under Stephen Frohn, the company's first leasing manager. Steve was an especially talented salesperson, but he quit the firm to do general real estate brokerage, leaving an unexpected vacuum, which Jamie soon filled.

When I moved from manufacturing fruit-drink concentrates to constructing and managing real estate, I quickly became concerned about the importance of preparing and training others to genuinely understand the entire business, and to effectively keep all the parts functioning harmoniously. I foresaw one of these people emerging as a "right arm" in the short term, and perhaps even a well-prepared successor in the long run.

Rapidly coming into his own, Jamie soon began figuring into that long-term planning. Owing to his extraordinary people skills, his strong work ethic, and his determination to learn everything he possibly could about business, the two of us gradually developed a close mentoring relationship. Within a year, it was clear that he would be the successor I had been looking for almost since I had started the firm a decade earlier. He would become the perfect first person to succeed me as president, before one of my own four children might, I then hoped, someday step in to succeed him.

Jamie's office was next to mine, and when routine business calls still used to come quite regularly to me, Jamie could, and did, pick up his phone and quietly monitor any of my calls, learning from everything he was hearing. He also received copies of every letter I wrote, to learn from those as well. Soon, he was writing those letters and handling the most challenging calls.

As a business prospers, entrepreneurs must disengage more and more from the "do it myself" mentality or risk strangulation of the business. Once any company reaches a sufficient size, in-house specialists will begin to be needed to handle many of the diverse responsibilities. With my office located directly adjacent to the main leasing conference room, I am today still often tempted to walk in and help out, but I rarely succumb. It is best when all the vital functions of a business can be capably handled by those whose responsibility it is to complete them.

Once they have proven everything they need to prove about themselves, successful entrepreneurs should be even more thrilled with their colleagues' successes than with their own. A business has reached a truly strategic plateau when the management team is deep enough and committed enough to ensure the continuing viability of the business even in the event of the unplanned loss or disability of the founder. Creating that type of corporate security was always a major concern for me.

In short, no one should even think of starting a business without believing he or she will love every hard-working minute of it. Additionally, I never started any new business without soon surrounding myself with competent people whom I respected for their values, their dedication, and their integrity as much as for their intellect.

> WHEN I HAVE opportunities to coach people about the joys and perils of entrepreneurship, the concept of needing to be a resourceful problem-solver is near the top of my list. It is also totally foolish, it seems to me, for anyone to own or operate a business if the work itself and the sense of accomplishment are not always a major part of the reward.

Most people who think they want to open a business will start out with little or no concept of how much is involved in the mechanics of doing so. The whole process of withholding and paying taxes, providing insurance, obtaining licenses, writing policies, performing government reporting, and conforming to a vast array of applicable regulations can easily become overwhelming. The intricacies of hiring, evaluating, and compensating workers can frighten many aspiring business owners, too, especially when it comes to meeting payrolls. Owners need to train employees, retrain them, and certainly replace them, sometimes much more frequently than they would like.

PURCHASING, TOO, IS AN extraordinarily vital part of any business, and buyers must know how to purchase what they need without spending money foolishly. Too often I have heard people describe their purchasing policy by saying, "We just get three bids for everything we purchase," or some other simplistic nonsense. There is so much more to it than that. Equally ill-advised is thinking one should never go with the low bidder, "because that bidder perhaps didn't bid enough." Buyers must recognize that a supplier's bid will often have much less to do with the sellers' cost than it does with what the bidder thinks he or she can get. And sometimes if a low bidder honestly bids too little, it may even be reasonable to help that supplier to be successful.

> Especially when it comes to purchasing things such as building or construction components, or whole buildings for that matter, there is a real art to buying at the right price. And just as anyone selling a product or service has a right to achieve as high a selling price as possible, so also does the buyer have the right to purchase the product or service at the lowest price. But the seller, of course, has no obligation whatsoever to easily give up his or her best price. Rather, the purchaser will usually need to actively negotiate and coax out that best price.

Getting back to the one-dimensional concept of simultaneously "seeking three quotes," when one is not dealing with a sealed-bid situation, there is nothing wrong with anyone using information from the first bid to help the next bidder get to a lower number. Once we have a quote in hand, say for $120,000 to install a new roof, our buyer might well advise bidder number two to not even type out any bid if he cannot beat, say, $110,000. It is amazing how rapidly and how far bids will drop when they are managed or even just allowed to "ripen." When there are significant value purchases to be made, buyers can use the bidding process to effectively set up "an auction" for the work, and there is absolutely nothing unethical about the process.

When making substantial purchases, we routinely use the concept of "ripening" the bids. If there are a half-dozen good prospective bidders for a job we need done, a piece of equipment we need to purchase, or an order of construction supplies, we routinely seek quotes from the first one or two and wait for those bids before we call two more bidders and seek lower quotes from them. A buyer may well wait until after the third and fourth quotes are received before then going to the last bidders on the list, knowing much more about the market by then.

Cost control must be an every day constant—there may be no greater direct influence on the profitability (or even the viability) of any enterprise. This especially applies to any kind of a production business, such as Old Medford, where reducing *the cost* of any product sold will have a far greater benefit than increasing its selling price. Assuming product quality is maintained, all of the cost reduction goes directly to the company's bottom line. Simply raising the selling price of a product is not nearly as beneficial, as a significant part of that increase may need to be shared with distributors and/or retailers. Additionally, inflating the price will usually also negatively affect how many consumers ultimately place the product in their shopping carts.

One thing that greatly helps Cummings Properties achieve consistently low quotes is that we have been buying so many of the same products and services for decades, and all of our regular suppliers know that we go out of our way to never quibble, or make frivolous claims, and we always pay everyone promptly. It is in our best interest to make sure sellers are convinced of these things *before* they start working with us, lest they add to their quote to offset the risk of incurring collection expenses, or worse, of perhaps not getting paid at all. It is uncanny how often subcontractors who have worked extensively with us have then taken on work elsewhere and been badly burned, especially by not getting promptly paid. Too many unscrupulous developer types get away with cheating subcontractors or suppliers in that manner all too often. How sickening it was to sometimes hear some building owners bragging about how skillfully they got away with cheating suppliers and investors.

Work to save money on every purchase, but then build a reputation for unusually prompt payment and abundantly fair treatment of suppliers. We also seek to treat *all* customers, suppliers, and clients with the utmost courtesy and respect. I have worked with thousands of suppliers and subcontractors over the last fifty years, and we have *never* gone to court with anyone for non-payment of any debt or for non-performance, nor has any business we have ever owned.

MANAGERS MUST DEAL with the exceptions. Managers must minimize losses when plans go awry. It is also crucial that executives analyze what caused failures so they can avoid making similar mistakes in the future. Managers who treat problems as challenges can thrive in dealing with them. They will teach others about what went wrong and help their colleagues see the lessons in the challenges. It will always be that extra effort—that makes the difference.

Business owners must be abundantly careful about establishing and enforcing company policies governing all aspects of their business. This is a hugely important aspect of entrepreneurship, and one that is frequently overlooked when new businesses are launched. One of Cummings Properties' important early policies was that, when dealing with large firms, or even small branches of national or sometimes worldwide firms, we would expect diligent compliance with all lease terms. For small businesses, on the other hand, we routinely try to take a far softer approach, especially regarding collection efforts in the event of a business default, at least when a defaulting client is being honest and straightforward in his or her dealings with our staff.

Those same executives who enjoy dealing with challenges will instinctively look to identify and solve small problems before they grow into larger issues. A competent manager always must be concerned with not leaving problems to fester. When things are going well, a manager's job is, of course, much easier, but good leaders will really shine in adversity. Yes, managers handle the exceptions, and they need to spend far more time spotting and resolving problems than they do gloating over the latest successes.

With institutions, as in business, incalculable money, time, and effort are thrown away by relying on inaccurate or misrepresented "facts." Top management in any organization must have the intuitive sense to know when it is presented with puffed-up or misinterpreted information as facts. Management must instead be sure that the information it utilizes is absolutely reliable, and that solid data, not some third party's suppositions, form the basis for decisions. Add up the real facts and then intuit from there.

Many people are given credit for the phrase "management by walking around." Among them is Abraham Lincoln, who was said to have used it to describe his staying in touch with and more fully understanding what his troops in the field were thinking. Make it a consistent business practice to keep senior officials in contact with the people in the organization's front-line operations.

The essence of managing in most businesses is *contact*. Many good executives greatly increase their effectiveness either by personally circulating throughout the physical work space or by being available at all times for brief comments or consultations to focus others or give them direction. Brief, unplanned interludes give a good manager the opportunity to react to work in progress so that shifts and adjustments can be made before effort is expended to complete a project or a product that must then be changed.

Another great concept is that of "catching people doing something right." Most good managers take note and likely say something when staff are behaving badly or performing inefficiently. But how much more valuable is it for managers to also offer kudos whenever they notice unusually good or caring workmanship or performance? Those certainly are the times to speak out publicly. I first read this notion many years ago in Tom Peters and Robert Waterman's *In Search of Excellence*.

I urge colleagues to remember what we call our "80 Percent Rule." Different from the well-known 80/20 Rule (or Pareto principle), our version simply suggests that one person's initial answer to any problem will likely represent, at most, 80 percent of the best solution. By collaborating with or bouncing the idea off others, we can so often make even a good first solution so much better.

> When time allows, it is especially important for managers to encourage their teams to improve on any solutions they (or others) may offer, and to be open to hearing suggestions for refinements. Some colleagues may instinctively react negatively at first if they think they are being "second-guessed," but cooperatively improving upon other people's initial thinking is exactly what teamwork is all about. We adopted and often mention this "80 Percent Rule" to strongly suggest that added collective input in most problem-solving situations will almost always result in either marginally or significantly better results.

Finally, at Cummings Properties we constantly preach to staff at all levels the need to go out of their way to smile and be friendly—to clients, visitors, colleagues, and passersby whom they encounter while working anywhere in or around any Cummings building. It is so much more enjoyable working in a place that is friendly and upbeat and where people will get into the habit of speaking and acknowledging others as their paths cross. This practice builds upon and perpetuates itself in giving Cummings Properties its reputation for friendly service. Doesn't this concept work with almost any business?

CUMMINGS PROPERTIES was becoming well established in commercial real estate immediately north of Boston, without ever doing any business in Boston itself. We were quite content in the near suburbs, along the northern portion of Route 128/Interstate 95, and along Interstate 93, from Andover down into Medford and Somerville—all solidly centered in Woburn. Growing rapidly, we were enjoying our role as the proverbial "big fish in a little pond."

Meanwhile, strangers routinely assumed in those early days that I could not be old enough to have built Cummings Park. "Is your father still active in the business?" asked many well-meaning folks. Or, "How long has your family been in the real estate [or construction] business?" Yes, it was old fashioned, but the business was beginning to accumulate great unrealized capital.

As a cohesive property-management team, we were becoming ever more adept at accumulating properties. We focused then on purchasing slightly distressed properties at bargain prices, and we always paid in cash, usually early-on using mortgage proceeds borrowed against other recently completed properties. In all cases, we either built or purchased rental properties and then continued to hold them. As I write this, we have still never once sold any of our major commercial buildings, nor have we ever partnered with other parties or participated in any of the syndications that seem so common.

Speculative builders sometimes invest their own money in projects, with serious risks, but they somehow "know" those risks will ultimately pay off if they work hard enough. Syndicators, on the other hand, often leave legacies of unfinished or even unneeded structures to be picked over by vultures. The syndicators suck so much profit out of a project that there is often little or nothing left to be divided among the "limited partners," other than the sometimes-questionable tax benefits. They often play the game fully prepared to leave their debt with some bankrupt shell at the end.

AS THE CUMMINGS FAMILY business prospered, so did my own family. During the late 1970s we owned a Chris Craft Sea Skiff. This fast twin-engine lapstrake boat frequently took us all to Provincetown or through the Cape Cod Canal into Narragansett Bay. We also traveled as far down east as Bar Harbor, Maine, and to so many picturesque spots along the way. Joyce and I enjoyed lots of day trips, often fishing with our kids, plus the occasional overnight trips alone, always sleeping on board. For six years we lived most of our summer weekends on this boat, the "Old Medford."

Our main living accommodations have certainly been more substantial sometimes than they needed to be, but they have never been too extravagant. In 1978, I built our second Winchester home, at 4 Fernway Terrace, using a classic iron-spot red brick exterior. This new contemporary home had six bedrooms and commanding views of Boston, especially from its upper floors. Though the house was larger than we needed for daily living, we were happy to have the extra space for the many times we hosted large charitable and personal events. Joyce and I greatly enjoyed this home for twenty-five years before downsizing to a much smaller third home in town in 2003.

It was also during this period that I spent many, many evenings as a volunteer in much different surroundings, working alongside my sister, Marian. She served as a part-time registered nurse volunteer at Pine Street Inn, a major Boston homeless shelter. She was on a remarkable team of volunteers who treated the many minor medical needs of destitute overnight residents of the shelter, while I and others stayed nearby to intervene if any situation got out of hand, which they sometimes did. That early personal experience benefits me, even today, in remembering the extraordinary good that so many magnificent not-for-profit institutions provide to untold throngs of highly disadvantaged citizens.

By 1981, Joyce and I, along with Doug Stephens and his wife, Carrol, frequently socialized with Jamie McKeown at company functions and elsewhere. Jamie would occasionally bring an eligible date-of-the-season, until Denise Arndt first appeared that year. According to Denise, Jamie's friends all thought he was a confirmed bachelor, because marriage would have interfered with his skiing. The common joke, after Denise continued showing up on Jamie's arm, was that "Rent-a-Date must have run out of girls for him because they kept sending the same one."

"Jamie was twenty-five years old when we met," recalls Denise, "when he was leasing manager for Cummings. He was a laid-back, easygoing guy who was always smiling. I thought at first it was just because I didn't know him that well, and eventually the smile would stop, and eventually I would see him lose his temper. I waited and waited, but it never happened. Sounds weird, I know. I thought, *Is this guy for real?*" I never once knew him to lose it either.

Their relationship blossomed quickly, especially after Denise moved from Chelmsford, Massachusetts, into a nearby apartment in Woburn, but then it seemed to stall for a couple of years. This was the most serious relationship Jamie had as an adult, but he was clearly in no rush to get married. Eventually, Joyce and I started nudging him not to let Denise get away. We may have been as happy as they were when they came to our home to celebrate the night of their engagement.

If I ever had any misgivings about the appropriateness of our bugging Jamie about getting married—in other words, about interfering in a colleague's personal life—Jamie later set me straight. Three nights before their May 1984 wedding, Joyce and I joined Jamie and Denise for dinner at Winchester Country Club. Just outside the clubhouse entrance, Jamie purposefully pulled me aside as Joyce and Denise went ahead. "You guys have both been so great. I want you to know that my marrying Denise will be absolutely the best thing that has ever happened to me."

| *Denise and Jamie McKeown at Sunday River, Maine*

Unrelated men did not hug each other much in those days, but that was how Jamie made his point that night. "There is nothing I won't do for the rest of my life but to try to make Denise happy," he told me. I had no more second thoughts about perhaps having become too personal.

Jamie was avidly athletic, but never seemed to have time for team sports or spectator sports. At a little over six feet tall and perhaps 170 pounds, he was always fitness conscious. He ran or swam almost every morning, and occasionally we did some great bike rides together, including our first one to Beverly when we had to work to find our way. He wanted to stay in shape for local triathlons, which he particularly enjoyed. We both logged notable events of the business day on simple steno pads, year after year. But virtually every single day, Jamie's first entry would be his start and stop times for whatever early morning workout he had done, only occasionally writing "off."

Knowing that Jamie's greatest enduring sports love was downhill skiing, I was relieved when he got married: Maybe now we could stop worrying about his someday taking off to live in the Rocky Mountains as he had sometimes fantasized about. After running and skiing, tennis was Jamie's next individual sport of choice. He was skilled at it, too, especially for someone who rarely played the game more than an hour or two a week. In time, however, as he steadily built his business and life skills, he also began to find great satisfaction in the pursuit of business, especially in putting together complicated leasing deals and property acquisitions. He had clearly learned by then that climbing a ladder of success requires our full effort and both hands.

In all my years working closely with Jamie, we never once had an argument or even a disagreeable conversation about anything. He never disappointed me, and he once told me that feeling was mutual. I was beyond happy when Jamie added, "I trust you more than any other person I have ever known." Then he thoughtfully added, "Except for Denise, of course."

WELL BEFORE THE phrase "bucket list" came into common usage, Joyce and I checked off one of our longstanding dreams: a piloted hot-air balloon ride. One lovely morning in May 1985, we gently floated over central Connecticut, up to about a thousand feet above the ground. Once we eavesdropped on a conversation on the ground as we silently floated low over farmland and other areas where there was no traffic. We startled two people who were deep in a private conversation by yelling out "Hello" as we drifted close overhead. Going wherever the breeze blew us, we felt almost no sense of movement through the nearly still air.

Then, about fifty minutes into our first and only balloon trip, however, the balloon's gas burner began sputtering and failed, and we quickly lost altitude. The excited aeronaut could not control the balloon's direction, but he had us frantically leaning over the left side of the basket, using our weight to guide us away from a house below us on our right that we were rapidly approaching. We missed the brick chimney by inches and then thumped down in the yard, with only a gash in the side of the balloon's big wicker basket. The family whose home we missed happily shared the champagne we had brought to celebrate our excursion while we waited for the chase car and trailer to figure out where we were and return us to our own car, twenty miles away.

About a year later, Joyce and I checked another adventure off our list with a pair of great glider flights near Truro, on Cape Cod. This time, Denise and Jamie accompanied us. Each glider was designed to carry a pilot and one or two passengers. We were dragged several thousand feet up in the air by small tow planes and then released to glide like hawks, using the air currents to sometimes soar high up over the ground. Remembering the angst we had experienced the previous year with the mild crash landing of our balloon ride, Jamie and I did a brief wife swap, just in case, before we packed into the narrow single seat directly behind each of the two pilots. It was a bit like riding on a motorcycle with two passengers lined up behind the driver.

Swooping along in a glider was more exhilarating than floating in the hot-air balloon, as we skimmed through the air with nothing propelling us, but both were terrific new experiences. Though we never thought about it this way at the time, the hot-air balloon and glider rides were the start of many exciting exploits all over the world with Joyce.

❈ *Creative people are highly selective in accepting what they are told at face value. They rarely assume that anyone's most recent idea or approach is necessarily the best or the last thing to be considered. They know that almost any good idea or process can be knocked around and improved, especially as more people focus creative attention toward that end.*

❈ *Managers must be constantly ready to recognize and react to whatever each day brings, and there is no possible way for anyone to imagine ahead of time what new conundrums may arise.*

❈ *To be intractably and vocally positive about something is sometimes just being mistaken at the top of your voice.*

[9]

Branching Out, But Still Only in Woburn

The 147-unit Place Lane Condominium in Woburn, Massachusetts, with the original Woburn Boys Club swimming pool and gym shown next door in the lower right corner

WOBURN RESIDENTS Douglas and June Brown contacted me through the then Woburn Boys Club in 1983 to say that they had decided to sell an undeveloped nine-acre parcel they owned adjacent to the west side of the club, at the end of Place Lane. Mr. Brown told me that his attorney "had checked the zoning map and told him [erroneously] that his land was undevelopable for anything significant, because it had only a single access point and just forty feet of frontage at the butt end of Place Lane," a few hundred feet off Main Street.

We immediately doubted the attorney's advice, however, and could readily see that the Place Lane acreage was properly zoned to allow office or research uses as a "matter of right," or residential condominiums with a special permit from Woburn City Council if it had more frontage on the street.

Indeed, the attorney's advice seemed preposterous, but there was no need for us to question the prospective seller. The needed frontage should have been easily achievable by utilizing a small portion of the twenty acres to create a cul-de-sac at the end of the street. With the latter in mind, we purchased the land in December 1983, and, as an increasingly skilled middle manager by then, Jamie took on the political challenge of acquiring the necessary permitting to enable solid use of this highly buildable and centrally located vacant parcel. The legal advice provided to the seller fell hugely short.

Aside from zoning or legal issues, though, there was an overriding neighborhood issue. "Greedy Mr. Brown," so the story went, was selling this previously undeveloped privately owned land to "the insatiable Mr. Cummings" from Winchester. "Why doesn't he build his condominiums in Winchester, instead?" was a frequently repeated refrain as Woburn's *Daily Times Chronicle* appeared to be working to get everyone agitated over the possibility of a residential development there. Unfortunately, this mood set up a long and acrimonious back-and-forth, and discussions quickly turned antagonistic, especially with the recently installed Planning Board. At the same time, I certainly knew how planning boards worked from my experience as a former member and chairman of the Winchester board. We were confident we could make the land much more usable than the prior owner thought it was.

It was, however, critical that we prevail, because in return for a modest purchase price of only $250,000 for the supposedly not-usable lot, we had taken title with no contingency for our ability to secure a building permit. Eventually, we submitted a Definitive Subdivision Plan to the Planning Board to simply extend the length of Place Lane into the property to gain the necessary legal frontage for whatever the Woburn Zoning Ordinance would then allow us to construct there. The timely submission also froze the zoning provisions for the next seven years and prevented any unreasonable rezoning attempt by the Planning Board, which we felt was a strong possibility, given its members' outwardly hostile attitudes toward us during that era.

This solution to the hypothetical major problem with lot frontage should have made the land developable, but our combative Planning Board at that time still did everything it could to challenge and delay approval of our fully compliant cul-de-sac plan. A break finally came when the former Planning Board dithered around so long that it lost track of its own legal calendar. Rather than simply approving or rejecting our Definitive Subdivision Plans, and delaying our efforts, the board inexplicably took no action at all within the allotted ninety days from the date of our submission. We knew it, but the board members seemed totally oblivious that Massachusetts laws provided a perfect legal remedy for such arbitrary behavior. Woburn's Planners at that time spent far more effort on character assassination than negotiating anything.

On the morning of the ninety-first day after our well-documented submission date, Woburn's city clerk, Attorney Jack Ryan, certified that the subdivision had become constructively approved by reason of the Planning Board's *failure to act* within ninety days. It was akin to recovering the other team's fumble in its own end zone to score in the final seconds of a tied football game.

Much of the lot consisted of a partially open grassy hill, known as Bucky's Hill, which had been used for decades for snow sledding and many other neighborhood activities. In retrospect, with all the flak thrown up to stop our development of the site, I was surprised no one tried to assert an adverse possession claim on the land. Once we created sufficient legal frontage and started building on the new cul-de-sac, there was little else anyone could do to stop our development of the property, and not surprisingly, there was no public disclosure by anyone about the board's glaring gaffe.

By that time, we had determined that residential condominiums were really the highest and best use for the lot, but since we had plans in a drawer for a small office building that fit easily on the lot, we requested and quickly received a building permit to construct the office structure. Immediately thereafter, Jamie went into his role as the designated Woburn native and submitted an alternative plan to build one hundred fifty high-end condominiums.

I made it my job to cobble together the complete set of condominium documents, using samples from other communities and making up new clauses as the need arose. This was a perfect example of entrepreneurs sometimes needing to play every position on the team in dealing with unexpected situations. There are so many scenarios in business when work commonly performed by so-called experts can be readily accomplished by laypeople.

Jamie and I then both came under repeated fire for supposedly "holding a gun to the city's head" to get the condos approved, but we soon earned the necessary city approval and built the residential condos. We really had a last laugh over the issue when the condo market reached a fever pitch in the fall of 1986, and the highly successful construction year perfectly meshed with a great sales effort just before the epic market collapse in 1987. We could hardly have asked for a better storybook ending.

We self-managed the unit sales at Place Lane and then managed the complex itself for ten years after the resident owners took over the board of trustees, though the more common practice was for condo owners to throw out the developers at the first opportunity. This often occurred in the 1980s shortly after a majority of the condominium units were sold and when the owners had enough membership votes to elect their own slate of trustees, but such action was never even considered by the Place Lane board. In fact, it was Cummings Properties that eventually informed the trustees, much to their disappointment, of our decision to give up our property-management role.

WHILE GROWING THE firm steadily in terms of both staff and square feet, we also became an early and vocal supporter of the campaign to eliminate smoking in the workplace. This was decades before it became a popular concern.

Jamie and a reporter during a television interview about the Great American Smokeout

From the mid-1980s, the firm paid annual cash bonuses of $500 per year to every employee who agreed not to smoke anywhere on company property or in any company vehicle, and we also all but stopped hiring smokers. Jamie was interviewed about this by a reporter from WBZ-TV who did a piece at Cummings Park in connection with the Great American Smokeout, arranged by Cummings and the American Cancer Society.

The TV report focused heavily on a former Cummings employee who filed what we, of course, felt was a frivolous lawsuit against the firm for "discriminating" against him because he was a smoker. Jamie had a good time pontificating about the great health risks of smoking at a time when many people still did not want to believe smoking was that harmful. The legal matter was thrown out after Jamie agreed that the employee had been discriminated against, but there was nothing wrong or illegal about this.

This anti-smoking campaign, coupled with the company's longstanding policy of overtly preferring non-smokers in its hiring practices, had a practical application as part of a whole collection of programs over the years to promote wellness among our staff. Certainly, it is not lost on corporate managers that healthy employees will generally perform better and will need less medical attention than those who do not make wise health decisions. Good employee health also means better lifestyles and lower health insurance premiums for both company and staff. The enemy in all cases has been tobacco—the most prominent legally manufactured product proven to cause disease and death when used as directed.

Illegal drugs and marijuana have been the other major targets in the workplace. The company and its corporate affiliates have conducted drug testing as part of the routine hiring process for all full-time employees at all levels for more than forty years, even though Massachusetts state law requires ongoing drug testing only for truck drivers and several other classes of employees. Random drug testing, plus targeted drug testing for cause, as well as the use of tobacco on the job, has always resulted in summary terminations if there is evidence of such usage.

For thirty years, we also have effectively used one-page business letters as editing exercises for all candidates for management or office-centered jobs. Many such applicants will be college graduates, but even then, it is truly remarkable how many prospective staff struggle with this test. The exercise consists of editing a single-page business letter that includes three dozen grammatical, spelling, or usage errors. A person whose job includes communications but who cannot compose a simple error-free business letter can be a huge liability. This comes at a time when most managers no longer have the luxury of a "secretary" at their disposal to make them look good. We also use the exercise to discover new hires who have particularly *good* writing and editing skills, which we can always use.

> For a half-century, I have preached at Cummings Properties about the need for all managers to express themselves well in writing. While that goal was not always fully realized, we have gradually pulled together more than our share of excellent writers. When it comes to achieving personal goals in business, being able to write down and share our good ideas with others is a crucial step. Another key consideration in hiring decisions at Cummings is that we are always much more interested in the potential, and the character, and the innate abilities of the applicant than we are in trying to hire the perfect résumé.

Skillful writers are also often especially good negotiators, even though they may agonize with draft after draft, as I often do, when structuring proposals or agreements. Strunk and White, in their classic book *The Elements of Style*, compare extra words in a sentence to extra parts in a lawn mower: Neither runs efficiently with extra pieces. The writer in any business communication must study all the words and know their meanings and their exact effects.

Fixing written words must be done carefully, especially anytime we run into communications that could become a factor in confrontations or legal issues. All staff are expected to seek peer review or legal review before transmitting significant written communications. Somewhat counterintuitively, staff at all levels must be even more careful to do this when sending off a "quick email." It is vital in business to recognize how damaging quick, casual responses can be when they subsequently resurface, sometimes years later, as discovery evidence in a legal matter.

When members of the management team must occasionally respond to captious correspondence, as inevitably comes our way from time to time, we find it is far better for us to be extremely temperate, careful, prompt, and accurate with any response. Since there are often many varied thoughts that might (or should) be incorporated, our response may easily involve three or more writers working together to clearly lay out fact patterns.

FROM ITS EARLIEST days, the company had a firm policy of allocating 10 percent of all net earnings (and later 10 percent of gross income) every year to support community activities and charities, especially in Woburn and Winchester. Joyce and I were personally active in a wide variety of volunteer roles and always found these activities highly rewarding. This spirit of giving ultimately inspired us to create Cummings Foundation in 1986.

We were both raised to do more than necessary and to "do good" for more than just ourselves. We realized early that there is a point at which it doesn't make a difference to earn more money. Rather, we were much more interested in helping the community, and we have found it highly satisfying to be able to do good things with what we have. It would be difficult to overstate how important our early upbringings were in our philanthropy today.

Cummings Foundation was created with a mission to invest in organizations that work to improve our society, and to mostly do it locally. The foundation emerged as a place to set aside meaningful philanthropy money for a later date, when we could better decide how to put it to work. Despite years of distributing funds to many different causes, we were still working on finalizing our ultimate long-term strategy, a process I will address in a later chapter.

Once the foundation was established, Cummings Properties and its affiliate companies all made annual financial contributions to it—as well as directly to many local organizations. Over time, however, we also gradually came to donate as many properties to the foundation as we found was legally allowed, providing a stable source of funding. The foundation now disburses funds derived from these properties primarily to community-based programs geared toward improving area residents' quality of life, particularly programs benefiting senior citizens and youth. Supporting such programs is a reinvestment in the communities that are central to Cummings Properties and its affiliate companies and employees.

| *Bill, Charles Gardner, and Jamie, 1986*

Although Cummings Properties operates the buildings owned by Cummings Foundation, federal law prohibits the company from receiving any remuneration or fees from the foundation for any of its "in-kind" services. The comparison has been made with the Newman's Own food-products brand, which also reportedly uses 100 percent of all its profits to support charitable work. That's the case here, including all sales proceeds from this book.

One of our earliest major gifts, in 1986, was a grant of $100,000 to the Boys Club of Woburn. That donation was specifically earmarked for the formation of the Charles H. Gardner Endowment Fund in honor of the years that Charlie had served the club as executive director. He had done so much to assist our work in Woburn, and we were thrilled to help support his legacy.

Twenty-eight years later, Cummings Foundation gave the club $1 million in cash for a major rebuilding project, along with an additional $2 million challenge grant to be paid when the club reached 80 percent of its $8.5 million goal to rebuild and enlarge its home directly adjacent to Place Lane Condominium. Joyce and I are so pleased to have played quiet but meaningful roles during many of the Boys Club's first fifty years, through some of its early struggles into periods of growth and great successes.

IN 1989, JOYCE AND I offered to purchase a home on several acres on Arlington Street in Winchester, directly across from Winchester Country Club and directly abutting our own home, for Hospice Care, Inc., now VNA Hospice Care. Joyce had been particularly involved with the organization for some years, including as a hospice home volunteer. After Hospice Care managers decided they were not yet prepared to operate a hospice home, we also considered creating a large assisted-living community on the property, in what was formerly a motherhouse of the Medical Missionaries of Mary.

But then we learned, in late October 1989, that Woburn's recently bankrupt Choate Memorial Hospital was closing, almost immediately, and that it would be auctioned off to the highest bidder. We were also told that any sale would be "consistent with the best interests of the city of Woburn." Our interests seemed to fit perfectly, and after several hearings, Judge Harold Lavian of the federal bankruptcy court awarded us the hospital for $3.1 million in January 1990, notwithstanding a competing higher bid of $3.21 million. When we decided to buy the hospital, Joyce was visiting her ill parents in Alabama and was more than a little shocked to hear we had purchased the community's hospital. We immediately began rebuilding the property as a one hundred-resident not-for-profit retirement community, creating our first major philanthropic presence, in the city where Cummings Properties had its beginning and its earliest successes.

Much more sensitive, we thought, than the past patients' medical records were some of their remaining body parts. There were several shelves full of preserved internal and external human specimens in what looked like large two-gallon pickle jars. There was also a refrigerator with many other "fresh" body parts in a secure area near the morgue. Symmes Arlington Hospital eventually retrieved those specimens, as it had agreed to do, but only after much finger-pointing and cajoling.

Having become a licensed auctioneer specifically so Cummings Properties could hold its own auctions after purchasing just such a property, I particularly enjoyed personally arranging and conducting a major public auction sale of all the hospital's furnishings and equipment, netting well over $400,000 in a mammoth one-day sale. Before people arrived for the auction, we updated the signs for the restrooms on the operating-room floor. Signs limiting usage to "Doctors Only" in one restroom and "Nurses Only" in the other told something of the hospital's outdated mindset as the time of its bankruptcy.

On February 6, 1990, a remarkably short time following the bankruptcy award, the Woburn City Council granted the special permit we needed to convert the hospital.

| *New Horizons at Choate, 1990*

Two council members who had been highly outspoken opponents of our Place Lane development unsurprisingly cast negative votes, but their behind-the-scenes efforts to delay this project had little effect. We rebuilt the entire hospital within seven months of the City Council vote.

Fortunately, there was no need for anything resembling a gut-out of the old building. Instead, we incorporated a careful, adaptive reuse of what existed to create an extraordinarily comfortable and cozy community.

WITH THE PASSING now of many years, it has been so gratifying to Joyce and me to see how many of our older personal and business acquaintances and their close relatives have opted to spend their final years at New Horizons at Choate. In addition, many early buyers from Place Lane Condominium have followed their friends or family members from Place Lane to the nearby New Horizons as their own living needs change.

There is no question that New Horizons is a truly marvelous place, but it is also an economical place. One of its most surprising features is that no resident has ever been asked to pay any type of an increase in his or her monthly rent or meals expense after moving in. Residency fees are adjusted only as new residents move in.

Choate Medical Center, which directly abuts New Horizons, houses medical practices and other health services on the ground floor of the former hospital. It is an eminently convenient provider of on-site medical care for many New Horizons residents. It enables residents to receive high-quality medical care without having to leave their building. The medical providers also serve others from all over the greater Woburn community. Residents can handily arrange visits with any of the many on-site physicians and other healthcare practices, which include a twenty-bed dialysis center. The substantial rental income derived from these medical and physical therapy facilities defrays almost all of New Horizons' food-service costs.

Recognizing how little extra it costs New Horizons in both Woburn and Marlborough to accommodate a second resident in most apartments, we made it highly attractive for couples to move in. Our additional charge for providing housing and three meals per day for a second person is extremely low. Partly for that reason, and because we offer special programs and activities for men, our gender ratio is typically about 30 percent male and 70 percent female, giving New Horizons a far higher ratio of men than most of the other top area communities.

The need for assisted and independent living units for Americans age eighty-five and beyond is expected to triple from perhaps 6 million in 2019 to 19 million by 2057. Most often, when couples consider moving to New Horizons, or any other similar group home, they do so because one of the two is in failing health. The more frail spouse is often keen to see his or her life partner settled into a new home before the ailing partner succumbs. Only rarely—indeed, almost never—does the surviving partner choose to leave New Horizons after the death of his or her spouse. Most importantly, the last months these couples have together are dramatically more comfortable and meaningful when they can be together in a highly supportive environment. This connectivity and support helps so many new residents flourish and thrive and truly enjoy their lives again.

We so frequently hear from residents, "We should have moved here sooner. Why did we wait so long?" We are proud that there hasn't been a single time in more than fifteen years when the Woburn community was not 100 percent occupied as of the first of each month.

By this time Doug and I had begun getting considerable experience working with David Leland as the foundation's principal financial advisor. David was particularly attentive to any financial or investment issues at our not-for-profit assisted living communities and later with Cummings family investments, for which I was so grateful. David was another key connection involving members of Winchester Country Club, as Joyce and I actually knew David's parents before we knew him. Decades later, David in turn met Darin Byrne, who became one of his standout younger team members, through Darin's parents at the club.

❀ *"Getting to yes" pithily summarizes the creative and committed problem-solving approach that led to our successes at Place Lane, New Horizons at Choate, and elsewhere. This requires strong analytical and negotiating skills, as well as scrupulous attention to key details to avoid unforced errors. Those businesses most able to "get to yes" are in a position to reinvest in the communities to which they often owe so much—a goal to which every business should aspire.*

❀ *One huge advantage of being a closely-held private firm is the ability to focus on long-term equity rather than short-term profitability.*

❀ *Business is never as much of a science as it is an artform.*

[10]

A New Generation Takes Over

STARTING IN the mid-1970s, I became increasingly active at Tufts under the omnivorously intelligent President Jean Mayer, whom I particularly admired. In addition to minor roles and committee work, I served on the Tufts Medical School board of overseers before accepting a ten-year appointment in 1986 as a charter trustee of the university.

As my extracurricular activities grew, and as Jamie—by then executive vice president of Cummings Properties— became an ever more esteemed colleague, it was

my special pleasure to nominate him to take my place on the board of directors of the Woburn Boys Club. That was particularly meaningful to Jamie, as he heavily attributed his success to his lifelong involvement with the Boys Club. He thus became the club's first former student member to serve on its board of directors. Before long, Jamie also became the first former student member to be elected president of the club, and he felt so honored to continue his long association with the place he cherished so much.

"Without exaggeration," Jamie's mother, Connie McKeown, recently told

Joyce and me in Florida, "from elementary school through his mid-teen years, Jamie spent almost all of his out-of-school waking hours at the club. He truly loved it. He was never home." When he was named Boy of the Year in 1974, it appeared as though he had reached the pinnacle of his Boys Club experience, but of course that honor turned out to be but a steppingstone. As the club's new president, Jamie—by then the father of two young daughters—quickly led the move to formally change the club from the Woburn Boys Club to the Woburn Boys & Girls Club.

1990 was a pivotal year for Jamie, beginning with his appointment as treasurer of the Woburn Industrial Development Finance Authority by Mayor Thomas Higgins. Then, in June, I named him president of Cummings Properties, twenty years after its founding and eleven years after he joined the company. Our company newsletter by that time bragged in its banner: "Serving 1,000 Firms in More Than 3 Million Square Feet." He was thirty-six years old.

I had no plans yet to go anywhere, but I was so pleased to see the company's next-generation leadership firmly in place. Still hoping that my children might have long-term interest in the firm, I felt it was important at that point for Jamie to be in position to someday help guide whichever of them might later best qualify for the job. With Jamie so firmly set in his new position as president, I could not possibly have felt any better about the reality and wisdom of my succession planning.

By then, Jamie was universally respected, and his appointment as president was extremely well received. People were drawn in by his natural charm. At thirty-four years old, he was surely young, but his maturity and commendable personal commitment seemed to safeguard him from negative feelings. He also had more time with the firm than anyone else who might have seen himself or herself taking over.

Thinking back, I know that the decision to have him succeed me at his young age was informed by my own earlier experience that caused me to abruptly leave Gorton's in 1964, when someone else was selected for an available post over me because of *my* age at the time. I was several years younger than Jamie was when his time came, and I had less seniority with my employer then than Jamie did, but still I was the right person to assume the new management position in the Cleveland subsidiary of Gorton's. At Cummings, Jamie never once pushed me for a new title, but I felt that he had in effect "trusted me" long enough, and he always appreciated my strong public display of confidence in him. Jamie truly cherished the respect he had earned from his peers, especially in his hometown of Woburn. This major management change came just as the final push was underway to open New Horizons at Choate. That effort consumed much of my time for a while, giving Jamie plenty of extra room to become established in his new role.

In the fall of 1991, Jamie was also elected as an early president of the Woburn Business Association, which was morphing into a highly effective voice for business interests in the community. Woburn businesses formerly had the North Suburban Chamber of Commerce, but many Woburn business people at the time believed that the so-called regional chamber was disproportionately interested in fighting off further reductions in the dwindling Air Force presence at Hanscom Field in nearby Bedford. Thus, the WBA came into being as a Woburn-centric business group, and it has enjoyed donated Cummings office space for decades.

| *Bill and Jamie in West Cummings Park, 1991*

AS IT TURNED out, three of our four children, Daniel, Kevin, and Patricia, occupied significant roles in the family business for a few years each, but each later chose a different career path. There never was a time, however, when anyone in the management team at Cummings had to compete with family members for career opportunities.

Our eldest son, Daniel, did well at Colby College, and he later worked closely with me for several years in various capacities at Cummings Properties. He always demonstrated exceptionally good business intuition, but he eventually chose to opt out while recovering from several major back surgeries following first a skiing accident and then a work-related accident in Florida.

Kevin received a bachelor's degree from the now closed New England Institute of Art and worked for several years at our large New Horizons retirement community in Marlborough, Massachusetts, which we opened shortly after New Horizons at Choate. Later, he started his own photography business.

Patricia graduated from Tufts University in 1997 and became a clinical psychologist in San Francisco, after first working for several years as associate director at our New Horizons at Marlborough. Although Patty, now a clinical psychologist in New York, had no Jewish connections, she later somehow also served for several years as the assistant dean at San Francisco Orthodox Hebrew Academy.

Marilyn, the only one of our children to work only part-time in the family business, was a 1992 Phi Beta Kappa graduate of Dartmouth College. After then graduating from Tufts Medical School, she completed a four-year fellowship to become an intensive care pediatrician at Children's Hospital of Philadelphia. She is currently medical director of the Clinical Trials Division of Columbia University Medical Center in New York and serves as chair of an institutional review board there.

Naturally, Joyce and I were proud of our children's successes in their chosen vocations, but I was still at least a little disheartened when none of them chose a career with the company. Their decisions forced me to continue making extremely careful selections of key managers who would eventually take over the business—but clearly, that process was coming together beautifully under Jamie.

BEYOND OUR TALENTED field staff, we manage all purchasing in-house and the company has been its own general contractor in every newly constructed building and in every major rehabilitation since its first building. That work includes almost all of the more than 10 million square feet we gradually developed and acquired over the last five decades. Among the hundred or so buildings we have built or purchased, the only buildings purchased that never required total makeovers were two small office buildings totaling about eighty thousand square feet between them, plus a recent direct acquisition of about one hundred thousand square feet in Andover, Massachusetts, from Boston

Properties in 2017.

The Jim Gillette era brought with it a much more organized set of written policies for dealing with suppliers of all sorts. Beyond simply paying vendors and contractors promptly, it is imperative for any company to work with vendors to help them reduce their cost of doing business with your firm. With suppliers of goods, especially, reduce the frequency of small orders, teach your team to get deliveries offloaded promptly, and avoid quibbling over trivial details. Be careful to always check the accuracy and condition of incoming orders, ideally as they are coming off the truck rather than making more time-consuming claims later, which may appear suspicious and will be difficult to verify. While occasional favors can appear harmless, be exceedingly firm about employees not accepting gratuities or special treatment from customers, clients, or vendors, and make the policy well-known to those who might offer gratuities.

| *Jim Gillette*

Cummings Properties' longtime designer, now chief design officer, Jim Trudeau, has a full-time in-house architectural group that rivals most small architectural firms.

Our Design Department handles building design, estimating, permitting, engineering, and project management, as well as graphics and web design. It constantly deals with multiple demands for its services from many different departments, including leasing, operations, facilities, construction, marketing, and communications.

In addition to the four attorneys who staff our busy Legal Department, we have been delighted to have a dozen lawyers who fill numerous other "non-legal" management roles on our sales, leasing, and operations teams. There may be more, but for no particular reason, I know of only one colleague who holds an MBA.

| *James "Jim" Trudeau*

PRIOR TO THE SUMMER of 1991, no one at our company had ever considered starting a newspaper to compete with Woburn's mostly excellent longtime newspaper, the *Daily Times Chronicle*. At that time, though, the "DTC," as we routinely called it, seemed to be publishing an increasing number of unflattering and sometimes anti-Cummings stories. They told me they could sell more newspapers by "stirring up" their readers, but that had the decided effect of feeding a vocal anti-business attitude in the community.

In September 1991, the long-time senior editor was pretty blunt with me. He said the paper's approach was "nothing personal," but "if you can't stand the heat, you'll have to get out of the kitchen." It was not clear how I was supposed to handle the remark, but within a week of that meeting in the DTC office, we began working to start a new Woburn newspaper. Joyce described this new endeavor as the perfect opportunity "to invent my own midlife crisis."

Prior to our paper's actual launch, however, we met one more time, again in the DTC office, to discuss whether that newspaper would possibly alter its dynamic. We were so much hoping it might move away from what we viewed as pandering to what was then a small but highly vocal group of naysayers.

> Unfortunately, the DTC was not open to any sort of accommodation. I was told that Woburn readers would not like "rich people from Winchester coming in and trying to tell them what to think." My response was that "this rich person from Winchester" had worked for every penny I had, and most certainly grew up with many fewer economic advantages than he had. Still, he made it clear the DTC saw no reason to change its highly populist posture.

The DTC team did not seem to believe we would move forward with a real newspaper of our own or that it would be any good, but we did, and it was. I made the final decision to start the *Woburn Advocate* during that second visit to the DTC office. Now we had to figure out how to build the first edition ten days later. No member of our original staff had worked a single day for a newspaper, and we had a great deal to learn.

We had no plans to tell anyone what to think, but we were intent on helping influence what our readers thought *about*. Rather than writing reports of who said what at each City Council or School Committee meeting, we wanted our reporters to discuss the issues with the many public officials who made sense and ignore the several who from time to time did not. They should concentrate on the back story when there was one, explore what was really going on, and write about the many highly successful businesses in Woburn and about the people behind them. Particularly, I requested that we conduct in-depth interviews and feature stories about the people who helped define the fabric of the town. I wanted us covering some of those who seemed as though they had been here forever but were never before visible.

I happily justified creating the *Woburn Advocate* as a way to keep myself busy so that Jamie would not see too much of me as he grew into his new role as Cummings Properties' president and then CEO. At the beginning, a *monthly* paper seemed like the right idea, but then a late friend who once published the nearby *Winchester Star*, C. Peter Jorgenson, convinced me we would be foolish to build anything but a weekly paper from the start. He further told me we should deliver it free on Thursdays, for no better reason, he said, than "Thursday is the day everyone publishes a weekly when they can."

Conveniently, Boston's now-noted author Neil Swidey was looking for his first real job when he responded to our line ad in *The Boston Globe* classified section. I immediately liked Neil, even though his only prior real-world experience was some part-time work at the *Providence Journal*, in addition to working on the *Tufts Observer* while in college. But he had indeed been the editor-in-chief at the *Observer*, and he performed brilliantly on our simple editing exercise. If I remember correctly, Neil started working the next day.

Once we settled on the paper's name, our senior designer, Jim Trudeau, produced a front-page banner design, which everyone liked. The paper was set for free delivery by U.S. mail to some eighteen thousand households in Woburn. For my part as publisher, I learned most of what I knew, including the U.S. Postal Service rules, from reading a small "how-to" book called something not too profound, like *Starting Your Own Newspaper*. That book showed me how easy and surprisingly inexpensive it was to acquire items like crossword puzzles, cartoons, and syndicated columns from writers whose views we respected. The first columnist we added was an old friend, Ralph Nader. With some extensive extra tutoring from a helpful postmaster in Woburn, we were fully operational on October 24, 1991, and never missed an on-time delivery.

We found many local people who were good writers, including several who had been regular or occasional DTC writers. Eventually, we also recruited several with experience in regional newspapers too.

Editor Neil Swidey, Fred Phinney, Josh Resnek, and Joyce Cummings are shown in the Harte-Hanks pressroom with the first edition of the **Woburn Advocate***, 1991*

Collectively, they did a superb job of showcasing city leaders and helping to break down some of the class stereotypes so liberally proffered by Woburn's anti-business activists. They also helped get us into less of a crisis mode at each week's deadline.

We never set out to overtly challenge or in any way embarrass the DTC. Stories about our own firm were extremely rare, and for reasons I just don't remember, I do not think we ever once used the paper to advertise our own rental properties. I think it is accurate to say that there was never a story about me, either. Getting out each new edition was our weekly miracle.

Starting the newspaper would help to greatly lessen my real estate involvement, even though everything was under one roof. Jamie rarely had time to think much about the newspaper, and I relied instead on Doug Stephens and Jim Trudeau as our editorial sounding board, at least until the new newspaper staff became acclimated. Jamie did, however, occasionally use his knowledge as a Woburn native to catch potential gaffes in stories about Woburn or Woburn people.

Neil was always "the professor" and the perfectionist of the group. If Josh Resnek—another new hire for the *Advocate*—was the bold activist I was trying to control, Neil was the idealist I wanted to both impress and teach. Rick Friedman was our philosopher, and he wrote many warm, thoughtful stories, often involving Woburn's delightful Horn Pond. His stories had great depth and genuine emotion, to the surprise of some readers. Our eldest son, Dan Cummings, became a highly competent newspaper photographer for the Advocate, and he built a nice personal following in Woburn, which still pays occasional dividends even today.

David Harvey, another Woburn native in his first real job, turned out to be a naturally gifted sports writer, even though he was hired as an advertising sales representative. He was the only original staff member to stay with the paper as long as I did. In many respects, he emulated the sincerity and sensitivity shown by Josh and Rick. After we sold the paper, David and Dan Cummings both became property managers for several years.

In 1991, we were still at the earliest stages of using computers to create our small newspaper. PageMaker software was the new thing, and seemingly fast computers were quickly outmoded by still faster ones. The first edition of the *Woburn Advocate* featured a front-page color photograph of Woburn's much beloved late multi-term mayor Thomas Higgins. Starting with that image, the *Woburn Advocate* became the first Woburn paper to regularly use full-color news photographs. Well before the arrival of digital printing, photographic color separations were expensive, but they gave us something special—a small edge, until the *Daily Times Chronicle* soon adopted color photos as well.

DENNIS CLARKE joined the *Advocate* in June 1992 as an advertising-sales representative and made a strong impression on me from the start. Dennis is the son of Dick and Nancy Clarke, our longtime friends who are now Woburn residents. Dennis grew up in Winchester, however, and graduated from Winchester High School, where he was prominently recognized as a *Boston Globe* scholar/athlete prior to attending Harvard. At six-foot-two with a strong build, Dennis also went on to be a Golden Gloves boxing champ. He gives great credit to his extra-long arms for his boxing success, but he would be the last person to ever throw his weight around, or to ever even mention his boxing days.

With only a year or so of corporate business experience when he joined us, Dennis was still pretty green in the art of business. During college, he sold fancy kitchen knives door-to-door in Winchester, and before that, he had cut grass, raked leaves, and shoveled driveways throughout his high school years, in addition to playing varsity football and basketball. But he rapidly came to know more about the newspaper business than I did, and I was delighted to appoint him as general manager of the entire newspaper operation by the end of his first year.

| *Jamie McKeown, Dennis Clarke, and Bill, 1992*

The DTC clearly did not appreciate us, but we consciously treated it with the complete respect we felt it deserved after so many decades of operation. Its publisher, Paul Haggerty, was one of Woburn's finest, most polished, and most distinguished citizens. When the DTC occasionally maligned us, we reacted quickly, but that was rare. Jim Haggerty Jr. once spelled out the situation quite succinctly with his "two straws in the punch bowl" analogy. The bottom line was always about not wanting to share the available advertising dollars—and certainly not with any hardly worthy newcomers.

> During my three years publishing the *Advocate*, it was not at all unusual for me to write stories with no byline, and I do not think my picture ever appeared in any issue, not did the words of any talk I ever gave. Thanks to strong encouragement from Josh, however, I did write one story with attribution, as an editorial. "From the Publisher" was a tribute to my dad, who lived in Woburn during his later years and died here in January 1992. Dad defined his life with his love of family and with his work: "Nowhere have I ever known anyone who ever worked harder at his job than Dad did, or with as great a sense of pride and accomplishment in trying always to do the right thing."

MEANWHILE, back at Cummings Properties, Jamie was as busy as ever. Between late 1992 and early 1993, we acquired eleven buildings during another huge slump in the Boston-area real estate market, adding more than a million square feet of mostly vacant property. Including properties in Wilmington, Medford, Somerville, Stoneham, and Sudbury, our total square footage now reached 4 million.

Despite the extraordinarily low purchase price of these properties—just under $10 per square foot of floor space on average—there seemed to be no one else with any appetite for purchasing such distressed properties. The most significant reason we acquired so many sites at practically giveaway prices was our ability to act immediately and to pay cash. We have many times assumed the risk of possible failure but have never thereafter failed to make something really good of any deal.

In April 1993, we created still another new buildable lot, this one at 17 Warren Avenue, Woburn, with some of New Horizons at Choate's unused land. We then donated this parcel to Supportive Living for the construction of a home for survivors of traumatic brain injuries. Supportive Living's fifteen-resident Warren House would be completed in 1997. The organization was formed by Doug and Carrol Stephens after their son, Scott, suffered a disabling brain injury in an auto accident when he was a teenager. Warren House became the first of what are now four free-standing Supportive Living residences. These not-for-profit homes offer long-term, semi-independent accommodations for their residents.

By mid-1993, Cummings Properties had reached a level of systemic success with all it had going on. Certainly, there were bumps—not the least of which was the wild economic upheaval of the early 1990s in the commercial real estate

Executive Committee, circa 1993: Dennis McClay, Bill Cummings, President Jamie McKeown, Treasurer Doug Stephens; seated: Vice President Michael Pascavage and General Counsel Susan Brand

market. As buyers of mildly neglected commercial real estate, however, we were in a comfortable position, having made the best of the economic downturn. I had achieved a long-cherished goal of maintaining debt-free status by then, and it was comforting never to worry about economic survival, while so many competitors seemed to be engulfed in old debt.

We opened New Horizons at Marlborough, formerly the thirty-two-acre home of Madonna Hall School for Girls, on October 1, 1994, three years after the Woburn New Horizons community. We purchased the defunct boarding school for $1.15 million from the Sisters of the Good Shepherd, a Roman Catholic religious order that operated the school there for thirty years. After investing approximately $12 million to renovate and rebuild the well-constructed Madonna Hall property, Joyce and I donated it, debt-free, including the entire highly successful assisted-living business, to Cummings Foundation, as we also eventually did with most of our commercial buildings.

Supported by about ninety mostly local employees, nonsectarian New Horizons at Marlborough currently houses more than 460 seniors on its beautiful forty-acre campus a dozen miles west of Interstate 95, just north of US Route 20.

While the real estate side of the company was firing on all cylinders, our fledgling newspaper venture was soon expanding too. Shortly after we started publishing the *Woburn Advocate*, we added the *Winchester Town Crier* and the *Stoneham Sun*. It was easy then to sell ads in all three papers. Sometimes it was even easier than it was to sell one town. Like the *Advocate*, the two new papers avoided devoting much space to topics such as auto accidents or who said what at public hearings. We sometimes covered such events, but only when they occurred on Tuesdays and we could appear somewhat current in reporting them Thursday mornings.

| *New Horizons at 400 Hemenway Street, Marlborough*

We mainly focused on positive developments in the business, educational, and not-for-profit spheres in each community. There were many in-depth feature stories about the people who were *doing* the talking and saying positive things at various events. We also concentrated on developing new advertising clients and were highly successful in this endeavor. Initially printing twenty-four pages a week, we were soon hitting a routine fifty-two to sixty-four ad-filled pages.

A MOST INTERESTING and highly profitable Cummings Properties side-story came up during our newspaper adventure, soon after we realized that none of the local Woburn residential real estate agencies would advertise with us. Realtor Joe Crowley, a good friend for many years, clued me in: "If one office starts using the *Woburn Advocate*, then they would all have to follow," which would increase their total spending for advertising. There was supposedly a clear understanding that none of the Woburn offices wanted to be the first. I did not blame any of them for not wanting to take a chance with us, but the situation still presented as a major challenge to our team.

Having greatly enhanced its success with the then-current condominium boom, Carlson Real Estate Company was at the time an impressive eastern Middlesex and Essex County chain of residential real estate offices, but with no Woburn office. So, I asked owner Dick Carlson to consider opening a Woburn office. He immediately told me Woburn might be a great location for him, but he had found that buying out an existing office was almost always a better pathway for him than building a new one. When I asked what his largest expense would be, he said that rental cost for an office was usually the greatest concern. He also said he was concerned that he might be stuck with a long-term lease if the office was not successful. I told him we had just the answer, and we had a deal within five minutes.

> It just so happened that Cummings Properties had one especially appropriate ground-floor space at 800 West Cummings Park all built out, and since we also still needed more advertising for the *Woburn Advocate*, we put those needs together. I offered Dick *free* office space for a year, and he in return quickly agreed to become a regular full-page advertiser in the *Advocate* every week for a year. Bingo, the lease was signed, and as expected, other Woburn real estate offices soon found the *Woburn Advocate* to be an attractive advertising vehicle.

The rent-free first year went by in no time, but the Carlson office remained at 800 West Cummings Park long thereafter. It became a regular rent-paying client, and soon it expanded this new Woburn office, which Dick told me was the single most successful all-new location he had ever opened. Not only did he expand in 800 West Cummings Park, but he also later moved his entire corporate headquarters to our newly constructed office building at 18 Commerce Way in Woburn.

As it turned out, that one tiny "free-rent" deal, in addition to gaining us a much-needed advertiser, produced substantially more net *rental* income for Cummings Properties than the million dollars we later received from the sale of the three newspapers. And then, instead of moving the newspapers out of 300 West Cummings Park when its initial lease with us ended, the *Advocate* purchaser brought others of its papers in and it, too, leased a much larger space for five more years. The synergies were magnificent.

We enjoyed our foray into the newspaper business, but when the end came, we were more than ready for it. We were waiting for it. It began in September 1994, when William "Bill" Elfers, representing a Fidelity Investments affiliate called Community Newspaper Company, knocked on our door and announced that his firm wanted to purchase our three local papers. This was exactly what we had been quietly hoping for and expecting.

It was perfect timing: During the bad economic period, Cummings Properties had acquired an increasing number of distressed buildings at low bargain prices, so the decision to lighten our management load by selling our three newspapers to CNC came easily. After publishing the papers for three years in the red, we sold them quietly and quickly, at the end of 1994. And as it happened, by the time of the sale, we were finally just breaking even each month, although we had accumulated $300,000 in earlier losses, not including my time.

In the end, CNC liked our product, and the quality of our advertising base, so much that it agreed to pay just over $1 million, plus a generous free-advertising allowance for Cummings Properties' use for decades to come. We would have up to a free full-page ad in each of the three papers each week for as long as I remained active in our business. As of 2020, we still advertise for free in our two remaining former papers and pay a greatly discounted rate to effectively advertise other local interests in a dozen or so of the parent company's other papers.

After twenty years of operating Cummings Properties almost exclusively within the city of Woburn, we had done extremely well. At the same time, before we published the *Advocate* there were few Woburn residents who knew much of anything about us. A large percentage of Woburnites knew only what was said by the naysayers who were so often quoted in the DTC. The *Advocate* routinely wrote about the positive actions and accomplishments of Woburn's *other* businesses. But readers did come to know our newspaper was a worthwhile public service coming to them free through Cummings Properties for more than three years, and attitudes toward the company seemed to change considerably.

WHEN I LOOK BACK on this newspaper adventure, my fondest memories are of the talented people I came to know through it. Neil Swidey remained at the *Advocate* long enough to help us build a solid foundation. He left and made a series of impressive moves, ultimately building his career with *The Boston Sunday Globe* and *Boston Globe Magazine*. Today, he is a senior *Globe* writer and has also authored several widely acclaimed books. Additionally, Neil in 2019 joined Cummings Foundation's grant-making volunteers.

Another prominent staff member at the newspapers was Mark Herlihy, who joined as a primary writer. He worked with at least a dozen other highly qualified full- and part-time reporters and stringers. Like Neil, Mark also had excelled academically at Tufts, and he also achieved first-team All-America recognition in high hurdles. He went on to earn a PhD in history from Brown University. As of 2020, he is chair of the Humanities Department and Associate Dean of Arts and Sciences at Endicott College, as well as an active member and former president of the New England Historical Association.

> *Here are a few recollections of my time at the* **Woburn Advocate:** *What made the* **Advocate** *successful was that it was a true community newspaper. A lot of community newspapers focus their coverage almost exclusively on*

things like the official business of City Hall and the school department. We certainly covered meetings of the City Council and the School Committee, as well as elections and crime stories—that's important—but we went beyond that. We went out into the community and talked to residents about the impact that events would have on their lives.

We went into schools and interviewed teachers and students about innovative programs. We found and wrote compelling human-interest stories about people in the city—unsung heroes, new immigrants, activists, individuals with interesting backgrounds, etc. And we put a spotlight on issues that had not been investigated previously.

The Advocate *was also notable for its photography, especially the work of Cheryl Miller and, later, Dan Cummings, both of whose creative and distinctive shots accompanied articles and were featured weekly in a two-page centerfold photo essay that focused on a theme or an event held in the city. Woburn residents responded positively to the paper, and it caught on quickly. I remember it growing in a span of a few months from thirty-two to forty-eight, and then to sixty-four pages.*

I joined the staff shortly after the paper was launched, selling advertising initially. My understanding was that Bill started the Advocate *to counter what he felt was an anti-business bias of the* Daily Times Chronicle, *which, until the creation of the* Advocate, *had been the town's only newspaper. But Bill realized that for readers to be open to hearing a different message, we had to offer things that readers would find in any other community paper, too—coverage of and commentary on major events, great sports news, plus obituaries, etc.*

And he hired great people to do that. Founding editor Neil Swidey, now a senior writer for Boston Globe Magazine *and a noted book author, was a terrific editor. Neil was also young and inexperienced, but he had high standards and his editing and his way with words gave the paper a certain flair without being pretentious. He made all of us look better. Neil knew the kinds of stories that would resonate with readers, and he encouraged us to go out and get them.*

Joshua Resnek had a talent for writing editorials and columns that were thoughtful and provocative. And he conveyed the pulse of the city and the personalities of its residents and officials in the weekly Around the Town section.

Staff writer and Woburn native Joseph McCool, who would later become a correspondent for the **Manchester Union-Leader**, *and also with a published book to his credit, reported on political developments and crime news in Woburn, and profiled business leaders and entrepreneurs in numerous Executive Corner profiles. Contributing writer Rick Friedman brought his thoughtful knowledge of Woburn history to bear on many memorable stories and columns.*

There were so many others like Marie Lingblom and Gail Carson who also made valuable contributions. It was a terrific team effort.

M.H.

Notwithstanding the two great ongoing rental relationships with Carlson Real Estate and with Community Newspapers, Dennis Clarke's later joining Cummings Properties turned out to be by far the most significant long-term benefit derived from our three-year newspaper experience. Dennis also ran the newspapers' transition to CNC for one year, as we had agreed, and then, after taking a three-month-long trip around the world with his still new bride, Alicia Angeles Clarke, Dennis returned to Cummings—just as planned, and just as we were taking on a giant new challenge in Beverly in January 1996.

❧ *Our experience with the* Woburn Advocate *taught us that an outlandish idea—like a real estate firm starting its own newspapers—can sometimes be the most effective one, especially when seeking to shake an entrenched status quo. An open mind and collaborative atmosphere will leave room for such an idea to emerge, and a thoughtfully assembled supporting cast will help realize it. These together may well also coax out further unexpected dividends—as we did with the important leases, free advertising, and brilliant colleagues we gained through the* Advocate *affair.*

❧ *A solid new business will make many more friends when coming across as the little guy, just trying to get by, than by bragging about how great it is. Running someone else down, or talking about putting someone else out of business can be the most fatal mistake of them all. It is far better for a new firm to overestimate the competition in every respect.*

❧ *One highly valuable new tool of Cummings Properties was the creation of our in-house distributorship of construction components and materials, Aberjona Valley Distributors, Inc. There are many manufacturing firms that will never sell directly to a user like Cummings, but* will *of course sell to a distributor like AVD.*

118 | *Starting Small and Making It Big*

❧ *One of the most satisfying things about building businesses is the simple act of creating jobs, and all the things which should go along with good jobs. Fair wages, healthcare, safety, growth opportunities, camaraderie, and job security are all vital, but not in any order.*

❧ *When bids are offered in response to any request, bidders' competitiveness will almost always improve when they are coaxed perhaps, but never rushed. A key element is giving bids time to fully ripen.*

❧ *The most valuable colleagues in any firm are typically those who quickly recognize problems when they occur, and then deal with them. Job candidates with intellectual curiosity and ingenuity can often do great work.*

Jerry McSweeney

As we move into Chapter 11 for the second half of this book, we move chronologically as well to 1995, the second half of Cummings Properties' 50-year history to date.

Starting off with one of the largest rebuilding projects in New England's history, this demolition picture opens the tale of the massive conversion of the former headquarters of United Shoe Machinery Corporation—one of America's most storied firms.

[11]

A Wholely Different League

Massachusetts Governor William Weld with Bill Cummings

HAVING RESOLUTELY avoided purchasing any property not in the immediate vicinity of Woburn, I was more than a little surprised when Jamie, in early February 1995, informed me that he planned to look at "somewhat of a monster" of a nearly vacant industrial property in Beverly, on Boston's North Shore. The one hundred-acre site, known as "The Shoe," had been the world headquarters of the once-proud but now almost-defunct United Shoe Machinery Corporation.

By this time, the former international corporate giant had been all but out of business for more than fifteen years. Effectively, the U.S. government eviscerated it following many decades of protracted antitrust actions in federal courts. There were reportedly attorneys on both sides who spent their entire careers working on nothing but the United Shoe antitrust cases between 1912 and 1979, when the hugely successful Beverly monopoly was finally forced to break itself apart.

One intriguing aspect of this case was the unorthodox role played by Louis Brandeis, who in 1916 would become an associate justice of the U.S. Supreme

Court. His brilliant legal career unfolding, Brandeis at one time represented early shoe manufacturers, including United Shoe. His law firm, now Nutter, McClennen & Fish, oversaw the merger that formed United Shoe Machinery Corporation, and Brandeis even joined United's board of directors and served as counsel to the already-giant budding monopoly. Any conflicts of interest notwithstanding, Brandeis was later one of the more notable antagonists to United Shoe while he was on the Supreme Court.

Jamie and I had not known much about it, but the mammoth Beverly property had been on and off the market since 1980. Jamie first described the building as "vacant" and certainly, with all the smashed glass on its vast expanses of window line, it did look the part. The property was so massive, so run-down, and so broken, that all efforts by others to make something worthwhile of it had quickly failed. Meanwhile, the asking price had gradually dropped from $78 million in 1980 all the way down to $10 million in 1995. Broker Bob Cronin told Jamie that he would be willing to present the seller an offer "even as low as $5 million, just to get you guys talking." Jamie convinced me to return to Beverly with him a week or so later.

UP TO THIS POINT, our proudest achievement was probably the one hundred thousand-square-foot office building at 92 Montvale Avenue in Stoneham, only two miles from our Woburn office. We bought it in a distressed sale by Eastland Savings Bank, paying $600,000 for the property in "as-is" condition. The deal yielded us a rugged, heavy-steel framework for what would turn out to be a unique upscale office building with an integral parking garage on four floors and a prime location abutting the Interstate 93 exit ramps. The concrete floors were in place for both the office and the garage, but the building had none of its exterior walls and windows, and no roof, nor, of course, any interior walls or finishes.

| *Rusting steel framework at 92 Montvale Avenue in 1991*

We received no architectural plans from the foreclosing bank, and our only lead on that front had been an angry architect in Lexington who was understandably bitter toward the original builder. In the end, Cummings

Properties' own in-house design staff created a complete set of plans to go with the massive skeleton. They did so within four weeks for about 20 percent of what the as-yet-unpaid architect demanded for the use of his original plans. Architecturally, the Stoneham building was a full cut above our other properties, and for a long time thereafter it was easily our most impressive structure, but the Beverly property was many orders of magnitude larger and more complex.

WITH THE USMC PROPERTY, Jamie was proposing that we greatly up the ante. On a frigid Saturday in February 1995, he and I visited The Shoe, joined by Fred Wilbur and Dennis McClay, who was then our construction superintendent. The property was indeed a monster. *Miles* of hallways and service tunnels crisscrossed through and under the 1.5 million square-foot interior of the main building alone. It was so large that employees in earlier days had regularly used bicycles to deliver mail inside the building. Built in 1903 by Ernest Leslie Ransome, a British engineer, The Shoe was one of the first large reinforced concrete buildings in the world—in fact, until the construction of Boulder Dam, it was reportedly also the largest reinforced concrete structure anywhere. In some places, we found concrete walls more than three feet thick, and we would later learn that the first phase of the structure, at the south end, had twisted square *iron* reinforcing rods that were as thick as one inch. Ransome's complex foreshadowed the later notable work of Mies van der Rohe in Detroit.

There were more than two thousand over-sized windows in these interconnected so-called "day-lit" buildings, almost all of them exactly ten feet square. Most of them were cracked or broken; many were completely smashed out, and the cold February wind streamed straight through. Even so, about thirty small businesses were clustered in areas where the massive oil-fired boilers still kept heat pulsing through ancient steam lines. Because the buildings were constructed before 1934, and because tenants collectively occupied less than 10 percent of the total floor area, the buildings could be treated as abandoned and were therefore eligible for significant federal tax credits. We gradually learned about substantial state and city benefits that were also available if we took on the unenviable task of becoming the property's saviors.

Jamie wanted to keep us in a strong growth mode, and once I admitted we could do the job, he became intent and determined in a way I had never known him before. Our conversations in early 1995 about the purchase of the Beverly property were some of the most serious and thoughtful meetings we ever had. He was so much the future of the company, and a successful conversion of this colossal asset would really put us in a different league.

> WE SOON FORMALIZED what some considered an almost laughable proposal of $500,000 to purchase the entire hundred or so acres of The Shoe, including more than 1.5 million square feet of historic concrete memories. There were no permitting or financing contingencies in the proposal other than the seller's guarantee that after the closing it would cost us no more than $1 million to clear the property of its waste petroleum and other contamination issues, as the seller's environmental firm had earlier represented to us would be the case. The seller was an affiliate of The Black & Decker Corporation, and the proposed purchase price was like asking for a gift.

Despite our exceedingly low offer, we believed through March and April 1995 that the deal was going to close on precisely those terms, but the paperwork seemed always a few days away. As is often the case, however, the environmental issues delayed any agreement month after month. Hundreds of voluminous softbound reports from Haley & Aldrich eventually revealed thousands of cubic yards of oil-soaked soil on The Shoe's property, accumulated during United Shoe's more than a century of heavy industrial use. There were some locations where oil had been allowed to slop into the sandy ground "just to get rid of it," as an older retiree from The Shoe later told me.

But we soon found out that there was great community goodwill toward United Shoe's possible successors, and that went a long way in awakening all of us to the real substance and significance of the property. In a communication to the Cummings Executive Committee on March 24, 1995, when we were still expecting each day to close on the purchase, Jamie wrote: "Although it will not negatively impact our staffing level if the Beverly sale does not close, the possible acquisition is a major wild card for the future growth and direction of the company. Also, if a sale is consummated, the project will obviously require great immediate attention on the construction side, and soon thereafter, an on-site leasing and operations presence. I think the odds favor the deal being finalized, but it will be another week or so before anything definitive can be resolved. The major obstacle concerns liability for future discovery of presently unknown environmental contamination (if any)."

IN THE MEANTIME, one of the best examples of our utilizing by now almost patented "extra buildability" on a newly acquired site arose in April 1995. We purchased a well-located 120,000-square-foot single-story property at 10 Commerce Way, Woburn. An affiliate of New York Life Insurance Company sold us this mostly leased property for a little more than $3 million. Located on a federal Superfund site, as were some of our other Woburn properties, it was only a few hundred yards from the Interstate 95/Washington Street interchange. The property did have upcoming exposure from expiring leases, but we considered that mostly as an opportunity to achieve higher rents. Most important, like so many other properties we have acquired, this one also had marvelous expansion capability, on which we soon built 18 Commerce Way.

| *10 Commerce Way, Woburn, after the construction of 18 Commerce Way*

This additional structure was designed to fit perfectly in the southeast corner of the existing paved parking lot of the original 10 Commerce Way building. A large water main, along with ample underground telephone, electric, gas, sewer, and storm drainage, all ran right across the east end of the property. Adequate striped parking already existed, greatly speeding up both the permitting and construction cycle and greatly reducing the construction costs for this new seven-story building. We had to do remarkably little excavation, and none of it was deeper than three or four feet. The 18 Commerce Way property was first occupied in early 1996, and it filled rapidly.

Not atypically, the new building we added at 18 Commerce Way shows up on our records as having a "zero" cost for its land. As I have already recounted, this ongoing philosophy of making judicious use of any extra land for future development has been a key to the firm's success and dates back to the first property we purchased at 10 Henshaw Street. All told, the organization today has built twenty-one major buildings on land for which sellers appeared to have established the price without their, or their brokers, in any way recognizing the future buildability. In all of these cases, the needed land was effectively "free."

We have also taken great advantage of unused buildability when assisting others in solving space needs on their already-owned properties. In addition to donating extra land at the former Choate Hospital for the use of Supportive Living, we helped guide and fund the permanent home for Winchester Community Music School. Also quite locally, I played significant roles in funding, designing, and engineering the major classroom addition at St. Eulalia Church in Winchester. I also did most of the design work for the new gym and sports center at Winchester Country Club, plus a large new maintenance building. We have helped to design and fund many other community improvements, including the new public restroom building at Horn Pond in Woburn.

I HAD NEVER DONE significant fundraising for not-for-profit organizations, but in 1997, after Joyce and I strongly encouraged founder Corie Nichols to somehow establish a permanent home for Winchester Community Music School, I knew we then had to help. Corie and her committee eventually identified the former estate home of the late nationally known comedian Frank Fontaine (a/k/a "Crazy Guggenheim" from the old Jackie Gleason Show) as an ideal location for the school. An interesting side story here is that my dad, who spent most of his working years as a house painter,

| Winchester Community Music School

single-handedly painted the entire interior and exterior of that structure for the Fontaine family before the family moved in decades earlier. He had previously also painted their former home, on nearby Winthrop Street, Medford.

Cummings Foundation gave the music school $500,000, and that made it easy for me to ask others for similar amounts. I enthusiastically approached only two Winchester friends to request their support, and they both quickly agreed to help. The late Sandra Rogers and J.P. Barger, with his wife, Mary B. Barger, each pledged the same $500,000 amount. I told each of them that I just did not have the time to collect $1,000 from each of one thousand other friends.

As far as I knew then, this endeavor both started and ended my fundraising career with an excellent batting average.

> Showing others that you perceive them in the way they hope to be viewed will engender positive feelings and a higher likelihood of a positive result. Bringing together a group of prospective donors and identifying them as "the most visible and generous leaders in a community" will be far more effective in getting their financial support for a good cause than calling them "prospects" for an upcoming campaign. In this case, it took only a tiny group.

BY LATE APRIL 1995, we were still interested in The Shoe, especially because there were strong signs that the recently disastrous real estate market was beginning to bounce back. But Black & Decker was now hedging on what was supposed to be its guarantee that all environmental issues could be resolved "for no more than $1 million." When we required that Black & Decker confirm such a broad guarantee in writing, its representatives at first refused.

We were disappointed as the deal all but fizzled out during late spring and early summer, but with the economy still recovering, other active projects were keeping us hopping. Jamie found time to train for and complete his second Boston Marathon in April, yet he stayed in regular contact with Bob Cronin, the broker for The Shoe site.

A Black & Decker on-site property manager in Beverly told us that his firm was losing $40,000 a week on the property, primarily because of its large crew of union-scale maintenance and security staff. It was also pouring money into operating three huge boilers in the power plant to provide heat and hot water for the drafty campus. Miles of ancient steel steam pipes, too, in the many tunnels and under the buildings spewed out energy, with breaches often appearing as fast as the maintenance technicians could correct them. The senescent system would need to be entirely replaced, as would the antiquated electrical distribution and all the HVAC components, and, of course, some two thousand windows and many *acres* of tired old roof. With clear-eyed knowledge of the unenviable work that awaited us should we acquire The Shoe, we still hoped the deal would be preserved. But we also knew that, with entrepreneurship, not every deal works out.

Hard work, risk-taking, and long hours pretty much define entrepreneurship, along with leadership abilities and surrounding oneself with other smart people who crave being part of a successful and worthwhile firm. Risk-taking should never mean betting the whole firm on any one thing, but being ready to take reasonable risks when we see opportunities with lopsided odds for success, and always-affordable losses should something go wrong.

Entrepreneurs must lead by example and truly be available with an open mind each time there are jobs to be done, including the less attractive ones. They must be constantly looking for and thinking of ways to make the company better and stronger. There are a few incredibly smart people who might be able to create legendary success in a forty-hour work week, but true entrepreneurs will feel deprived if they can't get the benefit of the innovative and extraordinary competitive results that extra effort can bring. And that was our situation.

Meager rents from the few dozen mostly small clients did almost nothing to help The Shoe's financial picture, which was bedeviled as well by real estate taxes, liability issues, and other major maintenance expenses. The Black & Decker on-site property manager in the meantime decried his company's resistance to making any new investment in the site to alleviate the city's legitimate concerns about life-safety issues. Although we would never indemnify Black & Decker for environmental issues, we could at least stop its huge monthly losses by taking the property off its hands, and in late August 1995 we resumed direct discussions with Dennis Adams, who was treasurer of Black & Decker.

Finally, instead of our resolving the contamination issue at The Shoe, we agreed to put $1 million cash into an escrow account. Black & Decker would then complete all necessary work and accept responsibility for possible future issues as well. After that proposed agreement, plus another couple of months, the sale was back on. We would still pay our same initial offer of $500,000, but we were guaranteed a clean hundred-acre property.

Shortly after we had decided to try again to move forward with the purchase, Jamie, who was known by all for his unaffected gracefulness, met on-site with two members of Beverly's Conservation Commission in an effort to learn that board's attitude toward the property. Later, Jamie told me that he was sure the commission leadership would help in any way it could to facilitate a real reclamation of this ugly remnant of Beverly's once-dynamic past, and as it turned out the members were absolutely true to their word. We had learned that the two ponds on the property were clean in terms of chemicals, but underwater, it turned out that they were like an uncharted minefield, with many *tons* of junk and debris that appeared to have been intentionally discarded into the water during the previous ninety years. In one spot next to the foundry building, there was a major coal spill from a railroad coal car that had somehow, many years earlier, spilled its entire load into Lower Shoe Pond. At that time, the Beverly Conservation Commission was both sympathetic and supportive.

CONVINCED THAT THE DEAL was almost done, however, there was a major media event to announce the sale, in a large on-site tent, just a few days before Beverly's 1995 municipal elections. An enthusiastic crowd of Mayor William Scanlon's supporters, along with dozens of other interested city officials, bolstered attendance. Massachusetts Governor William Weld was the keynote speaker. Officials from the city and Black & Decker also addressed the audience. Jamie and I spoke briefly as well, and the transformation was ready to begin.

Despite our decision to pursue this uncertain undertaking, I could not have felt more comfortable about where we were as a company, as I continued to plan my exit strategy with a target of about 2002. That plan mostly consisted of working thereafter with Joyce on our still-new family foundation. We had great confidence in the entire organization, especially as the local economy became increasingly active.

Dennis Clarke was due to return to the firm at year's end after his one-year commitment to Fidelity as part of our sale of the newspapers, and his post-wedding trip. By now Jamie and I knew that no one named Cummings would be interested in following Jamie. Instead, we decided that Dennis would one day become Jamie's successor, perhaps in another ten or fifteen years. Although we never told Dennis anything specifically to that effect, Jamie and I both knew Dennis, who was rarely underestimated, would be ideal for that role, just as Jamie was perfect following me. Jamie also made it quite clear that he was in no hurry for me to go anywhere while he trained Dennis, completing the second real step in the corporate succession plan.

Although I had expected Dennis to be working closely with me during the earliest stages of the Beverly project, just as he had done in Woburn as general manager of the newspapers, it turned out that Jamie wanted Dennis with him in Woburn, where the two of them could work side by side, the same way I had mentored Jamie. The extraordinary challenge of getting the colossal Beverly property under control, however, now loomed over us all.

AS THE SHOE PROJECT lumbered along, Joyce and I decided not to postpone a previously scheduled (and much needed) three-week vacation to Australia and New Zealand. We would visit our youngest daughter, Patricia, who was on a Tufts University junior-year-abroad program, studying at Monash University in

Melbourne, Australia. Built on a sixteen-hour non-stop flight from Los Angeles to beautiful Sydney, the trip thereafter gave us the best of so many things, like the rain forest, scuba diving on Great Barrier Reef, and climbing Ayers Rock. This visit to Australia was followed by an even more leisurely tour of the North and South Islands of New Zealand. We eventually arrived in Queenstown, New Zealand, which is billed as "the Adventure Capital of the World."

Although Patty and I had talked for more than a year about bungee jumping, I had not purchased tickets in advance. "Are you sure you want to do this?" I asked Patty, just before handing over my credit card for the booking.

After a half-hour ride the next morning, we arrived at the world's first and most infamous bungee-jump site, Kawarau Bridge, in time to stand among the crowd of observers watching three other people fly successively off the bridge before us. Then it was our time to jump. I did not feel one bit fearless, while Patty wasn't at all hesitant. "I love you," she said over her shoulder, and off she flew with near perfect form. My greatest relief was seeing her fly happily up and down a few times, and then watching as she was lowered into a rubber-bottomed raft in the Kawarau River, one hundred fifty feet below.

Now it was my turn to show off for my wife and daughter, but climbing onto the jump stand above the railing reminded me of perhaps climbing up on a gallows. I waited four or five seconds but as a cold fear washed over me, decided that I had not flown twelve thousand miles to show my wife and daughter that I was a coward. I did a rapid "Three, two, one, jump," and in no time at all the great elastic cord behind me was pulling against my legs, and just as I was about to become wet, the braided rubber cord yanked me ever so softly one hundred or so feet back up into the air, almost under the arch in the great old bridge. The three big gentle bounces that followed were even more fun. It was fantastic. In fact, both Patty and I felt that it was the single most exciting thing we had ever done.

Extreme sports seem to rule on New Zealand's South Island. Notwithstanding numerous signs reminding visitors about the inherent risks, local sources gloss over reports of how many people "routinely" die in and around Queenstown engaging in various dangerous offerings.

Our sixteen-passenger jet boat pushed every limit later that day, and in one case it cut off the sharp bend in the river by revving up its great jet engine and hurtling entirely out of the water and across a broad sandy beach, two or three feet in the air. What felt like a rip-off as the three of us climbed into that boat turned out to be another thrilling lifetime memory. Patty and Joyce then took the third adventure ride of the day, running off a mountain ledge and hang-gliding with two highly trained guides who kept them riding the strong mountain wind currents for more than thirty minutes.

> RETURNING TO MASSACHUSETTS, I found our interior cleanout and new construction in Beverly moving ahead nicely, *four months before we owned the site.* The essence of the unusual deal we put together with Black & Decker allowed us to completely take over the property, including the right to negotiate and sign leases, and to begin any necessary or desired construction. All of this began January 2, 1996, four months before the actual transfer of the property title. The final sale of the property needed to wait until after Black & Decker concluded some dealings with its union, which still represented about twenty remaining Beverly maintenance and security workers. The more than $2 million worth of work we did without owning the property was almost bizarre, and something of a risk, but we were confident the deal would go forward, and we had an equitable written agreement in place to unwind things in the event anything went seriously wrong, and it all worked beautifully.

But then, even as we closed in on actual ownership of this enduring piece of North Shore history in April 1996, we still had no idea what we would really do with it.

One of our key staff attorneys, David Moynihan, began working with an outstanding Beverly planning official, Tina Cassidy, putting together what is known in Massachusetts as a tax increment financing agreement, or a TIF. The TIF obligated us to invest at least $13.5 million in the property, to create twenty new full-time jobs, and to refrain from seeking a tax abatement for the excessive real estate taxes, which were based on an imagined property value many times higher than what we actually paid. Years later when Mayor Michael Cahill took over the administration in Beverly, Dennis Clarke was pleased to introduce Ms. Cassidy to Woburn Mayor Scott Galvin, who quickly invited her to Woburn City Hall in a similar management role.

Notwithstanding the size and complexity of the United Shoe property, the agreed broker's commission for the sale was 5 percent of the sales price—even though the final $500,000 purchase price was less than 1 percent of the original asking price—or a broker's bill of a mere $25,000. To our surprise, Black & Decker, on what its treasurer told me was a legal technicality, refused to pay Bob Cronin even this relatively paltry sum. In the end we paid the commission, just to avoid an awkward situation for all.

Black & Decker's treasurer, Dennis Adams, left, with Thomas Alperin and Jamie McKeown on October 26, 1995

We completed all our commitments (along with oh-so-many other improvements beneficial to the community) in return for the city's providing us a substantial ten-year reduction on real estate taxes and making us and client firms eligible for some meaningful state benefits as well. With the TIF, we ultimately, and happily, invested $73 million, rather than the promised $13.5 million, to rehabilitate and greatly expand the dilapidated complex.

> In addition to our runaway cash investment at The Shoe, we donated a new building for the North Shore YMCA in Beverly; we also donated land on opposite ends of our new hundred-acre campus for a new elementary school at the northwest corner, on Balch Street, and for the city's proposed new police headquarters at the southeast corner. We even gave additional land needed to widen Route 62 and made $2 million of cash contributions to various Beverly charities. Far more important, as I write this, we currently provide eighty of our own well-paid full-time jobs at the former United Shoe site, and we have facilitated 5,400 new high-quality jobs provided by Cummings client firms. The impact in Beverly has been truly gigantic.

Jamie and Attorney Moynihan also negotiated a "Covenant Not to Sue" with the Commonwealth, based on newly enacted legislation. Under the agreement, the state guaranteed it would never sue us for any additional environmental contamination found on the property following Black & Decker's cleanup. The covenant might not protect us from any possible federal or third-party claim, but we did have what we believed would be a reliable national firm (now Stanley Black & Decker) standing behind its cleanup of the property even if trust would later prove to be problematic. Two decades later, Attorney Moynihan had joined New Hampshire's largest law firm, McLane Law, and was instrumental in McLane becoming one of our largest clients at TradeCenter 128 in Woburn. Ongoing long-term relationships have been an important hallmark of my career in so many ways.

CUMMINGS PROPERTIES' OFFICIAL early arrival at 181 Elliott Street, Beverly, on January 2, 1996, was the start of a brand-new life for what had been widely proclaimed a useless relic of days long past. The former home of United Shoe was finally ready (once again) to become a major economic force on Boston's North Shore. As we were preparing for its return to life, no one, including us, knew where we were going. The $500,000 price to purchase the property, including its two ponds and 1.5 million square feet of solid concrete space, worked out to about eight cents per square foot for the land and the building. Yes, a purchase price of less than ten cents for each square foot of land and building, plus a million dollars to effectively receive a so-called clean certificate from the state.

Just finding our way around the immense facility was a task in itself, with its hundreds of secluded hallways, locked storage areas, and foreboding corners, not to mention the mammoth network of service tunnels carrying many miles of heavy copper cables, water mains, and steam pipes. Every so often, the dark, wet tunnels would open up into wide sepulchral rooms. They reminded me of the catacombs in Paris.

The money we paid up front to Black & Decker to remediate the site was well spent, especially

| *The United Shoe Machinery Corporation "hospital," circa 1915*

given the large volume of oil in the ground. United Shoe mostly leased its shoe machines, and then as they aged, they were returned to the factory by customers from all over the world, to be updated or scrapped. Routinely, we learned, the old machines were smashed with a large steel ball attached to a railroad crane car (which we also acquired) before being melted down in the on-site foundry. From all we could learn, there was little or no attempt to contain any of the lubricating oil from the machines. For decades, as the old machines were crushed up on the ground before being smelted in the foundry, the oil just "disappeared."

What would we do with this enormous decaying relic from America's golden age of manufacturing? We had no idea!

United Shoe had been "the Microsoft of its day." Sixty-four years earlier, Fortune magazine had pronounced United Shoe Machinery Corporation "the bluest of blue chip investments." Indeed, the company had been a giant in its day, but by 1996 it was all but dissolved, with only the hulking remainder of its glory days haunting this historic seaside city. There was significant community interest in what we would do with The Shoe, just as there was within our own offices. We had no idea but were determined from the onset that we could not possibly demolish it, as some people thought was our hidden plan. Those people didn't really know us. We felt there was simply too much value in the fine old buildings to blast it all down. Instead, we just nibbled away, establishing footholds of activity. Someday we would connect the dots.

The *Boston Herald* noted our progress and our unique approach in an April 19, 1996, news story: "One major factor in the development of Cummings' business has been its vertically integrated approach, in which all phases of project development are carried out in-house. Recent Cummings coups have included the renovations of the 1.5-million-square-foot United Shoe Machinery Corp in Beverly, and the conversion of the 170,000-square-foot former Northeast TradeCenter in Woburn."

We worked diligently through the summer of 1996 creating well-organized, newly paved parking lots throughout the entire southern half of the new Cummings campus. Landscaping was another major project. It included planting several hundred deciduous maple, birch, oak, and Bradford pear trees, plus thousands of shrubs of all sorts. Rather than planting maintenance-intensive grass lawns, we relied on hundreds of low shrubs, such as ground-clinging blue rug junipers, that require no sprinklers, little attention, and no bark mulch after a short time. The net effect would be a tidy and beautiful welcome for visitors to the new campus each spring.

Our crew also spent weeks that first summer clearing up the shorelines and dragging dozens of truckloads of junk and debris from the banks and waters of our on-site Upper and Lower Shoe Ponds. Undergrowth, junk, and brush had all but completely blocked any view of the now scenic ponds. We invested more and more to effect beneficial changes and received wide latitude in our extensive work. The relationship with a practical and highly supportive Beverly Conservation Commission at that time was truly outstanding, and as a direct result we completed an almost miraculous transformation.

Close to the concrete-core earthen dam that creates Upper Shoe Pond, an iconic yellow brick chimney towered over the gigantic complex. The corporate USMC initials were set in contrasting dark brown brick on the chimney sides. The 225-foot-tall radial brick structure had an interior diameter of twelve feet at its mouth, where the concrete top ring was seriously spalling following a hundred years of exposure to the elements. The chimney itself was not in any imminent danger of falling, but expensive repairs would have been required to keep it from occasionally (and quite dangerously) shedding small chunks onto the parking lot below, and we had no use for the impressive structure. The day we imploded it, a great carnival atmosphere prevailed, with hundreds of clients and local residents in attendance to witness this exciting highlight of the summer of 1996. In a few thundering instants, the historic USMC trademark no longer loomed over the property.

Implosion of The Shoe's 225-foot-tall chimney

AT NO TIME with Cummings Center, as we would soon call the United Shoe property, did we even pause to consider creating a master plan to lay out in advance where we were going next; we just did it, as the company had done so many times before on so many important but much smaller reclamation projects. Similarly, we had no budget whatsoever for the massive undertaking that had the potential to transform the whole region. If banks or other lenders had been involved in financing, we most certainly would have needed exhaustive detailed plans and budgets, but this project, because of the ongoing environmental issues, would never in those days have been financeable in the first place.

If we had ever engaged any brand of outside architects or designers to accomplish a grand plan ahead of time, we could surely have spent tens of millions of dollars for their efforts, and we would have totally lost two full building seasons. Soft costs for all of the pre-construction niceties would have killed us, just trying to figure out the hundred-acre complex.

We had purchased the property at a most propitious time. The great real estate recession was almost behind us, but the prices of essential materials such as steel, concrete, and drywall had not yet started to skyrocket. It was an exciting time. Anticipating the demand, we rebuilt four cavernous seventy-foot-high warehouse-type spaces, adding three new interstitial concrete floors within each space for another quarter-million square feet of floor space. Other buildings were so much refinished that they were all but unrecognizable. We also demolished more than one hundred thousand square feet of substandard original construction, which luckily was far from the norm in the otherwise solidly built complex.

We were off and running, and at this early stage it was already obvious to Jamie and everyone else that Cummings Center would become more than even he could have hoped, even though we had only just begun to realize the center's full potential. Following is Jamie's "President's Corner" feature from the July 1996 issue of our quarterly client newsletter:

"What a change a year makes. In the now-rebounding real estate market, many businesses have begun to realize measurable growth and increased potential for future expansion. Optimism abounds as our region enjoys a stronger economy and as the marketplace shows more willingness to take risks. In real estate, with the surplus of available space in the Boston area rapidly disappearing, future activity will depend mostly on the availability of new space to satisfy growing demand.

"Building the first speculative office building in Boston in the past five years, Cummings Properties is forging ahead with this optimism. Our brand-new seven-story, first-class complex at 18 Commerce Way in Woburn represents the company's investment in the future and an overall significant indicator for today's burgeoning economy.

"Additional substantial efforts are now being devoted toward the renovation of prime space at TradeCenter 128 (formerly Northeast Trade Center) in Woburn and at the giant new Cummings Center in Beverly. These two facilities combined will provide more than 2 million square feet of multiple-use space for diverse businesses of all sizes.

"Providing key access and visibility, abundant on-site parking, nearby amenities and services, full-service leases, and attractive leasing rates, these properties afford ideal opportunities designed to meet the needs of business today."

"How could they possibly ever fill it all?" was the common refrain around Beverly, but it was happening, and our neighbors were beginning to see it. We had not thought much about the impact our massive restoration would have, but for sure, home values were rising much faster in the Beverly area than in other metropolitan communities. Fortunately, the homes that were selling and the apartments being leased were mostly benefiting long time Beverly property owners, so the complaints about affordability and higher prices never caused too much concern.

By November 1996, businesses were clamoring for space, not only at Cummings Center in Beverly, but also in all the company's other Greater Boston communities. The Cummings Center staff was moving in new clients faster than we ever imagined. Soon, we had seventy newly hired employees of our own in Beverly, just twenty miles away from Woburn. These new colleagues focused exclusively on building and marketing Cummings Center. There were also dozens of mostly small subcontractors helping us complete the total makeover of this giant complex that Jamie had envisioned from the first day he visited the site. At one time, we had *eleven* local electrical contractors working on diverse projects in Beverly, along with eight or nine of our own in-house electricians.

REAL ESTATE developers are sometimes, and sometimes deservedly, maligned for their callous disregard of history. But to fast-forward for a bit, one of the things that makes us all most proud about Cummings Center is that people strolling through the hallways of today's sparkling office-and-research park can relive so much of the history of United Shoe Machinery Corporation, one of the true titans of twentieth-century industrial capitalism. Visiting the mammoth

Constructed in 1642, this tidal gristmill was in continuous operation at what is now Cummings Center until 1894

The former foundry of The Shoe, made of reinforced concrete, where most of the metal castings for USMC's shoe machines were created

Today, the restored 900 Cummings Center overlooks Lower Shoe Pond. Clients and visitors alike enjoy the picnic areas, parks, and a nature trail surrounding the two scenic ponds on campus

A desolate view of the south section of The Shoe, taken in the early spring of 1996. These three structures can be easily identified today when entering Cummings Center from Elliott Street

100 Cummings Center, a 1.3 million-square-foot building, is home to hundreds of businesses including corporate headquarters, medical offices, software firms, and research laboratories

engineering marvel that was, at its birth in 1905, the largest factory in the world, they can see dozens of modern glass display cases filled with memorabilia and mementos from a bygone era of industrial goodwill and plenty.

Before United Shoe assembled its Beverly campus in 1902 and 1903, most of the land, except for the mill site, had been used exclusively for farming. According to area historians, however, part of this historic industrial site is one of the oldest continuously used commercial properties in North America. The city clerk in Salem, Massachusetts, Deborah Berkinshaw, in response to in-house counsel David Moynihan, provided information about the fascinating history of our Beverly site. She sent David certified copies of many old, exquisitely handwritten Salem city records (the land was originally part of Salem), including evidence of a permit for Friend's Mill that was issued "about 1642," she wrote, though the city no longer had the complete record for that period. "The absence of many written records for that decade does not mean that government was suspended or that the construction did not then happen," she clarified in her letter to David. There was a great residuum of other evidence to document its history.

Dating back to the construction of John Friend's tidal gristmill in the 1640s, what later became the property of United Shoe originally straddled a branch of the Bass River, before the first dam was constructed there in the mid-seventeenth century. A second much higher concrete-core dam and a new tidal weir were constructed farther upstream near the center of the campus around 1900 to create Upper Shoe Pond and Lower Shoe Pond. Before the mill was constructed, this inlet was the documented landing area for farmers who traveled back and forth across the Bass River on tiny ferryboats from near the center of Salem.

The most prominent of several historic markers identifying the area of Planters Landing is an almost one hundred-year-old bronze plaque, loaned to Elliott Landing Condominium, which we opened on the site in November 2016 but was fully sold (or under agreement) by August 2017. I have sometimes imagined my eight-times-great grandfather, Isaac Cummings, landing in Salem in 1638 and perhaps traveling through this area on Planters Path, before he settled in Ipswich.

At about this same time, in 1643, John Friend's original tidal-powered gristmill was constructed directly on what is now the condominium property (but still closely connected to Cummings Center). The mill continuously operated there, and then about two hundred feet south of Elliott Landing, until the second location burned down on June 4, 1889. Dried corn was routinely shipped to Friend's Mill from Long Island, New York, and Newport, Rhode Island. The same ships then carried cargoes of corn meal and dried fish from Beverly to New York City. After the fire, the dock from the gristmill was used in connection with a small foundry, maintaining the continuum of commercial uses until the parcel was purchased by United Shoe around 1902. The submerged wooden piles of the last dock are still readily visible in the river bottom today, at low tide.

SINCE THE EARLIEST days of the company, our leadership team has held Monday night dinner meetings. Monday, November 11, 1996, was no exception; that night we were reviewing a brand-new set of third-quarter operating figures. Our focus then, as now, was on occupancy levels and monthly lease income, rather than net profits, which we simply never track. Our mantra has always been, "If we keep the buildings occupied, the profits will be there," and they always were. The foregoing statement may sound strange to many, but having no outside stockholders to satisfy, we found that it was and is absolutely true.

Everything I did as an entrepreneur has always been so simple and basic. By 1996, when we took over The Shoe property, a dozen great internet firms were bursting forth and beginning to change the entire world. We talked about how exciting it must have been for the whole generation of new computer and electronics entrepreneurs who were coming to the fore then, but no more exciting than it was for us with a real estate boom that defied our imaginations. Our real estate equity just sizzled, and the whole industry in the Northeast was on a roll, unlike anything experienced since the boom years following World War II.

We were also discussing our overall organization's recent much deeper involvement in financial equities investments with Advest under David Leland. Advest would later be acquired by Merrill Lynch, in May 2005, when the account still held only a small fraction of the value to which its assets would later grow.

But the big news this night was that our vacancy factor, calculated to include all buildings in service for more than six months, was under three percent for the first time ever. No one was happier to hear this than Jamie, because with my having worked almost totally at Cummings Center for the previous six months, these sparkling leasing figures from Woburn clearly reflected his strong leadership.

❦ *How to create business plans and budgets is surely considered an important aspect of an entrepreneur's education. Interestingly, however, I have never even one time created either of these "essential" documents. As with our purchase of The Shoe, we have—in all cases— opted to use the time and effort normally required for such planning and put it instead into actually getting started. Although often not possible when a third-party investor is involved, this practice is one of the great benefits of self-financing.*

[12]

Lowering the Flags

THE MORNING OF November 13, 1996 was the day we were paving large areas of some of the most visible new parking lots at Cummings Center in preparation for winter. Major excavations for drainage and utility improvements had been underway all summer, and although our construction work goes on reliably year-round, asphalt paving always seems to signal the end of our excavation projects until spring.

I was standing that morning exactly where Friend's Grist Mill stood in 1643, near the southwest corner of our soon to be sparkling new Beverly campus. I had arrived early to be there when the contractor's crew started spreading and rolling out the new surface over the last of the original parking areas being repaved. I took in all I could get of the scent of hot asphalt—it was such a great smell to me at the end of another wonderful building season. That's when my cell phone began vibrating.

November 13, 1996 became the worst day of my life.

In a heartbeat—that was a phrase Jamie so often used to describe how quickly life can change. I thought about that a few minutes later, as I was trying to process this call from Jamie and Denise's next-door neighbor. She tried to remain composed as she told me that Jamie had just been taken from his home to Winchester Hospital after an apparent heart attack. "You need to come back *now*. He was moaning some, but was not otherwise responsive," she said. She clearly conveyed the gravity of the situation.

The southbound rush-hour traffic leaving Beverly on Route 128 can be slow, but not on this day, and my drive to Winchester Hospital emergency room was under thirty minutes. The ER desk attendant happened to immediately recognize me. As she walked me inside, I heard the worst possible news.

Denise was waiting in a side room with one of her close friends. Both appeared to be in shock. Denise and I embraced for a long time. "Tell me what's happened, Den."

"He is gone," she said. "They did open-heart massage and everything they could, but he is gone."

TWENTY MINUTES AFTER my arrival at the hospital, Jamie's sister, Debbie Laudano, arrived. I knew Debbie well and was closest to the door when she came in. I felt her heart pounding as she clung to me, hoping that everything was somehow going to be okay. "How can this be? He was only forty one years old," Debbie said, sobbing so loudly, after learning there was nothing more anyone could do. (Jamie's parents experienced their second terrible tragedy when Debbie died from cancer several years later.)

After another hour or so, one of the nurses told us that the last two doctors had left, and that Jamie had been cleaned, if someone wished to go in to see him. Denise did not want to see Jamie in the hospital, but the nurse escorted me to where he was. After asking me to confirm his identity, she stepped outside.

I could barely kneel beside him next to the ER gurney. *Come back, Jamie, come back!*—a silent scream stuck in my throat. I tried to comprehend the enormity of what had happened. I first held his arm and then his hand. There was no mistaking the significance of his already cold fingers. My best ever male friend was gone…

WE ALL LEFT the hospital shortly before noon, and I headed directly to our nearby office at 200 West Cummings Park and asked everyone to gather outside Jamie's and my offices. Staff had just started to hear that "Jamie is in the hospital," but no one knew the extent of the situation.

The large open area was packed. My message was brief, and halting, to be sure: "I have the awful duty to tell you that Jamie suffered a heart attack this morning. He managed to complete his usual morning run, and he made it home. Denise thought she had heard him calling and found him just inside their rear entrance. Winchester EMTs responded quickly, but an hour or so later, at 8:40 AM, he was pronounced dead at Winchester Hospital."

There was a dreadful groan from the sixty or so friends and colleagues and an outburst of the rawest of emotions.

Doug Stephens was one of the first to react. As we retreated toward my office, he followed closely behind. "I'll have them lower all the flags," he said, referring to the dozen or so American flags we flew in prominent locations. We both wiped away tears. Everyone wiped away tears.

The Woburn office, where so many considered Jamie a good friend as well as an admired colleague, was in a state of stunned disbelief following my announcement. But soon the leadership team, spearheaded by Mike Pascavage, Doug, and Dennis, began sorting out what had to be done, such as notifying all staff members, clients, and other key relationships of Jamie's sudden passing. Dennis later told me they felt they were honoring Jamie by doing what needed to be done, in just the manner that Jamie would've expected them to do it, on this challenging and heartbreaking November day.

Joyce was at our Florida condo spending a few days with two of her golfing friends but was unreachable during my twenty-minute drive to the hospital from Beverly. I tried again after the staff meeting and then repeatedly for the next several hours. We finally connected late in the afternoon. It was a doubly emotional call—I needed her by my side so, so much. Joyce was on a plane early the next morning.

> Losing Jamie was more terrible than anything I had ever imagined. He was so much more than a good friend and colleague. Jamie had become a best friend to me and to our whole family, but he was also my successor. We had worked so closely and developed such an extraordinary bond, as I taught him everything I knew, over nearly eighteen years. My stomach ached for months with an unshakable agony. And how sad we all felt for Denise and for their young daughters, Molly and Kelly; for Jamie's parents, Connie and Leonard McKeown; and for Debbie and the rest of Jamie's devastated family.

JAMIE'S DEATH WAS covered on the front pages of the Woburn and Winchester newspapers, and as a news story in *The Boston Globe*. The *Winchester*

Star reported that more than two thousand people attended his wake, which continued until well after 11 PM. We were all surprised and deeply touched that volunteer honor guards from the *Woburn* Police Department arrived unexpectedly and stood at either side of the Winchester funeral home entrance for almost the entire time. During that evening, Jamie's dad left the funeral home twice when he heard how long the line still was. We later learned that he went to the far end of that line on his own to greet visitors he didn't know, introducing himself and thanking them for coming.

Woburn Police motorcycle officers returned the next morning to again honor Jamie by assisting Winchester police in escorting the procession from the funeral home to the church. Jamie was not Catholic, but three priests presided over his Mass of Christian Burial at St. Eulalia Church, in Winchester. Twenty-four members of the really excellent adult choir also surprised us with their gracious presence.

That Saturday morning, November 16, 1996, I delivered the single most important talk of my life. I don't know if it was my prayers beforehand or Joyce standing closely by my side in the pulpit that allowed me to hold myself together through all but the last few words:

> *Dear Friends,*
>
> *We came together today in this tremendous outpouring from all over Massachusetts, and from many other states as well, to honor in a singular way one of the finest people ever to live in this community. We came to celebrate Jamie McKeown's life, even though it is hard to even use the word "celebrate" when we feel such an immense sense of tragedy at his passing.*
>
> *When Denise sat down with Jamie's parents Thursday and selected the hymns in this musical service, they selected those hymns because of their relevance to Jamie, or to their lives together. And as we sing most of these hymns today, we are praying with them.*
>
> *No person in this church has a better sense of right and wrong than Jamie did, and no man I have ever met cared more about doing "the right thing." Earning the respect of his peers was an overriding tenet of Jamie's being.*
>
> *Jamie didn't do anything to excess. He loved to run, and ski, and play tennis, and golf and swim, and he did them all well, but each had its limited place—except when he could do them with his family.*
>
> *How often did Jamie ever get angry? Let me ask you—how many people*

in this congregation ever saw Jamie get angry, even once? He didn't get peeved or vexed at little things either, and he never pouted, or was snide, or called people names, or even implied them.

Jamie didn't preach, but he led by example. Most of Jamie's friends are better people because of him and because they wanted to earn his approval. I am certainly a better person because of him.

Jamie left us suddenly, but he left with no wrongs uncorrected. He had no fear or premonition of death, but he lived each day as though it could be his last.

We come here today from many Christian traditions, and certainly from other religions as well, but we all celebrate hope, and we celebrate God's boundless love for all. The Lord our God is one, and we know that Jamie is with Him now.

As many of you are aware, Jamie was a private person. He didn't know how to gossip or brag. He was a winner who didn't even think about it, he just did it. Quiet success was his way of life.

Jamie was a wonderful father, son, colleague, brother, and uncle, but Denise always told everyone that he was the best husband who ever lived. How many of his close friends didn't hear, at least once in a while, that our own wives wouldn't mind our "acting a little more like Jamie"? I certainly did.

Twelve years ago, while standing in the front entranceway of Winchester Country Club, just two nights before he was married, Jamie and I had a great talk: "There is nothing I won't do for the rest of my life to try to make Denise happy." He didn't just say that to me, however; he said it as though he was making a promise. We all know that he kept that promise.

When Kelly and Molly came along, Jamie then became the best father any man could be. He learned well from his own great parents, and from many of you, I'm sure.

Watching Jamie for over two decades, and closely working with him for more than seventeen years, I have had the truly unique pleasure of seeing him and knowing him all the way from Woburn Boys "Clubber" to seasoned corporate executive.

I told Jamie many times over the years how proud I was of him and all he had become… I only wish I could have told him, also, how much I loved him.

W.S.C.

Nothing could have prepared me to deal with the shock of Jamie's sudden death. He was a picture of health, and fitness was always on his mind. He exercised almost every day, whether by going on a long bike ride or run, playing tennis, or putting in an early morning session at Woburn's North Suburban YMCA. Staff at the Y a decade earlier honored him with a specially painted reserved locker in recognition of many things he had personally done to help the YMCA.

From November 13 through most of the next year, there was hardly a single day that I did not feel, at some point, shaken and depressed. I had never been one to reach for drink in times of stress, but just in case, I totally gave up all alcohol for many months.

In the story of this terrible tragedy, it was while doing something Jamie truly loved that his journey on this earth simply ended.

ALTHOUGH JAMIE MADE it home from his morning run that day, I learned many years later that a mutual acquaintance had noticed him earlier that fateful Wednesday morning sitting against a wall along Bacon Street in Winchester as the friend drove by. There was nothing alarming about Jamie's appearance, he told me, but it still seemed odd to see him resting. In hindsight, Jamie must have been in real trouble then. That was shortly before he would have crossed Route 3 and headed up Fernway to be with his family, in the home they had recently built just below the corner of Fernway and Arlington Street.

Jamie was hopeful that he might someday earn a place in Hawaii's Ironman Triathlon, but in the meantime, he said, the Boston Marathon would have to do. His times were not elite, but as his 1996 finish had been better than his previous race, he was hopeful that his 1997 results might be better still. Instead, a fatal heart attack ended his life. Every friend he had was saddened. The town was shocked. I was alternatively stricken and devastated.

I could only think how much Jamie had been all I wanted for the future of the company, especially after our own children had made it clear that they did not want careers in real estate. I had known Jamie well for twenty years, and he had reached the point of doing most things he took on either every bit as well as I did them, or better. Together, however, we had been extremely effective in a mutually gratifying relationship.

For several years prior to Jamie's death, my principal interest had increasingly been in solidifying the long-term succession plan, and it had so thoroughly come together. Jamie had progressed so well and was everything I could possibly have hoped for in my successor. Not only was he my successor as president, he would also have been the next chairman before he was fifty.

We had talked about it—about my stepping aside. It was too soon then, but we both had presumed by then that Dennis Clarke would move into the presidency when Jamie moved up to chairman, but what now? I fully expected to still be working, only it would have been full-time with Cummings Foundation.

Now, how would I—*we*—ever get through this situation? I knew we would deal with it, somehow. Working with an extraordinary team of colleagues at Cummings Properties, we resolved thousands of situations in our day-to-day activities, usually quite effectively. We almost always achieved good and fair results. But how profoundly I agonized. Losing Jamie was a problem for which there simply was no solution for me.

THE DAYS following the funeral, in November 1996, were grim for everyone who knew and cared for Jamie. We were all particularly concerned for Denise, whose emotional burden included not only her own overwhelming grief but also that of Kelly and Molly. Community support was everywhere, however, and Denise still had her parents close by. They brought enormous personal assistance through the most difficult years. Jamie had provided well for them financially, but there was no easy way to move beyond their collective grief.

Twenty years later, as I was working on this book, I asked Denise to share a few of her thoughts about Jamie. He was loved and respected by so many people, but most really only knew him as a leading business and civic figure. To honor Jamie appropriately here, and at the suggestion of author Bill Novak, I asked Denise to tell about Jamie the way she knew Jamie—as her husband, her soulmate, a father, a man:

> *Bill asked me to write a little something to further describe what Jamie was like in everyday life, besides what he was like at Cummings Properties.*

Family was so important to Jamie. The memory that really pulls at my heart is what an amazing father he was. Jamie was such an avid reader and really believed his children should be too. He was ever the schoolteacher he once aspired to be—so much so that he started reading to Kelly and Molly when they were days old. I remember hearing him reading aloud one day, and I went into the room to see our one-month-old baby lying in his arms while he read Time magazine out loud to her. I laughed and said, 'I don't think she gets it.' But she did. Both the girls must have turned out to have such a love of reading because of all that reading in the beginning. We always had to end the night with a story in bed, or no one would go to sleep. They loved reading and snuggling with their dad. To this day, they are both big readers. It was such a beautiful thing to watch and one of my fondest memories.

Spending time with me and our daughters was always a priority for Jamie. Late-night meetings for work and all the organizations that he volunteered for prevented us from having family time many evenings, but Jamie would balance those nights away with his dedication to us on weekends. On the weekends, he was 100 percent ours. We did things every Saturday and Sunday together as a family. I would steal him away on Saturday nights for our date night. It was important to me that we had a night to ourselves. I'm so glad I did that. We did that almost every Saturday until the weekend just preceding his death, and I shall be forever grateful.

The weekends were always such fun family outings. We always had a fun thing to do with the kids. Whether it be a swim, a bike ride, apple picking, museums, whatever, it was always about the girls. If Jamie wanted to do something for himself such as golf or workout, he would do it early in the morning before the kids woke up, and he would be back in time to be there when they did. They would wake up on Saturdays, get out of bed, go to the railing to look downstairs, and then start yelling, "Daddy, Daddy, come get us." They loved the weekends because they knew Daddy was around all the time to be their playmate. Somehow, I got forgotten, and he was the King. That's okay. I so thoroughly enjoyed it.

Jamie was a lover of sports. Not watching, but doing. He loved to bike and swim, and he ran almost every day. He was so healthy in his eating that his idea of a treat was an apple because it was sweet. He tried to instill these habits in his children. Even as toddlers, our girls went on the back of bikes for bike rides, or in jogging strollers to go for runs with Jamie. We taught them to ski at two years old. It was so important to him that his girls were active with him. He loved to take them swimming, sailing, canoeing. Anything that was moving. He used to be a swim instructor at the Woburn Boys & Girls Club, and he brought our daughters into the pool there at eight months old. Because of all this effort on Jamie's part, the girls were exposed to so many different activities, which they still enjoy as adults.

It is so sad they lost all of that so early, but he made a lifetime of love in the years they had him. That was the thing about Jamie. He lived his life to the fullest. I am grateful now that he was the way he was. We got so much time from him in his short years of fatherhood. The girls were six and eight when Jamie died, but they have memories as if he were here much longer. That comes from his dedication to them and to spending time with them. We have a lifetime of memories.

Jamie loved every day he lived—with his family, with his friends, with his coworkers. Who gets to go to bed every night knowing he did everything just the way he would have wanted that day, with no regrets? Jamie did.

D.P.M.

AFTER JAMIE'S SERVICES, several people commented to me that preparing and delivering the eulogy must have been extraordinarily challenging, and it was. But it was also part of the healing. Our youngest daughter, Patty, who was then a psychologist practicing in California, recently read my notes for this chapter and wrote to me: "I don't know if you want to add it, but I so clearly recall you struggling on the last few words of that eulogy, with Mom closely at your arm." My remembering Jamie that morning on behalf of so many people to whom he meant so much was cathartic to me, and was also an essential element of the respect I so much wanted to show him.

Looking back, my single most difficult task after leaving Winchester Hospital on November 13 was calling all our mutual friends and colleagues together at the office that dreadful morning. My announcement of Jamie's sudden death absolutely stunned the close-knit group. It felt so unfair and unnatural that someone so young and active and fit could so suddenly become only a cherished memory.

After a few months things were better for a while. But then, during the spring of 1997, I began feeling terrible again while trying my damnedest not to let it show. Some days it was extremely hard to focus. There were times when I just had to be alone, and I would drive to some secluded place to walk and think. For nearly all of the seventeen-plus years we worked together, I was teaching and mentoring him, and then we were clearly learning from each other. The loss of his presence was devastating to me, in so many ways.

The emotion was deeper than anything I could ever have imagined experiencing. Unlike the quiet grief upon losing my much-loved parents in 1986 and 1992, and later my sister, Jamie's death moved me to tears so many times. Patty also reminded me of something that Joyce mentioned to Patty at the time: The only thing that could have hurt me more would have been if something terrible had happened to Joyce or to one of our kids.

Despite my emotions over the loss of Jamie, it never occurred to me to seek professional help. I chose not to share much of what was happening, even though talk therapy or medication might have helped me get through the heartache more easily. After many times encouraging business colleagues and others to take advantage of professional counseling to help them through troubling issues, I did not do that in my own case.

The National Institutes of Health website was helpful regarding symptoms of depression, but they just did not fit me. I decided that grief was my problem, with symptoms of sadness certainly—and, in my case, a sense of profound loss. Never feeling hopeless or helpless or in any way incapable of coping with my responsibilities, I nevertheless coped with some of the symptoms for years before they finally passed.

UNRELATED TO ANYTHING else, in May 1997 I happily exercised my most enjoyable perk as a trustee at Tufts University. I had attended many Tufts graduations by that time, but this was the best one by far because both our daughters were graduating and I was able to present their degrees. Marilyn graduated from Tufts University School of Medicine while, at about the same hour, Patty received her undergraduate degree and conducted the

Bill at Tufts graduation with daughters Marilyn and Patricia

university band. There was a big logistical shuffle for Joyce and me to travel between the ceremonies, but it worked out and was certainly lots of fun.

People can become overwhelmed when good and bad things coincide in their lives, and may feel that they are not grieving properly. But despite Jamie's passing, I was quite able to take in and enjoy the many good things going on in our lives. They were slowly pulling me back to a good place. It was probably close to a year, however, before I stopped feeling a physical ache whenever my thoughts dwelled on Jamie. I credit the marvelous support I received from Joyce and our family as well as from so many colleagues and friends who were universally helpful and supportive.

Coinciding with the first anniversary of Jamie's death, I received a beautifully written anonymous letter from which I have several times directly borrowed when writing to friends and colleagues who are grieving. Instead of advising me to try putting Jamie out of my mind, the letter writer urged me to talk about him often to help preserve the memories. The writer quoted the long-passed German theologian Dietrich Bonhoeffer, who wrote that the loss of people we love creates enormous gaps, but as long as the gaps remain unfilled they preserve bonds between us. "God doesn't fill them, but on the contrary, keeps them empty," he wrote, "and so helps us to keep alive our communion with each other, even at the cost of pain."

This poignant letter gave me new meaning to the concept of how much it often helps when people can talk things out. That, of course, is the essence of counseling and therapy, and I was surprised by how much it helped when so many friends, some of whom barely knew Jamie, came by our office over the many months following his funeral. Each time I talked with someone who knew how close we were and recognized how deeply we all missed him, it was uplifting—and that is true even today, more than twenty-two years later.

Although Joyce and I had formed Cummings Foundation ten years before Jamie died, his death was a stark reminder to me that if we were to do meaningful good things, together with the foundation, we really needed to get started. I made fundamental commitments to myself to strengthen the company's executive team, and soon began reassigning more of Jamie's former responsibilities to other members, rather than back to myself.

Jamie and I, but especially Jamie, had already been actively mentoring Dennis. It was so fortuitous that Jamie prevailed in January 1996 when he pushed me repeatedly to make sure that he would be the one who would work most closely with Dennis. Jamie also longed to be in Beverly during the colossal effort there, but he wanted more to coach Dennis in Woburn. We had fully concurred about Dennis' potential just months after Dennis joined us through our *Woburn Advocate* team in June 1992. Jamie readily agreed with me then that Dennis should be groomed for the company's top spot.

During Dennis' year away with Fidelity in 1995, and then with Jamie through most of 1996, he had continued to grow his executive skills. But he had not yet picked up enough to take over Jamie's post when Jamie passed. Nor had there been enough of an opportunity for him to show others in the firm the considerable executive talent that he was rapidly developing. That last issue, it seemed, was especially critical, and Dennis fully realized that his work would be easier in the long run if he did not arouse feelings of resentment among his colleagues.

There had never been even a single moment when I ever considered hiring anyone from outside the firm. We had several possible successors to Jamie in-house, if one were needed quickly, the most prominent of whom was Mike Pascavage. But after much soul-searching, I decided to wait before taking any steps to directly fill Jamie's position. Jamie would always be my successor and our second president, of course, but here I was now succeeding him.

❊ *Investors must know all that they can, and must feel good about any investment before committing to it. The best investments, however, will rarely be the ones which everyone else feels good about, too. The smartest investors will make their independent judgments and have the confidence to seize whatever opportunities are available. Feelings and intuition will so often be far more important than calculations. The former United Shoe property required copious intuition.*

❊ *Whether due to death, changing market tides, new technology, or myriad other factors, life can and does oftentimes change in an instant. To the extent possible, entrepreneurs must prepare themselves for a business' inevitable ups and downs by thinking through a "plan B." Business leaders must be nimble, and they must always be ready to adapt to changing circumstances.*

❊ *Creativity is more instinctive than it is learned, and may have little to do with "intellectual intelligence." It is much more a product of how a person thinks about things than it is about what he or she knows, and may be fostered by a liberal education. Infinite curiosity about how things work will be a strong portent of creativity.*

❊ *The best decisions come from careful personal observation and intuitive business judgment.*

[13]

Carrying On

| *The main south side entrance drive into Cummings Center*

EVEN THOUGH WE were all weighed down with sorrow as we managed our way into 1997, Cummings Properties started gradually recovering its equilibrium—as we knew we had to do. It was helpful that we were all so busy. We carried into the new year the momentum of greatly increased leasing activity from 1996, and our commercial real estate leasing started off strong and remained that way through 1997 and beyond, especially as demand for biotech space was increasingly overflowing out of a greatly overheated Cambridge market. Office colleagues commented several times how much Jamie would have enjoyed this furiously busy period. I thought the same thing as business truly boomed. Each day was exciting and busy, but surely, nothing was the same.

Cummings Center continued to move forward with a mounting volume of activity. Construction costs were piling up more quickly than we ever imagined. "Just like Boston's Big Dig," we joked. But the more we invested to transform that historic complex into a fully restored, first-class business center, the more prospective clients showed up. Early on, we attracted biotech, medtech, and pharmaceutical start-ups, and Beverly Hospital opened our first walk-in medical clinic there. Many of these new Cummings Center clients became quickly connected to the large and talented North Shore labor pool, and their employees were happier for it. Hundreds of Beverly-area workers no longer had to make the difficult rush-hour trek into Cambridge and Boston, or to the increasingly crowded areas of Burlington, or to the now famous rush-hour gridlock so prevalent anywhere near Waltham.

We also started signing up dozens of independent medical practices. Area physicians needed a first-class central location to colonize near Beverly Hospital, and the growing reality of significant referral opportunities in Cummings Center became a major draw for an ever-widening base of medical specialties.

We were immediately earning new income from the improvements, and we continued investing more and more. Many of the expenditures generated substantial tax savings, including some major federal abandoned-building tax credits, as the buildings were built before 1934 and had been all but abandoned. Beverly provided us with a unique project on which to spend opportunistically. As a result, we improved and upgraded this vast complex far beyond anything we had imagined. By the end of 2010, we had invested—with no regrets—more than $73 million to improve our half-million-dollar Beverly complex.

| *A view from the south of a booming 2-million-square-foot Cummings Center*

FRED WILBUR TOOK over more of the management of the Cummings Center construction effort, capably assisted by Bruce Oveson, our main on-site staff architect there. Bruce worked only in Beverly, supervising details to accompany the larger plans produced in our main design headquarters in Woburn. He and several on-site designers in Beverly produced plans for individual fit-ups for smaller prospective tenants, as well as the more detailed plans needed for individual building permits for new clients as they quickly moved in. An important hallmark of our overall approach has been our ability from the company's earliest days to produce and focus on expediting the all in-house design and paperwork to facilitate prompt, easy leases. That vertical integration was growing rapidly.

One of the most consistent themes from my earliest days has always been saving money, and always knowing the cost of everything before I purchased it. Keenly establishing the cost vs. value ratio of any purchase goes a long way in helping to get a seller to his/her lowest price.

In my professional responsibilities it is hugely distressing to realize how often architects and engineers seem to completely ignore anything to do with the "value" of the sometimes senseless components they write into specifications for new buildings.

Some architects and certainly many engineers will roundly demean efforts of buyers to reduce building construction costs by editing out what are sometimes hugely excessive costs for over-designed building foundations, or structural steel, or roof assemblies.

Paying third parties to carefully review the cost of various major components in any proposed structure before contracts are awarded can sometimes pay huge dividends by flushing out extraordinarily conservative and wasteful over-design. Especially when engineers are engaged by architectural firms to design specific aspects of a new building, there is no incentive whatsoever for either one to be at all concerned about cost reduction.

For almost every aspect of any new building, there are uniformly strict state code requirements to ensure that all aspects of the structure will be first of all safe, and that it will comply with all requirements for things like environmental impact, energy consumption, and accessibility. The cost problems arise when designers—in an abundance of caution—spend to make the structure supposedly "better" than is required, with no known return.

From a purely "design" point of view, construction (both interior and exterior) should be simplified whenever it can be. Things like the dimensions of doors and windows being exactly the same whenever possible will yield much

Bill Cummings and Pulitzer Prize–winning author Ada Louise Huxtable at Cummings Center, August 1997. "Cummings Center is more than a success story; it is a dream come true"

greater cost efficiency and much lower costs. The savings will come not only from reduced manufacturers' costs but also from the builder's cost to create a minimum number of standard-sized openings, and then from the window or door installer in actually placing them in the structure.

I have long been a strong champion of our in-house design capabilities, but some people and organizations just do not get it. From my earliest active trustee involvement in construction affairs at Tufts, I strongly advocated in favor of the university's hiring on-campus architecture and design professionals. Instead, a constant progression of costly outside architects, designers, and engineers bill Tufts for the vast majority of even its smallest construction and maintenance needs. Universities, in my mind, do not need elite "figurehead" architects; strong on-campus design teams can do so much of the routine work themselves, at a small fraction of the cost.

> My viewpoint was vindicated, and then some, on October 2, 1997, when *The Wall Street Journal* ran a major feature story on Cummings Center written by its Pulitzer Prize–winning architecture critic, the late Ada Louise Huxtable. We greatly benefited from her abundant praise of Cummings Center, which she described as "the single most important, and generally unrecognized, concrete landmark in this country"—and she raved about our transformation of the property.

Before Ms. Huxtable first called us about writing a feature story, I frankly did not know who she was. When I told Bruce, our new Cummings Center architect, that Ms. Huxtable would be writing a feature story about our Beverly reconstruction, I asked him to tell me about her. Bruce was beside himself. "Bill," he said, "I was *weaned* on Ada Louise Huxtable in architecture school. *Everyone* knows Ada Louise." The winner of the first Pulitzer Prize for Distinguished Criticism, Ada Louise Huxtable was also a recipient of MacArthur and Guggenheim fellowships, and she wrote ten books.

Ada Louise spent a full day with me in August 1997, touring every corner of Cummings Center as part of her research for the article and was in touch for later follow-up. At the time, she was almost fully recovered from a recent hip surgery but was still a little concerned about not overdoing the tour. We resolved that situation nicely, using a golf cart to tour the perimeter of the buildings, our two large ponds, and then *inside* the main building itself, where the reconstruction was about 80 percent complete. We easily maneuvered the vehicle down the entire length of the wide, quarter-mile-long carpeted main hallway.

I learned that this celebrated author and preservationist had earlier written about The Shoe in five different decades—in at least two of her books and in both *The New York Times* and *The Wall Street Journal*. The most prominent architecture critic in the country was delighted that someone was finally making a serious effort to reclaim what she called "her building." She had come to know and love The Shoe through the many summers she spent in Marblehead, only a few miles from Cummings Center, and she seemed genuinely excited that we were "getting it right."

ADA LOUISE HUXTABLE was not the first person to speak or write about the fourth dimension of architecture, "the aesthetics," but she was the first person to ever talk with me about it.

Ada Louise, Joyce, and I were visiting in her charming long-term summer home in Marblehead, Massachusetts, and she went on at some length about how pleased she was with Cummings Properties' work creating our 2 million square foot Cummings Center. She summed it up by saying that we had handily passed the aesthetics test, and thanking us for "bringing dignity back" to what she had many times referred to as one of her favorite old buildings *anywhere*.

She was particularly complimentary about the four-story tall curved glass curtain walls we had added on the south-facing end of the quarter-mile-long main structure. Those striking new windows and more than nine hundred other individual new tinted windows were in dramatic contrast in every case with the juxtapositioned rough gray concrete walls of the hundred year-old landmark. The glasswork and the abundance of new trees and other greenery were what really sold Ada Louise as she planned her *Wall Street Journal* feature story about "The Shoe" and what she told us should be its next hundred years.

During our all-day tour of Cummings Center three weeks earlier, Ada Louise had been particularly impressed with how many old artifacts we had found, giving us materials with which to create splendid historical features throughout the interlacing interior hallways. Most of these artifacts are prominently displayed today in large custom-made glass and oak cabinets. We also talked about how many other things we salvaged and successfully reused, in what seemed like the unending reconstruction process. And all of this work was accomplished as the few inherited tenants and oh-so-many new clients quickly began operating in the grandly rebuilt complex.

We were extremely cost conscious as we invested $80 million to repurpose our original $500,000 property purchase. I tried without much success to interest Ada Louise in my theory that architects should pay more attention to the relationship of cost and value. I joked with her about adding "Value" as a fifth dimension.

She agreed with me that most architects probably do not focus much on the cost of materials or components of any given project, unless, perhaps, they have a financial interest in the final product. The market determines the price of the finished product, she said, and buyers or builders who want "the best" have usually abandoned any penchant for shopping the price or relative value of the components they specify. Ada Louise also pointed out how much architects and major builders rely on third parties to design so many systems, elements, and components of the buildings they crank out. And there is typically just no incentive whatsoever then to spend much time considering their cost.

We all so much appreciated Ada Louise's glowing architectural recognition in the *Journal*. Once again, our entire design and construction teams had distinguished themselves with their dexterity, blasting away many layers of grit and destruction, and completely transforming The Shoe. The Huxtable "Leisure and Arts" feature gave us the most meaningful media coverage we have ever enjoyed: "The Shoe is now Cummings Center," she wrote, "saved, restored and transformed, shrewdly and sympathetically, into nearly 1.4 million square feet of handsome commercial space for business and industry." (Today, Cummings Center contains 2 million square feet.) We were delighted with the piece and flattered by her effusive compliments.

> Ada Louise wrote of this pioneering reinforced concrete structure endearingly: "It is a building of outstanding utilitarian beauty. Its stunning glass-walled simplicity, the pleasing proportions based on its structural system, foreshadows the later modular designs of Mies van der Rohe, and one of the basic aesthetic principles of structure to style."
>
> She concluded her feature by calling our work "a miraculous rebirth" of The Shoe. "For those who prize an architecture still invisible to many and treated as expendable by most," she wrote, "Cummings Center is more than a success story; it is a dream come true."

Over the next several years, Joyce and I came to know Ada Louise quite well. The summer following the feature article, we were delighted to join her a second time for tea in her charming long-term summer home in Marblehead. She was such a dedicated and fascinating woman and a captivating conversationalist. Another later time, we visited her in her winter home at 969 Park Avenue, New York City, accompanied by our daughter Marilyn. I remember Ada Louise being so interested in everything she could learn from Marilyn's opinions about how architectural changes might better accommodate changes in healthcare delivery in New York.

Joyce and I were later pleased to establish a fellowship at Boston Architectural College "to pay tribute to Ada Louise's most memorable design leadership career." Subsequently, following a brief note, Ada Louise called to tell us how incredibly moved she was by this unexpected tribute. She also reiterated her personal thanks for "so carefully respecting the aesthetics of her forever favorite building" and she again reminded us how important it is to recognize aesthetics as the fourth dimension of architecture. In 2020, I was invited to spend a delightful day at BAC.

JAMIE WOULD HAVE been so proud—not just of Ada Louise Huxtable's high praise, but even more so of what Cummings Center has become. Today, the complex is home to hundreds of separate organizations, ranging from traditional business offices to cutting-edge research and technology firms, physicians, dentists, personal services, and seventy-three upscale residential condominiums. Once again, the entire site is bustling with activity—a vibrant economic engine for Boston's entire North Shore.

These key factors, and the center's proximity to nearby Beverly Hospital and North Shore Medical Center in Salem, have been particularly important in attracting the large number of medical, dental, social-service, and other health and wellness practices, too. In 2020, Cummings Center's general manager, Vice President Steve Drohosky, estimated that we now have more than two hundred physicians, dentists, surgeons, psychiatrists, therapists, and wellness practitioners operating daily at Cummings Center.

With all these tenants, Cummings Center offers an extraordinary array of conveniences at its bustling campus. In addition to the two full-service banks, there are several restaurants, a full-size Merrill Lynch branch, and the sparkling Beverly Athletic Club. Dozens of attorneys and accountants have located within the complex, along with numerous other business and personal amenities, including hair stylists for men and women, a sundry shop, two childcare centers, a U.S. Post Office, a veterinary center, and even a separate doggie daycare. In addition, there is a busy surgical-care center and an outstanding fifteen-bed in-patient rehabilitation hospital.

| *Stephen Drohosky*

Each of the four corners of the Cummings Center site now has its own large, multilevel covered parking garage. From two to four stories high, each one is equipped with a major solar-energy system. The northwest parking deck alone, adjacent to 500 Cummings Center, boasts more than 1,700 solar panels. Altogether, the four parking-garage systems include nearly 5,300 solar panels, producing nearly 1.8 million kWh per year of clean electrical energy. With the tax credits and the direct income, the systems were all fully paid off within five years. The "roofs," constructed separately after the garages were built and in use, qualified as solar support structures for substantially better tax treatment.

The Shoe's four original concrete buildings work perfectly with our brand-new 500 Cummings Center, an office building we constructed in the northwest quadrant of the campus to provide additional space as we approached capacity in the original Cummings Center buildings. Moving

ahead with this three hundred thousand-square-foot structure before we had a need for it proved to be a costly error when the city surprised us by taxing the building based on its cost rather than its rental income, during its extended rent up period.

The 500 Cummings Center building overlooks Upper Shoe Pond, providing marvelous scenic views. Aside from the four new parking garages, 500 was the only entirely new structure on the campus until recently, when we built our seventy-three-unit luxury residential condominium.

The Salem News has always been keenly aware and synoptic about our work in Beverly, and it has often gone out of its way to make complimentary editorial comments about Cummings Center. One such opinion piece, on May 15, 2016, concluded, "Those battling business development in Salem and elsewhere should take a look at the continuing success at Cummings Center in Beverly, which recently, and quietly, celebrated two decades as an economic driver in that city…Working with the city… the company transformed the site into something special. Today it is 90 percent occupied, housing more than 550 business and other organizations, making it the North Shore's largest business park. In recent years, Cummings Center has become a hub for innovation. It's a public private success story that's worth remembering."

And it all began with Jamie telling me he was going to look at "somewhat of a monster" of a property.

ONE ADVANTAGE SMALL companies have, but do not always use, is the capacity to hire a person based on attitude and personality, not just a résumé. Jamie had absolutely everything I hoped for in a successor, including being a native of Woburn who still lived only a mile from our office. I could give him the experience, but his personality was one of a kind.

In the months and years (now decades) after his passing, Jamie's memory was honored in many ways. Only four days before he died so suddenly, Jamie met with Beverly officials to discuss the city's proposed acquisition of several acres of Cummings Center land, on which Beverly's then mayor, William Scanlon, was determined to construct a replacement for the aging McKay Elementary School. Jamie quickly agreed in principle to swapping the old school site for the new land. Then, after Jamie suddenly died, we instead donated the needed land in consideration of the city's naming the new school in Jamie's memory.

There was some political pushback about our proposal to donate the land, but the oddest objection, I thought, came from a repeatedly unsuccessful mayoral candidate, Phil Dunkelbarger. He made the school naming an issue during his run against incumbent Scanlon. I wanted to laugh out loud when Dunkelbarger argued funnily that naming the new school "McKeown" would be too difficult for people to pronounce. In any case, the James L. McKeown Elementary School opened for its first students in September 1998.

| *Beverly's James L. McKeown Elementary School, 1998*

Somewhat inexplicably, however, and still under the Scanlon administration that built it, the city later decided that it did not need its almost brand-new school after all. It closed the school in 2008, only ten years after its dedication and opening. Still called the McKeown School, it was repurposed for other educational uses.

In 1997, Cummings Foundation established a formal scholarship plan called the McKeown Scholars Program for graduating seniors from nine local high schools. Each community determined its scholarship winners based on the students' performances on a writing assignment, which was graded anonymously by committees of teachers at each high school. The program distributed a total of more than $2 million divided among more than five hundred students. Beverly High School graduates received $430,000 under the program, and Woburn High School graduates received $502,000, before the fund ran itself out in 2015.

Still in 1997, State Representative Carol Donovan, of Woburn, a long-term trustee of Cummings Foundation and a consistent friend and supporter of Jamie's and mine, was also playing her own major role in memorializing Jamie. She and several of her friends in the Massachusetts legislature arranged to name the newly constructed Interstate 93 highway interchange in North Woburn in Jamie's memory. Jamie had been actively involved in lobbying for the creation of that interchange, including at least one personal appearance at a public hearing in the Massachusetts State House.

In one last tribute, in September 2014 the Woburn Boys & Girls Club announced its name change to the Jamie McKeown Boys & Girls Club, in honor of its cherished former Boy of the Year, board member, and club president.

EVEN AS WE honored Jamie's memory, we also honored his legacy by strengthening our leadership team to meet the challenges of the years ahead. In the summer of 1998, I was delighted to recognize Doug Stephens' twenty-five years of extraordinary loyalty and dedication by appointing him

| Doug Stephens and Bill Grant, 1998

as the company's second-ever executive vice president. Doug had been with me at Cummings Properties since 1973, and before that at Old Medford Foods since 1966. One of the company's best-known faces, Doug directed all of the firm's financial affairs from its single-property beginnings in East Woburn to its then 8 million or so square feet in nine Greater Boston communities, plus its rapidly growing investments in public securities.

In May 1998, William Grant, who had considerable experience as the chief financial officer of two large retail chains, joined the firm as our first CFO. Doug extensively coached and familiarized Bill on Cummings Properties' financial affairs as these continued to grow in complexity. Bill in turn then quickly focused on working with David Leland of Merrill Lynch in managing the burgeoning financial securities of the foundation and ceased working with a small investment-management firm previously used.

Merrill Lynch thereafter took custody of those then-modest assets, and in time David arranged with Merrill to open a highly successful North Shore office in Cummings Center as David and Bill Grant worked ever more closely and effectively. In what seemed like no time at all they grew the securities accounts from tens of millions to more than a *billion* dollars as Cummings Properties continued to do exceedingly well. David and his wife, Karen, were Winchester neighbors and had been personal friends of Joyce's and mine for many years.

Also that year, we purchased two more somewhat run-down buildings, at 30 and 50 Audubon Road, Wakefield, and another former Cabot, Cabot & Forbes building at 34 Commerce Way, Woburn. We quickly assimilated and leased these properties, converting them from single-user buildings to our typical multi-user buildings. We had fully morphed into a major North Shore developer, but we still had no interests at all in Boston *per se*.

In September 1999, I finally announced the appointments of *two* interim successors to Jamie, naming senior vice president Michael Pascavage and vice president of operations Dennis Clarke to serve as *co-presidents* of Cummings Properties. Although several other in-house candidates were worthy of consideration, Mike and Dennis were the most logical choices. This dynamic team allowed Mike's substantial company experience and management skills to complement Dennis' strong and developing people skills and strategic-management abilities.

"The decision to jointly fill this position also reflects our philosophy regarding teamwork, integrity, and ethics," I said, announcing the promotions. "Mike and Dennis share these traits, as well as a strong personal camaraderie. Their contributions to our company's success, the growing community support we enjoy, and our mission at Cummings Properties are extraordinary. As Dennis and Mike are appointed to this unusual position, where two people share the office of president, they honor the legacy of James L. McKeown." At the center of the company's evolution from a local area industrial real estate developer into the multi-disciplinary Cummings Properties, Mike continued to direct all design, purchasing, construction, and development efforts.

A Pennsylvania native, Mike earned a bachelor's and a master's degree in architecture from the University of Pennsylvania. Mike also holds an MBA from Northeastern University and is a member of the American Institute of Architects. Dennis, who was thirty-one at the time, is a Winchester native who graduated from Harvard and once served briefly as a licensed commercial insurance broker. Active in both Winchester and Woburn, Dennis became a director of Winchester Chamber of Commerce and had done considerable high-level behind-the-scenes volunteer work with Winchester Hospital.

▎ *Co-presidents Mike Pascavage and Dennis Clarke, outside 92 Montvale Avenue, Stoneham*

In 2004, five years after the appointment of Mike and Dennis as co-presidents, I turned over my chairman's position to Mike and, at the same time, appointed Dennis president and CEO, roles each had clearly earned.

Managing involves dealing with people and their often widely divergent personalities. Dennis had grown particularly good at this and at reading other people's egos, which is a huge advantage when dealing with generally successful people. I still remained active through 2019, but these moves allowed me to spend considerably more time with Cummings Foundation.

It was about this same time that Eric Anderson began to emerge as a rising star on the corporate management team, figuring prominently in planning for the future. A 1998 graduate of Colby College, Eric joined the firm in November 1999, first working in leasing and operations at Cummings Center. Single at the time, he lived in a small on-site manager's apartment adjacent to the main Beverly office and was the first resident of the former United Shoe property to ever become a registered voter in Beverly.

| Eric Anderson

A member of the United States Marine Corps Reserve, Eric was called back to active duty after the tragic events of September 11, 2001. He was called again in 2003, after he had transferred to Cummings' Operations Department in Woburn, where he worked as a property manager under Ernie Agresti. During his second call-up, Eric served in Iraq during Operation Iraqi Freedom. He left for active duty shortly after a rousing send-off party at the West Cummings Park office that included an on-site visit by the Woburn High School Jazz Band.

Shortly after his final return from Marine Corps service, Eric was named a division manager in the Woburn Operations Department. He became the youngest member of the Executive Committee in 2007. In 2013, Eric was selected as one of the "best and brightest of the area's emerging leaders" in *Boston Business Journal's* annual "40 Under 40" feature, and in 2018 I encouraged him to join the Boston chapter of Young Presidents' Organization.

MAY 2004 ALSO MARKED another tragic loss when Douglas Stephens died from pancreatic cancer at age sixty-four. Doug knew every person in the firm as well as or better than I did. He was the "mister nice guy" of our management team who always seemed to make the rest of us look good.

| *Douglas Stephens Teen Center, YMCA of the North Shore, Beverly, Massachusetts*

Doug warmly touched the lives of everyone with whom he dealt. He and I worked closely together a total of thirty-eight years. In Beverly, the foundation donated $1 million to create the Douglas Stephens YMCA Teen Center in Doug's memory. This brand-new combination teen-recreation-and-childcare center was dedicated in 2004.

❊ *Irrespective of anyone's concept of global warming, there is an incontrovertible truth that there are finite amounts of fossil fuels, and these are already becoming more and more difficult to access and harvest. Solar, wind, and water-source energy are all still much more expensive than "conventional" power without subsidies, but with greater usage and technological improvements they are becoming quickly more affordable.*

❊ *Entrepreneurs must focus not only on what is in front of them right now but also on what their business might become. The present state of a building, product, or company is not nearly as important as its potential. Although we never imagined that The Shoe would land us so prominently on the pages of* The Wall Street Journal, *we knew that the neglected site had enormous promise.*

❊ *Business owners and managers must of course deal with employees who do not fit in, but more importantly, they must recognize and* encourage *all of the people who really can fit in, and make a difference. That is what building a really good firm is all about.*

❊ *With today's photovoltaic solar panels capturing 10 to 20 percent of the energy to which they are exposed, there is enormously greater potential to massively further reduce our dependency on fossil fuel-produced electricity.*

[14]

Relocating the County Seat

ONE OF THE company's most important and visible developments is TradeCenter 128, a highly prominent office and research complex located broadside to Interstate 95, in Woburn. In October 1995 Jamie had fully negotiated and arranged the purchase of this eighteen-acre former manufacturing site of Sylvania Electric. Barely two miles from our Cummings Park headquarters, this much-abused property, then called Northeast Trade Center, was also only *yards* away from Jamie's childhood home on Pearl Street.

Our internal notes about the project describe that transaction as "likely the best purchase the company ever made." The delay in its major redevelopment was in part because of our later purchase of The Shoe, but it was more significantly due to the extreme political obstacles we were encountering with Woburn's planning board and its then highly caustic planning director. With all the political uncertainty and clamor about anything we attempted to build in Woburn during that period, it was just easier for us to invest in Beverly.

We swiftly renovated the existing one-and-a-half-story building at

TradeCenter 128, but we left the balance of that property undeveloped for ten years while we totally focused our attention on finishing Cummings Center. The work we did at "The Shoe" immediately built up Beverly's assessed values by more than $100 million, greatly benefiting Beverly for its receptiveness to our responsible redevelopment of the former United Shoe site.

Ten years later, in August 2006, Ernie Agresti, a key member of Cummings Properties' Executive Committee, suggested that we accept an invitation to bid on, design, construct, and lease a "temporary" replacement for the former high-rise Middlesex County Superior Court in Cambridge. Officials had determined that the court's existing building was no longer safe for occupancy, so the commonwealth of Massachusetts needed a new 150,000-square-foot courthouse to be built "immediately." Ernie first proposed our TradeCenter 128 as the site of this new "temporary" courthouse.

| *Ernie Agresti*

The state's Division of Capital Assets Management and Maintenance (DCAMM) published exhaustive specs detailing precisely what the court would need, and it turned out that we not only had the building-site availability but also the in-house financial and design capability to move quickly enough to satisfy DCAMM's highly accelerated timetable. The state wanted all costs incorporated into the rent, but there were numerous aspects of the building interior that needed to be treated as non-standard construction if they were to be amortized into the lease.

For example, our courthouse would have to include an entirely separate parking area and an elevator for the exclusive use of judges, and a separate stairway, too, so judges could avoid face-to-face encounters with anyone having business in the court. There were also countless specialized finishes and furniture including judges' benches, jury boxes, built-in seating, individual holding cells on each floor, plus large central holding cells for dozens of male and female detainees, and a sallyport on the ground floor. We bid it to make money on the project, but our winning bid to build and lease their temporary courthouse was still millions of dollars lower than the next lowest bid. We also took the extra step with the court's construction specifications to add expensive granite details. We decided that if we got to build the place, we wanted the users to really like it and hopefully remain for many years more than "temporarily."

State officials at first believed the old Cambridge courthouse might take two years to clean up and modernize, but Ernie had told me even DCAMM was confident that even if we built a replacement, the renovation of the old courthouse could never be complete in only two years. Furthermore, DCAMM would write requests for proposals in such a way that we could be comfortably responsive. In contrast to the twenty-story building the court was vacating, our building would be only six stories tall, with fourteen courtrooms on its upper four floors. The building could also be readily repurposed for general office or research use if ever that became necessary, greatly reducing some of the risk on our end. Our general superintendent, Greg Ahearn, would be the key to delivering the structure "on time."

| Greg Ahearn

The Commonwealth agreed to separately amortize the cost of required court-specific furniture, and many special items, such as the extra elevator, extra stairway, and the detention cells, over the first three years, so we were covered for at least this significant part of the up-front special investment. Many people still thought we were crazy to risk so much in such a customized structure that could lose its only possible client after just three years. As it turned out, however, the old courthouse was soon deemed too expensive to either repair or tear down. (It was still in place in 2020, appearing to be totally unused and largely unchanged in appearance since 2008, although some commercial redevelopment proposals were still being discussed for it.) The first long-term lease for the Woburn courthouse was signed in 2020.

> There is always a feeling of accomplishment when new clients leave Cambridge for us, but attracting a classic gem of a tenant like the Middlesex County Superior Court, and later the Probate Court, too, was truly special. By any standards, the county seat had been moved to Woburn.

Before the "temporary" lease was signed, we already had the building-permit application in process. The permit was promptly issued immediately after Christmas 2006, following direct involvement from Chief Justice for Administration Robert Mulligan. His intervention became appropriate after Woburn's old vocal minority started organizing opposition to the court's moving from Cambridge to Woburn. What was really a magnificent coup for Woburn, as well as for our firm, was barely tolerated by the city's highly controversial building commissioner at that time.

| *Aerial view of TradeCenter 128, facing Interstate 95 in Woburn*

ON JANUARY 2, 2007, we started laying out the entire project's six hundred thousand square feet of office space, plus a three hundred thousand-square-foot five-story parking garage. Construction of what Cummings Properties perceives as its largest, most prominent, and most intricate new structure began with the driving of the first steel pile the next day. We completed the entire garage and all the exterior walls and floors of three interconnected structures in record time with massive pre-cast concrete panels, including horizontal sections for the garage floors. There were hundreds of truckloads of individually pre-cast concrete panels, support columns and beams, plus the enormous concrete "double tees" for the floors of the garage. It was like the entire project was on steroids.

I marvel at Cummings Properties' longtime structural engineer, Greg Flaherty, who has designed the concrete foundations and steel framework for all our new buildings since 1998. Greg once admitted to me how nervous he feels every time the large construction cranes pull in, followed by trailers loaded with steel beams. And no wonder: Every piece of steel has to click precisely into place in each enormous three-dimensional jigsaw puzzle we build. Any left-out or mis-cut beam during the typical two- to ten-week erection process can cause chaos, but that has never happened. Greg views a plan for every single piece beforehand, and he just does not miss. Our largest built-from-scratch structure at TradeCenter 128 started out in a frozen windswept field, and

| *Greg Flaherty on site*

not a single beam or bolt hole had to be corrected or altered.

Twelve months later, to ensure that we were ready on our end, we worked until well after nightfall on December 31, 2007, completing the final touches of the courthouse carpeting before celebrating the New Year. The court took a little time moving in, as we imagined it would, in part because we surprised virtually everyone with our speedy delivery, and the Commonwealth was not quite prepared to start its big move. There was a long way to go with the balance of the building at 300 and 400 TradeCenter 128, but the entire court building was fully complete in exactly one year, and all we needed was an occupancy permit from the building commissioner, which we received in a timely manner.

Our design team, with no outside engineering or architectural assistance except for the design of the pre-cast concrete, completed this gemstone among our properties: TradeCenter 128. As with all our structures, we designed this extraordinary nine hundred thousand-square-foot office complex (with garage) entirely in-house, and then as always we were our own general contractor. If, as I mentioned above, moving the Superior Court to Woburn was a real coup, our also moving the Probate Court to Woburn in 2020 was an even bigger one.

We made exceedingly few errors during the TradeCenter project on anything, but I personally made the most costly one when I considered the total size of the complex and decided that our plans called for too many parking spaces. Without really studying the situation, I arbitrarily reduced the size of the pre-cast concrete parking garage from six stories to five, just before the deadline, thinking that we were saving perhaps a half-million dollars. It was less than a year later that we built a small *additional* garage to *put back* the spaces I earlier rejected—at a substantially greater cost than that of the original garage plan. It is important for managers at any level to be aware of all errors, but it is even more important for them to recognize and own up to their own.

Another more general error we made over a period of years was to sometimes over-protect a few workers who were persistently disgruntled and who also seemed to perform that way. Notwithstanding the high cost of worker replacement, managers of smaller organizations must also be careful when really necessary to remove workers who are or who become consistent negative voices within any otherwise smooth running organization.

SOON AFTER TradeCenter 128, our entire staff was shocked when Mike Pascavage was recruited to leave the company for the second time. He had served eighteen years during his second stint, most recently as chairman, and he left, with nothing less than mutual best wishes, to join the Swedish construction giant Skanska International. In a way, we were perhaps even a little proud that a world-class powerhouse with tens of thousands of employees would come to a comparatively tiny firm like ours to supplement its top executives.

Although Mike's colleagues and I were disappointed about his departure, Mike once confided to me that he had a dream and a vision about someday altering the Boston skyline. I told Mike several times that we had no difficulty understanding that dream, or why he might take the chance he did, even in what turned out to be such economically perilous times. Mostly, I was relieved to learn from Mike that he had not been looking for another job, nor did he leave because of any unhappiness with our firm.

Several years after he left Cummings, Mike left Skanska and founded his own architectural-services firm, also here in Woburn. We were pleased to provide complimentary accommodations for him for several years at TradeCenter 128, where a prominent lobby plaque identifies Mike as chief architect of the complex. In 2016, the directors of the newly named Jamie McKeown Boys & Girls Club selected Mike's firm to design and oversee the development of the club's new $10 million structure.

For this book, I asked Mike to share some more of his most pertinent reflections concerning his two decades of important leadership positions with Cummings Properties. Because Mike was so integral to our entire operation for such a long time, I shall, with great thanks, use much of his response here:

> *The most striking recollection of my time at CPL is of the people who made up the company. Cummings employees ultimately were a true reflection of the work ethic and attitude that started at the top. Many folks cycled through, and the self-selection process generally weeded out those who did not fit the mold. I take pride in having known every employee in the company (over 260 at the time) and to this day still recognize and care about the CPL employees I encounter.*
>
> *There is no question as to the impact that you, personally, Bill, had on me throughout my career. My growth in the organization was measured, culminating in significant authority and responsibility, only after having been vetted through every conceivable design, development, construction, personnel, and cultural aspect of*

| Michael H. Pascavage

your personal philosophy.

Relative to individuals, working alongside Jamie McKeown was a true highlight—vibrant, smart, charismatic, and holding your highest confidence, he was the gateway to the future. To now have the opportunity, as its independent architect, to recast the former Woburn Boys & Girls Club facility in his name and memory is truly special. Doug Stephens, totally understated, but truly loyal, dedicated and a saint in his own right, is similarly missed.

Being in control of your own destiny in every aspect of the development process was, I believe, the key ingredient to CPL success. Controlling the design, financing, construction, legal, leasing, and property-management aspects of the total real estate process was truly unique in the field and continues to be a defining premise of CPL. It became our calling card for uniqueness in the industry.

My initial Cummings involvement blended well with my personal work ethic and approach. While oft overused, the firm was truly a 'hands-on' organization. Complete involvement in every minute decision, direction, and process insured the success of each effort. The Cummings attitude of 'do-it-yourself' across all corporate functions was key. We did not rely on third-party consultants to do critical path components of the work that were both time sensitive and expensive.

Bill, the biggest, always understated, achievement of your career has been the establishment of Cummings Foundation. It needs no endorsement from me, I say thank you for the trust you had in me to allow me to serve for a time on the Board of Trustees of this amazing new Massachusetts institution. It continues to serve so many organizations that will most benefit from the largesse, and I am most proud of the involvement I had with CF.

M.H.P.

After a year-long closing of what is now the Jamie McKeown Boys & Girls Club, Joyce and I were so pleased to see the totally rebuilt and enlarged club operating again directly next to Place Lane Condominium, in September 2016. Still serving such a broad base of primarily Woburn families, and now with a fine new regulation-size swimming pool, it seems so fitting that the directors voted to rename the club in Jamie's honor.

Although Cummings Foundation has since made more than $260 million in local area grants of $100,000 or more, we will always remember that the foundation's first $100,000 grant was presented by Jamie to the former Woburn Boys Club in 1986.

> ONE OF THE MOST endearing and enduring aspects of our organization is the outstanding level of corporate respect within. Throughout the company, the pride and loyalty of the staff are obvious at every turn. The single most apparent sentiment from our most experienced colleagues is how greatly they value the friendly collegial environment of the entire firm. Our team members have heard many times that solid professional and personal ethics must absolutely define how we do business, and for the vast majority of times they do. Staff have also heard how important it is that we think of corporate and individual success as a lifetime journey and not a destination.

Among our early decisions about TradeCenter 128 was that we needed a full-service, white-tablecloth restaurant to serve both our own local business community and the general population along Route 128/I-95. It was not at all the Company's plan to become involved with operating any such venture on-site, but when no viable prospects emerged with the interest and ability to build a premier restaurant on our timetable, we moved forward and opened a first-class destination restaurant on our own. We called it Beacon Grille. Desiring to give the restaurant a Boston theme, which was already implied in the "Beacon" name, the Cummings in-house design team created oversized Boston photo art, including my favorite picture of Boston's Leonard Zakim Bunker Hill Bridge, taken from Bunker Hill by our son Kevin.

| Boston's Leonard Zakim Bunker Hill Bridge

Kevin Cummings

As a company, we thoroughly enjoyed working out all the complicated details for the complete build-out of this three hundred-seat restaurant prior to its opening in January 2010. Our staffing issues at Beacon Grille, however, were in stark contrast to my decades of personnel experience at Cummings Properties, where our management team has always been so strong. We recently calculated that the thirty or so people filling our highest management and executive positions at Cummings Properties have an average seniority of more than twenty-two years with the firm. Our nine most senior field managers average slightly more than twenty-seven years. At the restaurant, however, for one good reason or another, it seemed no one on the management team lasted much more than a single year.

With this contrast in mind, and the chronic Beacon Grille issues so disproportionally occupying our senior corporate management time, we were clearly ready, after three years, to sell the restaurant. In traditional terms, the restaurant had been an unqualified success. With annual sales having grown to $4.5 million in 2012, we proved that TradeCenter 128 was a viable site for a first-class dining venue. But selling it would relieve us of a significant distraction and perpetual angst about what *might* happen next at Beacon. We also learned firsthand about the remarkably outsized profits restaurants and others realize from unredeemed gift certificates. Fortunately, nothing serious ever went wrong, but for years we were concerned that our collective inability to recruit and retain the right staff might somehow cause us great embarrassment, or worse.

So, we all felt great when Nick Varano, sole owner of The Varano Group, agreed to buy us out. Nick had built a great name with his high-end Strega restaurants in Boston, and now he wanted his first suburban presence. He was as motivated to buy Beacon as we were to sell it. No matter how well it was doing, and how proud we were of the overall project, it was time to turn it over to some real professionals.

Nick Varano with Bill Cummings, May 2013

But even though we had a firm oral agreement with Nick, he came in near the end of the process with a push for us to either reduce the price by $300,000 or lose the deal. We certainly could have agreed to his price, after a "split the difference" proposal didn't work, because Nick was pretty convincing with his "last and final" statement: "Take it or leave it," he said, "but I'm out the door if you don't take it now." And we did want Strega there.

Then I remembered how much Nick had sometimes talked about gambling. "Instead of splitting the difference," I said, "how about we toss a coin to decide?" Nick thought about that for about three seconds, and then he agreed.

I reached in my pocket and pulled out a coin and flipped it. Nick called "Tails" with the coin in the air. The $300,000 coin landed heads up.

The sale to The Varano Group then closed in May 2013, and Strega Prime opened, with its brand-new glitzy décor and considerably fancier menu, to great acclaim in early August. For those who want and can afford the flourish and frills of such high-end dining, Strega Prime at 400 TradeCenter 128, like Boston's Strega restaurants, is always a sure bet for a memorable meal. In January 2020, Strega Prime and the other largest Stregas were sold to the Irish chain Smith & Wollensky, just a month or so before the devastating effects of the COVID-19 outbreak shut down all restaurant dining rooms.

BEYOND THE excitement and occasional exasperations of permitting and constructing TradeCenter 128, there was the challenge in an exceedingly slow market for leasing it all out—that is, the remaining half-million square feet not leased to the court. As has always been our custom, we built the balance of the complex entirely "on spec," with no clients or even prospective clients for any of it.

I have long believed that most people who get things done have to be inherently gamblers of a sort. They sometimes come up short, because there are downturns in any game. Such people, if they are smart, will usually have a reasonable fallback position, and in the long run they will rarely lose, unless they walk off the field. TradeCenter 128 was such a gamble, especially the courthouse building. In the end, however, this gamble paid brilliant dividends.

With its unique three-story archway directly facing Interstate 95, between its 300 and 400 wings, TradeCenter

Michael Lamothe

128 is distinctive, and the structure deserves all the acclaim it has received for its fine in-house architectural design. Despite the financial crisis in 2008, the building began filling immediately after it was ready for move-ins, undoubtedly benefiting from our creative marketing.

One of our central marketing objectives is always to bring amenities—banks, health clubs, restaurants, dry cleaners, childcare centers, and the like—to each major building complex as soon as possible. These make a campus highly attractive to many prospective clients, because they and their employees have access to so much more than merely a place to work.

Amenity-rich TradeCenter 128 has a large YMCA daycare as well as My Montessori School on campus, and direct-to-door MBTA public bus service to and from the Wellington "Orange Line" station in the historic Boston rapid transit (subway) system. In addition to its upscale Strega Prime steak house, TradeCenter has a busy Dunkin' Donuts, plus a terrific sandwich shop and an excellent small gift shop in the central lobby. There are also a thousand fully covered free garage parking spaces. The complex is additionally home to a large number of medical and legal practices, and, of course, the fourteen courtrooms of the Middlesex County Superior Court at the far northern end of the campus.

Another major point that helps us when we are negotiating with prospective clients is the uncommonly strong financial condition of Cummings Properties and the foundation that has come to own so many Cummings buildings.

Described by many in the industry as one of the most financially solid real estate firms in New England, Cummings Properties has often been informally identified as the "owner and operator" of millions of square feet of mostly office and research space in ten metropolitan Boston communities. In reality, Cummings Properties, as our operating entity, has never owned *any* real estate or much of anything else besides tools, service vehicles, and an enormous collection of heavy-duty snow equipment. All land and buildings have, for the most part, been owned by separate corporate entities, more and more of which are themselves now owned by Cummings Foundation, and all are debt-free.

The separate entities have mostly to do with limiting exposure in the event of any sort of catastrophic liability claim. If, for instance, an accident occurred involving an underinsured vehicle carrying dangerous cargo onto one of our properties, separate ownership of adjacent lots could keep one property owner from becoming exposed to claims generated from another property.

SINCE 2007, our in-house Legal Department has been directed by Craig Ziady, our senior vice president and general counsel. Craig joining our firm was another highly serendipitous personal connection. Before Craig and his wife, Joan, joined Winchester Country Club, I met them, in my role as a director of the club, during their membership-application process. Craig and Joan were both working at a major Boston law firm, where Craig had made a name for himself as a highly successful environmental and real estate litigator.

Craig told me during his interview at the club that he might sometime explore professional opportunities outside the city. Shortly after the family joined the club, he responded favorably to my invitation to also consider joining Cummings Properties, and since June 2007, we have had a marvelous relationship. Interestingly, Cummings Properties typically has more than a dozen full-time attorneys, with all but four of them filling important management roles *outside* the legal department. Our legal department also serves Cummings Foundation on a strictly *pro bono* basis. IRS regulations prohibit payments from the foundation to any related for-profit entity, no matter how reasonable the payments might be.

| Craig Ziady

We try hard to avoid legal skirmishes unless absolutely necessary, and we strive for clear and thoughtful documents, letters, and emails. Communication is imperative, and those with the greatest literary skills tend to be the most effective communicators. True empathy toward others, as well as to their needs, desires, and personal dignity, will also enable good entrepreneurs to communicate effectively. Entrepreneurs who do well rely on facts to support their points, and they will expect others to do the same.

> When court proceedings are necessary—and they most frequently develop when client firms cannot meet their rent obligations—it is so extraordinarily helpful to have a solid in-house legal team. With literally thousands of client firms, we tend to see the same fact patterns repeat themselves, so often, and there are so many major benefits to always having the same legal team for each case.

We have also argued more than a few precedent-setting legal issues, and our in-house team has done outstandingly well. Susan Brand, during her eighteen years as counsel and general counsel, had several notable and significant cases, including her only trip to the Massachusetts Supreme Judicial Court (SJC): Cummings Properties, LLC v. National Communications Corp. The SJC, of its own volition, selected that case after we first won in the trial court but then lost in the Massachusetts Appeals Court. The SJC determined that an accelerated rent provision negotiated in a commercial lease between sophisticated parties was an enforceable liquidated-damages clause, and the ruling has since been cited effectively in other cases. An unrelated but analogous case held the holder of a New England Patriots luxury box ticket contract liable for the full multi-year contract amount after an earlier default, even though all of the seats had been resold to others at higher prices.

In another precedent-setting case for our legal department, our senior litigator, Joseph Mingolla, spent years finally earning a win on an important right-of-way case. Effectively, he established in the Massachusetts Supreme Judicial Court that the rights of an owner of "registered land" in Massachusetts are similar to those associated with unregistered land when it comes to adjusting or relocating a recorded right of way. In both situations the rights to use a right of way may be changed by a property owner so long as the beneficiaries of the rights are not materially disadvantaged.

Joseph Mingolla

Another particularly significant Cummings case, also in the SJC, established the rights of landowners and tenants to protect both parties with insurance against losses or claims including those that might allege negligence by the owner/lessor of the property.

After having installed and benefited from video-recording devices at many of our properties, we first installed cameras in a systematic way at TradeCenter 128. This was partly due to our involvement with the elaborate camera systems in our adjacent Middlesex County Superior Court building, where the State reportedly installed about three hundred digital recording cameras. We initially planned two hundred cameras for the rest of the TradeCenter 128 complex but ended up operating a total of almost three hundred interior digital cameras ourselves, plus another twenty exterior cameras.

One of our earliest successes with exterior video involved footage of two felony suspects stopping in front of a remote trash dumpster to discard items linked to a crime. After being alerted by Cummings watch staff, police checked the trash container and found freshly bloodied clothes. Prosecutors were able to use the video as conclusive evidence in an attempted-murder case in a nearby town. The video cameras have come into play in literally dozens of incidents, fully justifying our expenditures of several hundred thousand dollars on the systems.

In 2003, Joyce and I decided it was time to downsize from our large Fernway home, where we had lived for twenty-five years. We moved from Myopia Hill to a more modest home in the not-so-elegantly-named Winchester Flats. Denise McKeown was our broker, during her affiliation with Winchester's Century 21 Fortin Real Estate. Shortly after Denise managed our new home purchase, we were delighted to welcome her to the Cummings team on the management and leasing staff of our TradeCenter 128 Executive Office Suites.

AS THE YEARS have passed, Joyce and I have been fortunate enough to become increasingly involved in hugely satisfying situations and causes—many of which have nothing whatsoever to do with the company or the foundation. As a Tufts trustee *emeritus*, for instance, I somehow became the designated emissary for a significant church issue—one that again involved obtaining an unusual approval from the Archdiocese of Boston.

This time, Tufts sought to have Father David O'Leary appointed by the diocese to serve a ten-year term as the *university* chaplain. Father O'Leary would become what appears to have been the first American Roman Catholic priest to ever officially serve in a nondenominational religious role at a public or other non-secular university. Father O'Leary held a doctorate in philosophy and had earlier served as Tufts' Catholic chaplain. Following a long line of largely, if not exclusively, Unitarian Universalist clergy in that role, this highly respected Roman Catholic priest contributed much to the university community during his ten-year appointment.

ONE OF THE most meaningful of all our many international trips was my second and Joyce's first visit to Israel, in 2009, when we joined a superb Tufts University Travel-Learn group for two weeks there and in Jordan. I visited Israel in 1964, as part of my solo adventure around Europe and the Mediterranean, but this later trip was planned

| Joyce and Bill at Golan Heights, 2009

to give us a real sense of the immense importance of the region from the earliest of recorded times, particularly its spectacular role in the development of world civilizations.

Our bus tour looped clockwise through Israel, beginning northward along the coast from Tel Aviv, and included a multi-day stay in and around a large kibbutz with many farming and dairy operations. The kibbutz also makes highly customized wood pews and other seating for churches and synagogues all over the world. We visited vast areas of carefully planted and irrigated new pine forests around the kibbutz, learning how they are reforesting several other species, as well.

Our crossing of the Sea of Galilee, visits to the areas along the Jordan River, and learning about the massive reforestation efforts were all interesting and educational, as were our attempts to understand the complicated water issues associated with the Jordan. We saw up-close that this river is but a narrow stream and only a few inches deep at the point where it enters the Dead Sea. At that exact location, I easily stepped across the five-foot-wide river without getting my shoes wet.

Every day, we enjoyed sites of biblical history and came to better understand places and events that would have taken years of study to truly comprehend. We read literature provided by the Tufts Travel-Learn office, but a book given to us by our son-in-law, Jason, stood out from the rest. We both found *History of Modern Israel*, by Colin Shindler, to be superb and particularly useful, placing so much of what we saw and witnessed in the context of what Israel is today.

Although *History of Modern Israel* provides some details about the Palestinian issues in Israel, more current sources like Jewishvoiceforpeace.org advocate strongly against human rights violations there against Palestinians. Decade after decade of international talks have gone nowhere through 2019, while recent actions to recognize a Jewish Jerusalem as the capital city of Israel may have greatly set back whatever progress there might have been.

One issue that particularly fascinated me concerned the potential good that would come from a replenishment of the Dead Sea, as envisioned with the proposed so-called "Red to Dead" project which would use enormous siphon lines to bring billions of gallons of water to slowly refill the Dead Sea.

One of the most surprising aspects of our 2009 visit along the Jordan River was the extent to which the "average people" in the regions we visited appeared to fully embrace the notion of peaceful coexistence and mutual support. Tourism benefits both lands enormously, and both peoples seem intent on preserving cooperative policies. More moderate voices in Israel are also working toward more equitable solutions with the Palestinians, but that will take enormous efforts.

Near the end of our journey, just before we crossed into Jordan for a fascinating stop in the ancient carved city of Petra, we visited Yad Vashem, the Holocaust museum in Jerusalem. Following a four-hour tour, our forty-person group met Holocaust survivor Eliezer Ayalon for a moving ninety-minute talk about his experiences in five concentration camps. Joyce and I consider ourselves fairly well read and thought we knew quite a bit about the Holocaust. After touring Yad Vashem and hearing Elie, we realized how little we really knew.

| *Eliezer Ayalon, 2010, while speaking at Tufts*

He told a riveting story of arriving in Israel as a survivor, but being suspected by some of being a Nazi collaborator. Many mistreated him, as they simply would not accept that he survived the Nazi horrors without conspiring with the despicable regime. He learned quickly that, even as he began to locate family members in this new land, he had to fabricate an entirely different story about how he got to Israel.

> We later came to three powerful realizations: First, the lessons of the Holocaust are far too vital to be forgotten or denied. Second, genocides are still occurring throughout the world. And finally, thinking people cannot simply sit quietly and let more genocides happen. While flying home, Joyce and I determined almost simultaneously, "We have to do something."

ONE OF OUR first steps after returning to Boston was to invite Elie Ayalon to Massachusetts. Joyce and I had learned so much from him and were so grateful for our ten days in Israel. We wanted to help him share his experience with others. We met with Tufts then president Larry Bacow, who lost family members in concentration camps, and with longtime friend Rabbi Jeffrey Summit of Tufts Hillel. Together, we arranged for Elie to come and speak to Tufts students, which he did in 2010. That was the beginning of Tufts' interfaith Cummings/Hillel Program for Holocaust and Genocide Education. Elie stayed two nights in our home. During his visit, he met and spoke with two large

Tufts students fill the auditorium for a Cummings Foundation talk about the Holocaust

groups at Tufts, and he particularly enjoyed meeting informally with many active and acutely interested students before and after his formal presentations.

Following Elie's visit, the foundation established two long-term programs in Holocaust and genocide education, each with a $1 million commitment. One of these was at Tufts University and the other at Salem State University with Professors Robert McAndrews and Chris Mauriello. We also began supporting substantial programming at the United States Holocaust Memorial Museum in Washington, D.C. at about this same time.

Our earliest interest in Rwanda arose from our support of Tufts students who traveled to Agahoza Shalom Youth Village in Rwanda. We learned so much about the Village, which was originally founded to help high school-aged victims of the terrible Rwandan Genocide of 1994.

"Bill and Joyce's commitment transcends particular religious affiliation," Rabbi Summit noted in a May 2014 *Chronicle of Philanthropy* article. "To join hands across religious traditions to look at these issues is extremely important." Convinced that real change can come from the next generation of world citizens, we created and then formalized our programs. It is our hope that through academic courses, immersion-travel experiences, meetings with genocide survivors, and much more, these students will be sensitized to the early warning signs of genocide and become strong and passionate enough to stand up against genocidal forces.

❦ *Deal-making in business can often be quite similar to playing chess, or bridge, or even billiards, in terms of knowing how and when to take advantage of situations as they develop. Careful planning ahead, and sometimes a little bluffing—not lying—are often part of any serious game and must be anticipated. And like experts at chess, bridge, or football for that matter, the negotiating expert must always be thinking ahead, and anticipating the opponents' next move, as well as his or her own.*

[15]

Cummings Foundation Matures

Trustees of Cummings Foundation, 2019. Shown left to right (front): Hon. Margot Botsford; Dr. Marilyn Cummings Morris; Dr. Deborah Kochevar; Joyce Vyriotes, a director of Cummings Properties; Joyce Cummings; Carol Donovan; and Laurie Gabriel. Second row: Cummings Properties CFO and senior vice president Bill Grant*; Cummings Properties chairman and CEO Dennis Clarke; Tufts University president Anthony Monaco; Cummings Foundation executive director Joel Swets*; Dr. Joseph Abate; Dr. Arlan Fuller, Jr.; Bill Cummings; Richard Ockerbloom; Paul Casey; Union College president David Harris; and Cummings Properties president Eric Anderson. Not shown, Dr. Patricia Cummings. **ex-officio trustee*

FIRST FOUNDED AS Cummings Properties Foundation, Inc., in 1986, our foundation was created to become a meaningful philanthropic presence, hopefully during our lifetimes. We expressly organized it to "give back" within the communities where Cummings Properties does business and where most of its employees and clients live. In large part these communities were the source from which our assets were derived.

We established this charitable entity as a private operating foundation, as distinguished from a private grant-making foundation. Unlike grant-making foundations, which grant funds to other organizations that then put those funds to work for their charitable purposes, an operating foundation is required to concentrate the vast majority of its expenditures on sponsoring and managing its own programs. Cummings Foundation has evolved to now have four operating divisions. We later created a separate, but related, foundation to act as a grant-maker with the capacity to make more and larger grants to public charities than our operating foundation would be permitted to grant under the tax laws governing private operating foundations.

Although Cummings Foundation's first $100,000 gift was made to the Woburn Boys Club, as described earlier, it was a quarter century later that we established our first programmatic plan for giving. Joyce and I determined that if we worked first at building an endowment for this new financial entity, we might be able to create a truly meaningful organization by the end of our productive years. And that was exactly what we set out to do.

There were, of course, many other things we were able to quietly support as we chose to, and did, but mostly we worked to create a substantial net worth for the foundation, and we handled our ongoing philanthropy through personal funds, or through Cummings Properties, as time went on.

In business, I always sought to surround myself with people who were smarter than I am and who brought diverse experiences and perspectives to their work. Cummings Properties owes its success largely to the synergies resulting from so many dozens of talented, caring, honest individuals working so beautifully together. Joyce and I approached the foundation in a similar way, inviting trusted friends and respected community leaders to serve as trustees, with a strong majority being *non*-family.

The community trustees of Cummings Foundation who have no company or family relationship are Dr. Joseph Abate; the honorable Margo Botsford; former state representatives Paul Casey and Carol Donovan; Dr. Arlan Fuller Jr.; retired Wellington Management partner Laurie Gabriel; Union College president Dr. David Harriss; Dr. Deborah Kochevar; Tufts University president Dr. Anthony Monaco; and retired Boston Globe president Richard Ockerbloom. The six charter trustees, who are family members or company officers, are Joyce Cummings, Dr. Marilyn Morris, Dr. Patricia

Foundation executive director Joel Swets with pro bono *deputy director Joyce Vyriotes, 2015*

Cummings, Dennis Clarke, Eric Anderson, and myself.

In addition to the six charter trustees and ten community trustees, Harvard University president Lawrence Bacow and Michael Pascavage are trustees *emeriti*. William Grant and Joel Swets are *ex officio* community trustees by reason of their positions as CFO of Cummings Properties and executive director of Cummings Foundation, respectively. No person is paid to be a trustee.

Cummings Foundation also benefits greatly from *pro bono* management help from its trustees and from so many colleagues of Cummings Properties. Joyce Vyriotes, the long-term communications director for Cummings Properties and a 1996 graduate of Mount Holyoke College, joined the Cummings Properties Executive Committee in 2019 and also serves as the *pro bono* deputy director of the foundation.

Joel B. Swets, a 1976 graduate of Colby College, also has a degree from Suffolk University Law School, as well as a master's degree in taxation from Boston University School of Law. He joined the foundation in October 2006 as the foundation's executive director. Joel is still its only administrative employee.

In addition, Cummings Foundation benefits magnificently from more than one hundred twenty-five otherwise unaffiliated volunteer professionals and so many others. These volunteers diligently read and process many hundreds of grant applications and conduct site visits with grant recipients.

"The plan for the grant-making foundation was to depersonalize the giving side and to gradually move all that activity away from Joyce and me," I told a reporter for "Chronicle," a popular Boston television news series. "It works so much better now that we have some really well organized systems in place. In fact, we are almost completely beyond our personal involvement, because we are surely not going to be here thirty years from now." We are both still feeling great, but our runways are, of course, becoming ever shorter.

ONE OF THE FOUNDATION'S most significant relationships began with a rather plebeian meal. In early 2002, when former Tufts president Larry Bacow was still the new guy on Tufts' campus, he invited me to join him for lunch. By that time, Joyce and I were significant donors having recently endowed the Cummings Family Chair in Entrepreneurship. I remember going to that lunch visit with a somewhat self-satisfied

| *Pres. Lawrence Bacow*

sense of immunity from any kind of solicitation.

Although we were initially going to dine at Boston's Four Seasons Hotel, I suggested the on-campus Dewick Dining Hall instead. That particular student venue had served many times as a convenient testing site for me decades prior, when I was developing Old Medford beverage bases, and Tufts Dining Service was Old Medford's first new college account. It would be a nostalgic treat for me to have lunch there with Tufts' new president. Because there was no agenda for that "get acquainted" meeting, I could particularly enjoy what we now refer to as our "veggie burger lunch." But following that casual meal, we had one of the most instantly productive advancement conversations any two people could imagine.

Founded in 1978, the School of Veterinary Medicine, the only such school in New England, was building a magnificent reputation for itself, but severe budget constraints were limiting its further improvement.

After walking back up the hill to Larry's office in Ballou Hall, he and I scoped out a "what if" agreement for Cummings Foundation to acquire operating responsibility for the School of Veterinary Medicine and then hire the university to run it for us. The foundation would effectively adopt the educational component of the school, which is located in North Grafton, Massachusetts, and then invest at least $50 million to significantly stabilize its future growth. Through 2020, actual contributions exceed $75 million.

The school, which had recently taken a major wallop in its contracted annual state appropriation, stood to benefit greatly from the foundation's financial assistance, as well as from some occasional management and consulting participation of the sort we could readily supply. The school would also be renamed Cummings School of Veterinary Medicine, and its teaching component would be legally merged into the foundation.

Neither Larry nor I anticipated this complicated proposal, and yet it came together in substance in about forty minutes. Tufts' trustees effortlessly approved the agreement in principle, but it then took all of a year and a half before all the required regulatory and accrediting approvals came through. In the end, however, the basic understanding was almost exactly as Larry and I had arranged it following that fortuitous meal. After also serving as a trustee of Cummings Foundation, President Bacow later went on, in October 2018, to become the twenty-ninth president of Harvard University.

The Tufts trustees soon announced our commitment to Cummings School as Tufts' largest gift ever, and it has since grown to almost $80 million. It was also the first naming gift for a veterinary school in the United States. In 2005, we were told that our gift helped to inspire an even more innovative $100 million gift from fellow Tufts alumni and fellow Giving Pledge members Pam and Pierre Omidyar, the 1995 founders of eBay. Their wonderful contribution made us feel even better.

> Most unusually, Attorney Michael Bohnen of the Boston law firm Nutter, McClennen & Fish represented both the university and the foundation in the $50 million transaction, handling not only the acquisition agreement itself, but also the federal tax and regulatory considerations, for both entities, as well as the renaming of the school. Not surprisingly, we developed a strong working relationship with President Bacow and his wife, Adele Fleet Bacow, who also did so much for Tufts.

The agreement with Tufts University that resulted in the renaming was highly original and unusual in other respects too. Cummings Foundation was beginning to dramatically grow its net worth, and it determined to also grow its operational side beyond the scope of its not-for-profit assisted living facilities. To continue to qualify as an operating foundation, current IRS regulations require that the foundation must *spend* approximately 4.25 percent of its endowment value each year on its "operations." The intention of the regulation is to ensure that the foundation substantially conducts its exempt activities *directly*, rather than through grants to other organizations.

Joyce and I have directly collaborated with the school on several major projects in Rwanda. One of the most significant of these has been helping Cummings School introduce the One Health concept promoted by United States Agency for International Development throughout Africa, including at the University of Global Health Equity (UGHE) in Rwanda. Joyce and I attended the formal opening of this new university campus in February 2019 along with Alice and Skip Fuller and doctors Zoia and Tony Monaco, in Butaro, Rwanda.

Not long after our relationship with Cummings School began, its dean of nearly ten years, Dr. Philip C. Kosch, stepped down. Since then, we greatly enjoyed working with Dean Deborah Kochevar, who is an extremely bright, dedicated, and down-to-earth scholar and leader. Only the fourth woman in the United States to head a veterinary college, Dean Kochevar came to Cummings School from Texas A&M University, where she served as associate dean.

| *Dean Deborah T. Kochevar*

| *Joyce and Bill Cummings delivering the commencement address for the tenth class to graduate from the Cummings School of Veterinary Medicine, May 2015*

Debbie, as we know her, has been a true partner, both at the North Grafton campus and in relation to our mutual work in Rwanda. She has also served as a trustee of Cummings Foundation. Joyce and I were delighted when she invited us to jointly address the tenth commencement class since the renaming to Cummings School, in 2015.

❈ *As much as entrepreneurs might like to think they are going it alone (or that their teams are going it alone), companies do not exist in bubbles; they coexist as part of communities. In the spirit of the saying, "A rising tide lifts all boats," remember that money spent improving the lives of local residents will pay dividends by enhancing the entire community as a place to live, visit, and do business.*

❈ *Good managers must constantly optimize combinations of quality and cost, and they must constantly teach others how to do the same. Well-trained, caring, long-term colleagues who understand what their company is all about and want it to be a great firm are the greatest asset in any firm.*

❈ *Success is much more a journey than it is a destination.*

[16]

The Giving Pledge

Joyce and Bill during a Guadalupe sailing vacation

IN EARLY 2011, JOYCE and I began to greatly broaden our philanthropic commitment when we joined the Giving Pledge, the international organization founded in 2010 by Bill and Melinda Gates and Warren Buffett. There are numerous excellent groups around the United States and abroad dedicated to high-level philanthropy, but we have never become involved with any others.

Neither Cummings Foundation nor Cummings Properties has enough staff members for them to be joiners or to attend non-essential meetings or events. In the forty-five-year history of Cummings Properties, we also almost never needed to attend conventions, trade shows, or similar gatherings. Joyce and I have traveled extensively all over the world in more than eighty nations for personal enrichment and enjoyment, and now for philanthropic purposes, too, but business travel *per se* has been all but nonexistent.

The Giving Pledge is loosely organized and except for occasional references to the three "founders," I have never seen or heard of any member of the group holding a title. Neither have we ever heard of votes being taken for any purpose, and there are no dues or membership fees. All these aspects help to make the group unlike any "club" we have ever known.

The group does not promote any particular charities or causes, and it does not set up or organize joint or collective contributions. It also appears to be entirely non-political, although we, along with the Gates, Warren Buffett, and two dozen or so other Giving Pledge members, did meet with President Obama in the White House, in July 2011. For two hours, the President chaired the meeting, which included considerable give-and-take discussion about how philanthropies might better work with government agencies to accomplish more.

> SHORTLY AFTER BECOMING Giving Pledge members, Joyce and I attended the first annual meeting, which brought together dozens of billionaires as guests of a delightful southwestern resort. It was startling to realize that every participant in the hall had not only the interest but also the desire *and the ability* to meaningfully improve the lives of *millions* of people. Bill and Melinda have likely already *saved* millions of lives through their philanthropy. Looking over the large group of guests, we realized that while we fully qualified as members, we were among the "poorest" members there.

Although the participants tend to be extremely pleasant and friendly, it would be wrong to think of the Giving Pledge as a social organization. Its sole purpose is to promote philanthropy and share knowledge, techniques, and strategies for making a positive impact in our varied world. To that end, there is an annual meeting each spring and occasional regional meetings dedicated to specific topics. The meetings often feature member-led panels.

These events, as well as periodic communications from the Giving Pledge, are extraordinarily well planned and implemented. Bill and Melinda Gates Foundation capably arranges activities, and numerous members serve as hosts, speakers, and facilitators, rather than employing outside speakers. The annual gatherings are typically hardworking two-day, three-night meetings, with full agendas from 7 AM through after-dinner hours. As I write this, Joyce and I have attended all but one of the Giving Pledge's first eight annual meetings. The members, each one an all-star of world philanthropy, participate to discuss and learn about philanthropy and have little time for amenities. Not that we have sacrificed in any way—the accommodations, service, and cuisine at each meeting have been beyond superb.

Just a few of the more well-known Giving Pledge members who joined early included: AOL founders Steve and Jean Case, Chuck Feeney of Duty Free Shops, Ted Turner, George Lucas, Carl Icahn, Lyda Hill, David Rubenstein, Elie and Edyth Broad, and eBay's Pierre and Pam Omidyar. Also, Jeff Skoll, Mark Zuckerberg and Priscilla Chan, and former New York mayor, Michael Bloomberg, as well as T. Boone Pickins, David Rockefeller, and Jon Huntsman. Bill and Melinda Gates and Warren Buffett are an impressive trio, and we have found them to be as genuinely smart, friendly, and caring as they are rich and powerful, whatever "powerful" means.

| *Framed photo hanging in Bill's hotel room in Virunga National Park, near the northern edge of Rwanda*

A national news source once quoted Bill when he jokingly bragged that he was valedictorian of his Harvard class—"the dropout class." From reading Warren's biography from a quarter-century ago, I learned that my earliest background is in many ways similar to parts of his, particularly our predilections for self-made part-time jobs. And we tell strikingly similar stories about being rejected ("deferred") by Harvard Business School. I have heard that at one time the only plaque on Warren's office wall was one he received years ago for completing a Dale Carnegie course. My office wall, on the other hand, is loaded with family pictures and other memorabilia, but they do not include even a single "political photo" or any other photo autographed by anyone.

In January 2012, during our first visit to Rwanda, we enjoyed a good example of how well-known Bill and Melinda Gates are in so many corners of the world. The majority of that trip was dedicated to foundation business, but we took two days to visit the highly endangered mountain gorillas in Virunga National Park, which required several hours of exceedingly bumpy driving north of Kigali. As we were settling into our mountain hotel, some familiar faces in a framed photo caught our eyes. Hanging right there in George Washington-slept-here style was a nice picture of past hotel guests Bill and Melinda, flanked by Dr. Paul Farmer, second from the left, and some others we did not know.

We should not have been too surprised to learn that Bill and Melinda had visited this place, as we were well aware of their many philanthropic interests in Rwanda. Looking back, I remember a private conversation with Pledge members during the 2012 annual gathering of the Giving Pledge that gave us the reassurance we needed to commit to making a significant charitable investment in Rwanda. We were in the earliest stages of discussing—with Boston-based Partners In Health—what would eventually become the first outpatient center for cancer treatments anywhere in Rwanda. We had little experience with international philanthropy, but after the informal chat with Bill, we felt confident that Rwanda would be the ideal place for us to try to make a meaningful impact. And Joyce and I had already decided that Partners In Health was the perfect partner with which to do it.

This anecdote demonstrates what I think many Giving Pledge members find to be the most beneficial aspect of the organization: the opportunity to learn from others' experiences. As is shown on its website and elsewhere, the Giving Pledge has grown from about seventy American members to a roster, as of mid 2018, of more than one hundred eighty members from fourteen countries. Joyce and I were delighted when three additional couples from Massachusetts appeared on the published list of members. Most members are well-known, either regionally or nationally, and almost all are interesting and smart, and much like "regular" people. They demonstrate what appears to be a great and genuine care and concern for doing important, good things for the world, and considerable information about the members is readily available on The Giving Pledge website.

Warren Buffett, in particular, was a helpful sounding board for me as I struggled with being simultaneously engaged in the seemingly contradictory activities of making money and giving it away. From my earliest days, my parents instilled in me the importance of *saving* money. And having run businesses for so long, I know all too well how difficult it can be to earn a dollar. Yet, no one needs to look hard to see the urgent needs in our own community and throughout the world that will benefit from our financial support. Warren readily related to the mental tug-of-war inherent in concurrently managing enormous assets and doing massive grant making.

Warren's solution, as he publicly shared in 2006, seemed to be to pick one primary activity: running his business. He effectively delegated much of the giving-it-away part to Bill and Melinda Gates, donating upwards of $30 *billion* worth of Berkshire Hathaway stock to *their* foundation, according to a June 26, 2006, *Wall Street Journal* article.

Joyce and I do not see ourselves sunsetting or outsourcing our philanthropy. The act of giving hard-earned dollars to help improve other people's lives fulfills me not only as a human being but also as a son. My parents and Joyce's parents were intimately acquainted with both sides of that equation—the discipline and ingenuity necessary to earn a dollar and the selflessness to help others in any way they could. Collectively, they are at the root of my story. Nevertheless, it was reassuring to hear Warren's perspective, and we hold him in extraordinarily high regard.

Another Giving Pledge member whose work I greatly admire is Michael Bloomberg, a 2020 candidate for the U.S. Presidency and founder of the eponymously named global financial data and media company. Michael is also a former resident of Medford and a fellow graduate of Medford High School. While our alma mater recently noted that two of its graduates went on to become members of this unique group, it is unlikely that many other public high schools will ever make the same observation. His Honor was several years behind me at Medford High. We did not know each other at all at the time, but we lived two miles apart and had friends in common.

Medford also has at least one more, less-direct tie to the Giving Pledge: Tufts University graduates Pam and Pierre Omidyar hung around Medford for four years as Tufts undergraduates. After studying computer science at Tufts, Pierre went on to found the groundbreaking online auction company eBay. Although this talented and generous couple attended Tufts three decades after I did, our paths crossed in later years at trustee meetings and during major university events, including at Tufts' European campus in Talloires, France. Bloomberg, both of the Omidyars, Joyce and I all hold honorary degrees from Tufts and continue to be involved with and supportive of the institution that played such significant roles during our formative years. The Omidyars' $100 million grant to Tufts, in 2005, is still the university's largest-ever single grant.

Until we joined the Giving Pledge, Joyce and I had done most of our giving quietly; even our major philanthropic activities were known only in a relatively small geographic area. We have never been a part of Boston society circles, and rather than attending fundraising galas or museum openings, we far more often spent our evenings with the same friends we have enjoyed since our kids and theirs were all in their infancies. Our lives are much the same today, except that our participation in the Giving Pledge and other foundation-related activities does provide some fascinating experiences. Most of our friends pretty much knew that we were comfortable financially, but none had guessed that our assets or those of the foundation had grown enough to put us in this particular company.

Although membership in the Giving Pledge comes with no other requirements beyond net worth and committing at least half of one's wealth for philanthropic purposes, members often help educate potential new members about the organization and its activities. As the first Massachusetts couple to join, Joyce and I were pleased to co-host an intimate dinner with Bill Gates for some Boston-area residents whose assets were believed to meet the billion-dollar threshold. Given that Joyce and I were not well-acquainted with many people who fit this description, the Giving Pledge provided a prospective guest list, and we assisted by providing a great venue and making personal phone calls to follow up on formal invitations. This dinner, in February 2012, took place during the time we owned and operated Beacon Grille Restaurant at our TradeCenter 128 office campus in Woburn.

By the time the Giving Pledge dinner came together, Joyce had already made plans to be with friends in Florida. Our eldest daughter, Marilyn, therefore served as my co-host, driving from New York to help me welcome Bill Gates, his staff members, and our local guests, which included one Boston couple who did later join the Giving Pledge.

As one might imagine, everyone present was extremely interested in what Bill Gates had to say. He openly shared his and Melinda's thinking about many aspects of philanthropy, but he also showed much attention

Dr. Marilyn Cummings Morris and Bill Gates, immediately following the 2012 Giving Pledge dinner at TradeCenter 128

and genuine interest in every other guest's charitable activities and thoughts about how to make the largest impact through giving.

> We never particularly liked the expression "Give until it hurts." We thought the better goal would be "Give until it feels good and then keep on giving." The Giving Pledge feels really good to us, and we applaud the vision and leadership of its three founders: Warren Buffett and Bill and Melinda Gates.

BOLSTERED WITH encouraging information from Giving Pledge associates, we began our first Rwandan trip in Kigali in 2012. Kigali is a modern city in the center of a landlocked sub-Saharan country about the size of Vermont. There is a rapidly growing airport and major roads leading out of the city in several directions, but even some of these spoke roads soon run out of pavement, and the country has little yet in the way of connecting highways.

Our good friends Alice and Skip Fuller joined us for this first trip, after learning that we planned to include a visit to Rwanda's Volcanoes National Park for up-close encounters with families of the rare mountain gorillas. In addition to visiting Agahozo-Shalom Youth Village and the gorillas, we toured two rural hospitals operated by Partners In Health, the Boston-based organization founded by Dr. Paul Farmer, Ophelia Dahl, and others.

There are reportedly fewer than eight hundred mountain gorillas in the world. All are now highly protected, and most dwell in the contiguous national parks of Rwanda, Uganda, and the Democratic Republic of Congo. These parks meet on the side of a high volcano in the Virunga Mountains, north of Kigali. The gorillas typically roam at high altitudes, eating as much as seventy-five pounds of vegetation daily.

Our first trek to visit with the gorillas began after our Land Rover bumped us violently up to about six thousand feet above sea level. Then we climbed to a spot at more than eight thousand feet, where, higher up than our guide expected to find them, the guide's scout located the family

Bill took this photo of a seven hundred-pound silverback in the wild from about nine feet away

we would visit that day. We had already become somewhat acclimated to the lower oxygen level because all of Rwanda is high above sea level, so the altitude did not seem to be much of an additional factor for any of our prescribed eight-person group.

THIS BOOK CANNOT begin to devote appropriate space or attention to the historical and political events surrounding the horrendous Rwandan genocide. Instead, here is just a bit of context for our trip to Rwanda, and Cummings Foundation's philanthropy there: The genocide officially began in April 1994, although sporadic massacres had been occurring for several years prior, and it lasted for one hundred days, during which the Tutsi people of Rwanda and their sympathizers were singled out for death. Altogether, the horrifying atrocities claimed the lives of more than eight hundred thousand Rwandans.

In 2001, the Rwandan government invited Aegis Trust, a charity dedicated to the prediction, prevention, and ultimately, elimination of genocide, to establish a memorial and museum in partnership with the Kigali City Council. The memorial opened in 2004, at the time of the tenth anniversary of the genocide. More than 250,000 victims of the genocide were buried on the museum grounds, many in respectful glass-topped crypts surrounded by beautiful gardens.

Skulls of victims killed in a Kigali church are lined up and displayed on steel racks

The museum's main exhibit tells the history of Rwanda leading up to the genocide, and it catalogues the details of the genocide through personal testimonies, photographs, videos, and artifacts. There is also a small room dedicated to children, the most innocent victims of the genocide. On another floor, the exhibit "Wasted Lives" reflects on other genocides of the past, including the massacres in Armenia, southwest Africa, Bosnia, and Cambodia, and of course, the Holocaust.

The day after visiting Kigali Genocide Memorial, we toured Kigali and also traveled out of the city to visit two former churches where thousands of people had sought refuge during the massacres. When there were troubles in

1959, the church supposedly protected anyone who was able to get to it, but not so in 1994. Many priests and ministers had reportedly left the country and were simply not there to provide sanctuary. Emotionally, this was the single most difficult part of the trip.

At the two former churches, we viewed walls gruesomely splattered with blood, where babies had reportedly been thrown against the walls to kill them. Each church also has hundreds of victims' bloody clothes, turned brown with time and carefully laid out on pews and kneelers. Even altar cloths were heavily stained with splashed blood. We repeatedly heard stories of women who were raped and then further violated with poles thrust into their sex organs. Like in a horrific nightmare, rows and rows of skulls are displayed on steel racks with piles of the victims' other bones just beneath. "This one was killed by a machete," the guides pointed out. "This one by a club..."

> The Holocaust is the most readily recognized example of genocide and the most atrocious outbreak of this recurring madness that has infected our world throughout history. But from the tribal groups in Darfur today to Rwanda and Armenia to the Native Americans during the European colonization of the Americas, and even long before that, history provides all too many examples of the persecution, displacement, and murder of entire populations.

IN 2007, in Rubona, Rwanda, the late Anne Heyman, a South African–born woman from Long Island, New York, and her family began building what would become a wonderful residential high school called Agahozo-Shalom Youth Village. They used basic, quality materials and good workmanship, and the complex is beautiful in its no-frills simplicity. In 2008, it opened with one class of one hundred twenty-five students and added similar-sized classes each of the next three years. By 2012, it was at its full occupancy of five hundred students as a marvelous four-year facility for the most needy young people in the country.

The "mayor" in each of Rwanda's thirty districts submits to the school a list of the ten most vulnerable children between the ages of fifteen and nineteen in the district, from which a list of three hundred children is created. The list is culled to around two hundred, at which point "home" visits are made to determine which children will be chosen to attend Agahozo-Shalom. "Home" is in quotation marks because some have no family and are living on the streets. Others have no parents but live with a relative. Some have one parent, often a

Agahozo-Shalom Youth Village with Bill and Joyce in 2019

mother who has HIV from being raped during the genocide. (The HIV rate in Rwanda is substantial but still reportedly among the lowest in Africa.) Still other prospective students are effectively heads of households, taking care of younger siblings. Most new students pick up some English before they arrive, but all are soon fluent.

While many of the school's graduates go on to college, including many who have already come to the United States and Canada, the overriding goal is to give students tools to be responsible citizens with the ability to earn a living, be good parents, think straight, and contribute to a peaceful society.

Throughout the country, there is a fervent policy not only of reconciliation but also of retraining people to not blindly follow anyone. Still, the question remains: How much will it take to change a culture that condoned the massacre of hundreds upon hundreds of thousands of friends, neighbors, and even family members in the horrific genocide of 1994? How will Rwandans eventually overcome this disastrous tragedy?

ON ONE OF our mornings in Kigali, Joyce wrote, "Looking out the hotel window at a beautiful large swimming pool, listening to soothing sounds of a fountain, drinking in the clean air, and enjoying large tropical plants…This is the way God intended Rwanda to be." From its 1994 image as the worst country on earth, Rwanda has come magnificently far. There are many organizations with smart, energetic, dedicated people who are working hard every day to help return Rwanda to its natural beauty and its peaceful way of life. Partners In Health is one of the most important and effective such organizations.

Dr. Paul Farmer, Ophelia Dahl, Dr. Jim Yong Kim, Thomas J. White, and Todd McCormack all worked to found PIH in 1987, originally to support

| *Joyce and Bill Cummings with Alice Fuller in a rural Rwandan village*

schools and healthcare in Haiti. Although well-known for its ongoing work there through Tracy Kidder's renowned best-selling book *Mountains Beyond Mountains*, PIH has expanded its services throughout the world, creating medical centers in the United States, Russia, Peru, Mexico, Guatemala, and several African countries. We visited two of the three PIH hospitals in Rwanda.

We had a morning meeting at Rwinkwavu Hospital with all levels of the hospital management and healthcare providers and received an extensive tour of the facility. In the afternoon, we went with a nurse and social worker for some home visits. It took more than an hour to get to the first village, far off the paved road, where the many children who greeted us all wanted the wazungu ("white people") to take their photos. The kids were excited when they saw their pictures on a digital camera.

Butaro Hospital, in northern Rwanda, was built through a collaboration between PIH, Rwanda's Ministry of Health, and private North American financial contributions. The flagship one hundred fifty-bed facility is the first permanent hospital in Burera District, which previously had only one doctor to serve more than three hundred thousand people. Plans are under way to make Butaro Hospital the cancer center for the entire country and the hospital component for the first phase of this new medical university.

Dr. Peter Drobac,* the former director for PIH in Rwanda, who also holds

| Dr. Peter Drobac

an appointment at Brigham and Women's Hospital in Boston, described the neonatal intensive-care unit at Butaro as just one example of the new services the hospital is now offering. "Prematurity and low birth weight are incredibly common here because of malnutrition, malaria, and other factors associated with poverty," Dr. Drobac said. "Even babies born full-term frequently look like preemies, and many babies are still dying. Although we now have incubators and other equipment, simple things can also be done to prevent these deaths."

In 2013 Cummings Foundation built the first outpatient cancer clinic in the country, adjacent to Butaro Hospital. A year later we would be highly instrumental in working with PIH to begin the first phase of University of Global Health Equity there as well.

❈ While almost all people mentioned in this book are exactly who they appear to be, a few names have been intentionally left out, or situations altered to disguise the identity of people who might be offended or hurt if their names were revealed. Additionally, in several instances I have withheld completely the names of prominent, well-known people with whom Joyce and I have dealt in connection with The Giving Pledge, because mutual confidentiality is such an important aspect of membership and participation.

❈ To accelerate the learning process, seek out opportunities to learn from the experiences of others. Our joining the Giving Pledge allowed Joyce and me to hear about different philanthropic practices and philosophies, albeit often from vastly different perspectives. Although what works for other members—even Warren Buffett—may not work for us, being aware of the many possible paths helps us to make better, more confident decisions.

❈ Most people do not lack the strength to succeed nearly as often as they lack the will.

---

* Dr. Drobac and his wife, Dr. Neo Tapela, along with their two young daughters, left PIH in October 2017 for England, where Peter became director of the Skoll Center for Social Entrepreneurship at The University of Oxford. I was honored in late 2018 to accept a speaking engagement at the Saïd Business School Entrepreneurship Forum in March 2019.

[17]

Real-Life Monopoly

ERIC S. ANDERSON became our fourth president and COO on July 1, 2018. A Colby College graduate and a Connecticut native, Eric took over the key position from Dennis A. Clarke, who remains CEO, and assumed the chairmanship from me. A colleague since 1999, Eric has proven to be an outstanding leader with a strong knack for building and strengthening relationships with both clients and colleagues. His distinguished

Cummings Properties' president, Eric Anderson (left), founder Bill Cummings, and CEO and chairman, Dennis Clarke (seated)

military service, early in his career, prepared him well for many of the various roles he has filled with the company.

When Dennis Clarke earlier committed us to purchasing the fifty-four-acre former headquarters of Parker Brothers and Atari games, before I ever saw the property, we effectively acquired the local-area legacy of this famed Massachusetts firm. We would be successors, in a way, to a choice bit of the iconic and most genuine Monopoly patrimony, on Dunham Road in Beverly.

The older I grew, the less important it seemed to accumulate more square feet, but this opportunity we could not ignore. On the other hand, I still enjoy the game of Monopoly, and as a firm we greatly enjoyed the opportunity to play real-life Monopoly in Beverly, and what an opportunity that was. At first, we joked about calling it "Ultra Monopoly."

With massive unlocked potential and eight hundred feet of frontage abutting Massachusetts' famed Technology Highway (Route 128), just off exit 19, this project let me play yet again with real-life Erector sets and huge Tonka trucks—hundreds of them. Founded in Massachusetts in 1883, Parker Brothers was a family-owned company that General Mills purchased in 1968 and operated as a subsidiary for several decades. Later it was purchased by Tonka, and then Hasbro.

Purchasing this site was the sweetheart deal that Dennis, in his tenure as president and CEO of Cummings Properties, found and determined we could not pass up. It truly was a unique opportunity to purchase an existing one hundred thousand-square-foot first-class office building on fifty-four bucolic and conveniently located acres. This lone structure was neatly centered among the tall trees, hills, and streams, and overlooked beautiful Norwood Pond.

Eastern Bank facilitated our purchase by signing off on a deeply discounted short sale, thus waiving its $9 million mortgage loan balance on the property. The asset, with its almost empty building, was lovely, but as with The Shoe, there had supposedly been no other interested buyers for years. Luckily, we were able to do another all-cash close for a rock-bottom $2.3 million purchase price in December 2011. Once any property like this remains on the market or "available" for multiple years its perceived value can plummet.

This property had stunning but totally unrecognized additional buildability for six large office or other light-industrial buildings. The most important and difficult and expensive project was creating a gorgeous "shovel-ready" five-acre site at the top of West Hill after we removed a heavy forest of fifty- and sixty-foot-tall pine and oak trees, and leveled the hill off at thirty-two feet below its original elevation. We were able to accomplish this at minimal cost by allowing others to load and carry away the massive quantity of trees and fill for free.

Real estate investors will do well to remember that December is the best time to be looking for deals on problem real estate. Banks tend to be much more motivated to rid their balance sheets of loans gone bad before each calendar year ends, often giving buyers who offer no-nonsense purchase proposals much improved buying opportunities. The cost for financial institutions to maintain under-producing assets on their books can be truly staggering. Fast, decisive moves can consummate such transactions and secure the most attractive deals.

Having the ability to do all-cash proposals, as we always have done, or at least having enough cash to fully qualify for a conventional mortgage, can put any buyer in a great position.

WHEN OUR DEVELOPMENT TEAM first arrived at Dunham Road, we were surprised to learn about some exceedingly limiting wetlands restrictions at what we otherwise found to be an ideal new location. The Beverly Conservation Commission had mistakenly and somewhat arbitrarily classified several large areas of the Dunham property as "vernal pools," a type of protected seasonal wetland. What we viewed as the commission's overreaching measures totally confounded our initial long-term development thoughts.

After being rebuffed during meetings with the commission, we took the matter to Essex County Superior Court but lost. The court effectively ruled that irrespective of the wording of Beverly's wetlands regulations, it was the intent of the conservation commission regulations that mattered and not the exact wording of the published regulation. More specifically, the Superior Court determined that several wet areas on the property did not have to completely dry up each summer to be classified as vernal pools, even if the plain English of Beverly's regulations clearly stated otherwise. There was abundant evidence proving that the supposed vernal pools retained water year-round and, therefore, were not vernal pools, but our position was totally rejected.

One of our top in-house attorneys, Jonathan "Bo" Lamb, immediately appealed the case in the higher Massachusetts Appeals Court, however, and in April 2015, a portion of the Superior Court's decision was quickly reversed in our favor. In a summary decision, Judges Green, Wolohojian, and Blake remanded the case back to the Beverly commission for further proceedings after finding that its omission of a portion of its own regulation was in error as a matter of law. Most importantly, the Appeals Court effectively ruled that the Beverly regulations could only be interpreted in accord with the common and customary use of the English language.

Nevertheless, following this important Appeals Court decision, Dunham Road became dramatically more developable and is already delivering meaningfully increased municipal real estate taxes and good jobs to the city. To facilitate this development more quickly we then created Dunham Ridge Condominium, thus converting the site to a six-unit *land* condominium, including twenty-five acres of unusable wetlands. At first it appeared that this novel subdivision approach might not work with the local registry of deeds, however, unless there was a building associated with each new lot to be conveyed.

54 Dunham Ridge, Beverly

I personally had never heard of a land-only condominium before we decided to create one and thereby avoid the somewhat cumbersome process of filing for a new lot under what Massachusetts calls its Definitive Subdivision Control process. And, as it turns out, our local registry of deeds had never heard of such a thing either, unless the surveyor's plan also included a plan showing a properly located "building."

Since buyers were standing by with $6 million in hand to acquire this new six-acre "Lot 54," we added a twelve-foot square metal building on a concrete pad to the master plan, and promptly received a permit to construct that tiny building. We then purchased the small metal yard house and assembled it on the site the next day (as shown). On the third day the surveyor returned to certify the completed "structure" on the site, and the document and a quitclaim deed were successfully recorded.

Construction is nearing completion for one additional new office and research structure at 52 Dunham Ridge Road following the completion of 48 Dunham Ridge in 2019. Another brand new robotic manufacturing center for Harmonic Drive Company is also complete at 42 Dunham Ridge, and the land at 54 Dunham Ridge has been sold to a West Coast developer. Altogether, the site will support eight hundred thousand square feet of mid-rise buildings on a total of fifty-four acres of woodlands and scenic ponds.

Still a giant factor in the success of the company is our ability to occasionally acquire occupied but undeveloped or grossly underdeveloped properties and then build one or more new buildings adjacent. New space created in this manner—often with effectively no cost for the land and with adequate utilities, parking, and other amenities available at little or no additional cost—has helped us build two dozen new buildings and major additions to others at a fraction of the usual cost. This has been the ongoing and hugely successful operational mode of Cummings Properties, greatly benefiting several host cities as well.

Putting aside much of my personal work at Cummings Foundation, I had what will probably be my last big fling of fieldwork during the summer of 2015 at Dunham Road. We had trucks, bulldozers, a giant rock crusher, and huge excavators going in every direction as we totally reordered almost thirty acres for these new projects. I have taken no salary from any source for eleven years now; my work at Dunham has been a labor of love, with 100 percent of all corporate profit, in one way or another, benefiting Cummings Foundation.

Newly completed 48 Dunham Ridge

We blasted untold thousands of tons of granite, and then excavated and crushed the broken granite every day for a month. This would have been a small project for a big land-development company, perhaps, but it was quite significant for us. Doing it all in-house with our own team of a dozen staff members, a few small subcontractors, and lots of heavy-duty rental equipment was perfect. From my view, I had a bonus vacation playing with all the equipment for a whole season. To boot, I lost a beneficial dozen pounds during the process. I chased earth-moving equipment all over the site from 7:01 AM every day and loved every minute of it.

> "UNUSED BUILDABILITY" has now been a common denominator among so many of our real estate transactions for five decades. Such buildability is among the most significant features real estate developers should seek when acquiring new properties, yet it is so often ignored. What "extras" are there that other prospective buyers may have overlooked? The value implications of unused or underused land can be astonishing and can make a dramatic difference in the long-term success of any real estate investment.

Reportedly the largest taxpayer in both Woburn and Beverly, we are as concerned as every appointed or elected official should be about each city's fiscal health and about responsibly building the tax base of the city. We seek cooperative, open relationships with local administrators, and we try hard to work with all of our host communities in a mutually respectful manner. Going to court to establish such relationships is never the perfect outcome for us, and certainly not for the municipality, either. Making use of the court system is, however, sometimes a necessity. Woburn is one of fewer than ten of Massachusetts' three hundred fifty-one communities with a bond rating of AAA.

Recognizing that we might be creating more commercial space than greater Beverly needs, we decided to build only one more office building at Dunham Ridge for our own account. Although all profits earned by Cummings Properties eventually goes to support the philanthropic work of Cummings Foundation too, all buildings owned by either entity still pay their full fair share of real estate taxes in each host community. We also work to donate earnings to the best charities in the communities where the buildings are located, especially when we are not pressured to do so. We remain careful about *not* donating when it might appear that we are attempting to win imbalance in any community by making large contributions.

For the remainder of the beautiful Dunham property, we now expect to sell or lease most parcels for independent, freestanding businesses. Indeed, in February 2017, we sold off the newly laid-out 54 Dunham Ridge parcel to Vitality Senior Living. The six-acre portion is expected to be developed in 2020 as an upscale, independent memory-care and assisted living complex with approximately one hundred eighteen units. Vitality is a new national chain of memory-care and assisted living homes being developed by affiliates of the Gary and Mary West Foundation. In connection with that broker-free sale we were pleased to arrange a direct 1031 Exchange with Boston Properties to acquire our first office building in Andover. In another brokerless direct sale we sold off 42 Dunham Ridge in 2018 to Harmonic Drive Technologies, which has since built its U.S. headquarters there.

THE ELLIOTT LANDING condominium project, meanwhile, is one of our latest major building developments. This seventy-three-home property is located in Beverly at the extreme southwest corner of Cummings Center. Although we had always expected that this now ninety-acre site would continue to be redeveloped entirely for commercial and public-service uses (including, we thought, a hotel), we determined in 2014 that adding high-end residences to Cummings Center would work especially well.

With thoughts of providing good housing in areas convenient to great workplaces and public transportation, we determined that luxury residential units are the perfect bookend for the south side of Cummings Center. The city of Beverly, meanwhile, is completing its all-new Beverly Police headquarters at

| Elliott Landing condominiums at Cummings Center, Beverly, 2019

the extreme southeast corner of Cummings Center, opposite Elliott Landing. The entire parcel was acquired from Cummings at no cost to the City.

Already being recognized as an established Beverly community, Cummings Center, after twenty years, had everything but residents. But now, the new condominiums have brought in about one hundred forty new Beverly citizens to enjoy magnificent water views over the Bass River to the south and Cummings Center's own urban environment to the north.

We already had the steel piles and concrete foundation in the ground there when we decided to give up plans for a Cummings Center hotel, and it was not difficult to enlarge the footprint and build the six-story condominium building instead. Although I did not realize it at the time, my last-minute decision to add two feet to the new building's ground-floor elevation, in anticipation of global warming, proved to be highly beneficial when it came time to certify that we were not in a defined flood zone. Selling the Elliott Landing homes as condominiums was, of course, consistent with beginning to reduce our commitment to and our exposure in Beverly. The real estate tax revenue for FY 2019 from this seventy-three-unit structure alone was reportedly about $500,000, with no school age children in the schools.

About half of the Elliott Landing buyers are retirement-age couples or individuals who are downsizing from large local homes they no longer need. The other half are people of all other ages, a few of whom are now walking to work in Cummings Center or to nearby MBTA stops. The lack of grounds maintenance required by owners is highly appealing to those no longer interested in cutting grass, raking leaves, and shoveling snow.

> Highly attractive also to many buyers at Elliott Landing is the Cummings Center neighborhood itself, which has a half-dozen good dining options, two of which include full-service lounges, and the eighteen-hole Beverly Golf and Tennis Club. There is a mile-long circular walkway, with twenty-four cast-aluminum historic markers, around our two beautiful on-site ponds, plus Beverly Athletic Club and several smaller fitness facilities. Cummings Center's robust health and wellness community includes on-site physicians with approximately twenty distinct medical specialties, which also greatly appeal to many local residents. Our "Live, Work, and Play" theme of Elliott Landing and so many of our office and research parks is such an important consideration wherever new real estate investments are planned. On-site amenities are an incredible attraction.

We decided to provide housing, rather than more office space or a hotel, on this newly laid-out lot after determining that Cummings Center, like Dunham Ridge, has enough office space. Building more offices there would further delay our ability to enjoy a fully leased office complex. In fact, across most of Beverly, there is no longer an insatiable need for more office, laboratory, or marketing space, and if we continued to build commercial space, we would soon be competing mostly with ourselves and hurting other commercial owners, too.

In relieving a chronic housing shortage, by the way, it just doesn't make much difference what type of housing is built. With Greater Boston's chronic shortage, new housing units at *any* level will ultimately benefit *all* levels of housing needs. Even the most expensive new units will help to free up other less expensive housing, thus trickling down to lower housing costs for even the least affluent buyers. The seventy-three Elliott Landing homes sold out in 2017 at prices from around $400,000 to just over $800,000.

Construction of Elliott Landing went along exceedingly well, and we moved in the first residents during Thanksgiving week 2016, just thirty years after we completed our on hundred fifty-unit Place Lane Condominium in Woburn. As of August 2017, all the Elliott Landing homes were sold or were under written agreement. Cummings Center is now truly Beverly's newest neighborhood and, as our sales theme states, thousands of people now "Live, Work, and Play in Cummings Center."

After spending six months designing Elliott Landing and fully constructing all of the foundation walls, we made a last minute change to raise the building foundation by two feet, to better meet the likely effects of global warming. Yes, global warming is surely coming, and even if we were not in any imminent danger

Tide Mill Institute Conference, 2015 at Cummings Center

of flooding otherwise, we are on the water and will likely appear much smarter if someone looks back, say in 2050.

Eight or nine months later soon after the marketing of Elliott Landing began, I ruffled many feathers among the sales team of our seventy-three homes there. I realized we were making a huge error. We had already encouraged a dozen new buyers to make a broad range of selections, like eight or nine varieties of natural inlaid wood flooring, and carpeting, paint colors, etc. Buyers could also select which appliances they wanted, and which bathroom fixtures, and even wall tile colors. The sales team seemed to think it should be in charge but the confusion would have been totally stifling if that process had been allowed to continue.

We experienced every bit of the consternation I had imagined with the small number of new owners who signed up under the original agreements. The trouble was that while we were delivering a highly superior product to our local area competition anyway, our production team was simply not experienced enough to handle the multitudinous different specifications, and then what seemed like interminable change orders at every turn. We made an error, for sure, but by stepping in and dictating a necessary major change in our offering we were able to make the large preponderance of the buyers happier because our designers thereafter made all of the design decisions before buyers ever got close at all. All that the buyers had to do then, was to select which unit they preferred.

Work on a much smaller building for moderate-income housing at 33 Balch Street, at the extreme northern end of the property, is separately pending municipal approval as I complete this chapter. Building housing at the otherwise unused areas at each end of Cummings Center was the correct approach to finishing those two areas, which will soon be totally repurposed twenty-four years after we acquired the massive hundred plus acre site.

According to knowledgeable local historians, the seventy-three Elliott Landing homes are located exactly where the original Friend's Grist Mill stood during the 1650s, when this area of Beverly was a part of the city of Salem.

We celebrated the history of this seventeenth-century mill that launched an uninterrupted series of commercial uses for the site that is now Cummings Center. An actual millstone believed to be from Friend's Mill, and on loan from Beverly Historic Commission, is prominently displayed along the walking trail adjacent to Acapulco's Restaurant.

Cummings Properties' management was pleased to host the 2015 Tide Mill Institute Conference in the Community Conference Room at Cummings Center. John Goff, a local representative of the Tide Mill Institute, recently discovered an additional millstone from Friend's Mill at the edge of Bass River, partially buried just above the high-water line. This newly discovered stone is visible near the terminus of the crosswalk, fewer than one hundred yards from Elliott Landing.

❧ *All people have differing skills and abilities just as we all have our unique flaws and shortcomings. We need to recognize what they are, trying always to make good use of whatever special abilities God has given us, while avoiding the temptations that may lead us toward our failures. Work regularly at developing a system of strong values, even though we may regularly fall short of those values in our daily lives.*

❧ *Acquiring commercial properties with "unused buildability" has been an oft-repeated theme in this book for real estate success. With the cost of purchasing and developing land typically representing 20 to 40 percent of a building project's total cost, buying a property capable of supporting additional square feet can be like finding free money.*

❧ *Corporate community responsibility is one of the most integral facets of Cummings Properties' makeup. Completed grants from the Company and Cummings Foundation together total more than $260 million through 2019.*

❧ *Good leaders will spend their days, and often their nights, too, figuring out ways to better serve customers or clients. If we don't work harder to stay ahead and keep our clients happy right where they are, we may soon be talking about former clients.*

❧ *Hire for "nice," and then promote the people with ingenuity who can deal with problem solving and make things happen.*

❧ *To be positive about something is sometimes just being mistaken at the top of your voice.*

[18]

Back to Africa

An intrepid Dr. Skip Fuller jumping into Devil's Pool at the top edge of the breathtaking three hundred fifty-foot-high Victoria Falls, in the Zambezi River, 2013

AFTER OUR FIRST exciting and highly successful trip to Rwanda, Joyce and I were delighted to return in August 2013, again with Alice and Arlan Fuller, for an even more stirring and productive visit.

On this journey, we took a more scenic route to Rwanda, from London via South Africa, and then enjoyed three days in Zimbabwe and Zambia and at Victoria Falls, the highest and largest water drop in the world, on the Zambezi River. After observing the majestic mile-long falls from all the conventional viewing trails, and then from a helicopter, Alice, Skip, and I signed up for a guided water-level view from Devil's Pool *in the water* directly at the upper edge of the falls. This is surely one of the most dangerous tourist attractions in the world, and we knew it.

From late August through January, a carefully regulated small number of tourists are able to travel by boat every hour or so across the open water to Livingston Island at the upper edge of Victoria Falls. Our guide's sixteen-foot-long aluminum boat had a new-looking single outboard motor, but anyone who has spent any time around small boats knows that outboards will sometimes stop running at inopportune times. The possibility of being washed over these colossal waterfalls to certain death before we even neared Devil's Pool was the first real danger of the day.

Once there, we needed to hike upstream along the edge of the Zambezi River from Livingston Island. Then we swam to an outcropping of ledge just above the edge of the falls, near the midpoint of this spectacular natural wonder. The greatest danger during the swim seemed to me to be the possibility of becoming mesmerized by the fast downstream flow and missing the tiny island. Although neither guide asked if anyone wanted to back out, he did ask us a second time if we still self-identified as "strong swimmers." I wondered what that question really meant in a life-or-death setting like this one, but after a vigorous swim across the rapidly moving current, we all scrambled safely onto the rocks near the center of the falls.

> Upon arriving on the tiny island near the center of the Falls, there was nothing to do but throw all caution to the wind and leap into the deep, water-filled depression. The pool itself is about thirty feet square, and, we were told, twelve feet deep. The natural rock formation defined the outer edge of Devil's Pool and the edge of the chasm wall, and was about eighteen inches thick. The flowing water over the wall's edge there is about six inches deep during the dry season when access is allowed.
>
> While resting in the water on the top of this shallow lip of rock, and with the guide holding us by our ankles, we leaned out, oh so carefully, and looked three hundred fifty feet straight down into the thundering mist!

After the visit to the pool, with millions of tons of water cascading down all around us, we swam with the current safely back across where the flow was slow. There the guides escorted us individually to where Joyce held our wallets and watches on Livingston Island. Dozens of people have reportedly been swept over the falls to horrific deaths over the last fifty years, including one guide who had died just a year earlier. Three elephants were also swept over the year before. In one manner or another the deceased tourists had been doing exactly the same thing we were doing. This was adventure tourism at its most extreme, with no expectation of safety for anyone. The awe and majesty of this gem of south-central Africa were breathtaking.

Flying down into the Pennsylvania coal mine on the high speed conveyor belt five decades earlier, and bungee jumping in Queenstown, New Zealand eleven years before, were both more scary, but swimming at the brink of Victoria Falls was by far the most dangerous thing any of us had ever done, or likely ever will do again.

WE TIMED the rest of this second African journey to coincide with the dedication of Butaro Ambulatory Cancer Center. During our visit the previous year, Joyce and I had committed several million dollars to fund the construction of this important new center. Although Rwanda had made impressive strides in healthcare since the genocide, the foundation's new facility was still the first outpatient cancer-treatment clinic in the country.

Shown at the Butaro Outpatient Center are (left to right): Burera Mayor Samuel Sembagare, Joyce Cummings, Patricia Campbell, Bill Cummings, Dr. Paul Farmer, and Dr. Agnes Binagwaho

We spent considerable time during this dedication visit becoming better acquainted with representatives of PIH and the government of Rwanda. Paul Farmer and his wife, Didi, hosted a lovely dinner in their then Kigali home. We also greatly enjoyed the company that day of Dr. Peter Drobac and his wife, Dr. Neo Tapela, who lived then in Botswana with their two young children.

Later we were also honored to share an elegant lunch with Paul, Peter, and their wives with His Excellency, President Paul Kagame and Madam First Lady Jeannette Kagame at the presidential residence. I continue to exchange occasional emails with President Kagame, and we were delighted to see him again in 2014 at Tufts University, where he lectured and spent time with students. Later, I spent a morning with him in Boston, in February 2016.

Over a short few months, we came to know and highly respect Paul Farmer and his truly remarkable organization, which was then regularly operating in eight countries around the world. Likewise, we admired President Kagame for how well he used his keen intellect and business mindset to completely turn around the economy of his country and the quality of life of its citizens. Any political leader trying to prevent a country from annihilating itself has a moral obligation to fairly use all power at his disposal to restore order. Kagame must be admired and honored for his work.

> While some may portray President Kagame as a tyrant, he is better described as the transcendent leader who suppressed the madness of a nation, then in violent chaos. He has proven to be a smart, courageous, and highly effective president. Rwanda managed to find a heroic and trustworthy leader with enormous competence who also appears to be creating an honest and graft-free society. Those who would malign President Kagame for his desperately needed strong methods in stopping an unfathomable genocide do him and the republic a great disservice.

Another great book by Tracy Kidder, *Strength in What Remains*, is certainly an outstanding resource for understanding how the great genocide materialized and was then brought under control by Kagame and other leaders. I asked President Kagame what he thought about *Strength in What Remains*, and he told me he did not agree with Kidder on *every*thing he wrote, but on balance, His Excellency told me, "I am glad he wrote the book."

OUR 2013 TRIP to Africa was most notable for providing an opportunity for Joyce and me to spawn the notion that the significant upgrades under discussion for Rwanda's health sciences schools could become something much greater. A fortuitous conversation developed in Kigali during a meeting billed as an Oral Health Stakeholders Meeting—a session that brought us together with Rwandan experts in the field of dentistry and healthcare delivery, along with Dr. Drobac and several key educators from National University of Rwanda, Tufts University, and Harvard University. In addition to Peter, and Skip and Alice Fuller, Joyce and I were joined during this meeting by Tufts University's executive vice president, Patricia Campbell, and Dr. John Morgan of Tufts University School of Dentistry. Most significantly, John had been conducting a review of Tufts' involvements in Tanzania and elsewhere that included an epic study of African dental health (which was completed in 2016). Professor Philip Cotton, formerly of the University of Glasgow, is the newly elected Vice-Chancellor of the University of Rwanda who chaired much of the program.

Earlier this same day, Cummings Foundation had offered to assist in building a dental clinic in Butaro, in the same area where the foundation had funded the outpatient cancer clinic. Upon learning that a new medical school was then under consideration, however, we set aside the dental school offer. We suggested to the group of distinguished attendees that, with the backing of the renowned PIH organization, Cummings Foundation could help develop a world-class pan-African—not just Rwandan—multidisciplinary medical university in Rwanda. The whole concept of the new international health sciences university first materialized that afternoon during a ninety-minute meeting.

After we returned to Boston, our overwhelmingly positive experiences in Rwanda, combined with our confidence in PIH's ability to work well with President Kagame's administration to bring about meaningful change, prompted us to move forward quickly.

A few weeks later, on October 4, 2013, Joyce and I reached out to several interested parties at PIH and Tufts, as well as in Rwanda, to confirm our thoughts on what we first called Pan-African College of Health Sciences. We envisioned a university that would attract the best students from all over Africa—and well beyond—and that would help Rwanda fulfill its potential to become an economic and educational hub for Africa.

By early 2014, we formalized our offer of a $15 million matching grant from Cummings Foundation to build the first phase of a major new health sciences university. Beyond the condition that matching funds be raised, we specified only three contingencies: The new university would not bear the name of any person, now or in the future; the Rwandan government would assemble and provide all needed land; and everything needed for the construction and continuation of the new school would be free of value-added or sales taxes. We (I) also fussed vociferously about the absolute need for the long-planned new road between Kigali and Butaro.

The enthusiastically received report immediately generated these responses from Partners In Health: "What a great vision," said co-founder Dr. Paul Farmer, "and one that squares with the Rwandan vision of pulling people up by

UGHE's main campus, under construction in Butaro, was designed by Shepley Bulfinch, the firm founded by the original designer of the Woburn Public Library

building a 'knowledge' economy while delivering care—and what better way to promote peace, justice, and development in the region."

Ophelia Dahl, PIH co-founder and board chair, wrote, "This will be transformative in ways we cannot yet even imagine."

Shortly thereafter, Skip Fuller, who had by then become a Cummings Foundation trustee, and I traveled to Seattle and requested the matching grant from Bill and Melinda Gates Foundation on behalf of PIH to fully fund the first phase of what was ultimately named and accredited as University of Global Health Equity. This fine new university formally opened its campus in rural Butaro on January 25, 2019, after earlier conferring its first master's degrees in Global Health Delivery in Kigali, beginning in May 2017.

Phase I of the main UGHE campus is adjacent to a beautiful valley and directly across from Butaro Hospital and the Butaro Outpatient Cancer Clinic. The ninety-acre campus features classrooms, labs, housing, food service, sports, visitor housing, and other amenities. The university will grow in phases, eventually creating an academic community of more than a thousand Rwandan and international students, faculty, and staff. There were reportedly more than twelve hundred applicants for the entering class of future physicians and dentists, which arrived in September 2019, coming from twenty-three nations.

There were two days of ceremonies and seminars in Butaro and at the brand new Kigali Marriott Hotel for the school's grand opening. Notable delegations from Harvard and Tufts University and a throng of major Partners in Health supporters included Dean George Daley from Harvard Medical School plus Tufts University President Anthony Monaco and his wife Dr. Zoia Monaco and Dr. Peter Drobac, both from University of Oxford.

Shortly before the end of the opening program, Cummings Foundation responded to a well-orchestrated pitch to the assembled major benefactors with a surprise $10 million gift offer if the other supporters present would commit to match the foundation total. The other attendees responded spectacularly, giving a total of an additional $11 million in additional funding. CNBC Africa broadcasted several TV segments throughout the continent, and *New York Times* reporter Donald McNeil was there for two days.

UGHE will likely soon also have a smaller city campus in Masaka, near Kigali and the new international air hub already planned there. The government of Rwanda has enthusiastically supported UGHE from its earliest phases. Government officials recognize its potential to provide high-quality education and a well-trained healthcare workforce. This fine new school will also help bolster Rwanda's international standing and attract businesses to locate or invest within its borders, all while strengthening its economy. Rwanda seems to be the perfect nation in which to locate UGHE.

The Rwandan government acquired the land for the second campus on UGHE's behalf, and while its construction is moving rapidly, the government is making the major much-needed improvements to the surrounding infrastructure. We most surely anticipate that the enhancements to the area, along with the construction-related and educational activities taking place at the new campus, will greatly benefit the entire Butaro region in the form of job opportunities, vocational training, and higher living standards. The new national highway is also now nearing completion from Kigali to Butaro, near one of Rwanda's most stunningly beautiful lakes areas.

Former Rwandan Minister of Health Dr. Agnes Binagwaho, who has done so much to help her nation become a recognized healthcare leader for all of Africa, is vice chancellor. Dr. Hellen Amuguni, DVM, PhD, MA, of Cummings School of Veterinary Medicine, is the first full-time Tufts addition to the fledgling UGHE staff in Rwanda. As soon as the new campus became operational in 2019, it began training physicians, dentists, nurses, post-graduate veterinarians, public-health workers, and other healthcare practitioners. UGHE will be much more than an

Dr. Hellen Amuguni

African version of a Western medical school. It has been conceived as a fully accredited groundbreaking international university. It will teach not only the science of healthcare, but even more significantly, the *delivery* of it, even in the world's poorest and most underserved regions. Often overlooked by teaching institutions, remote healthcare delivery requires a good understanding of applicable social forces, the ability to marshal political will, and the capacity to manage and refine dynamic, multifaceted operations.

There will be a strong emphasis from the beginning on the concept of "One Health." This interdisciplinary approach focuses on the linkages between animal, environmental, and human health, and it will encourage far greater collaboration and cooperation among all different types of healthcare providers. This starts with common classes to teach basic sciences to all students so that there is a uniform core of knowledge, which is terribly lacking in many societies. With a goal of improving health outcomes by emphasizing practical solutions, One Health breaks down the traditional boundaries between academic disciplines. With One Health as a foundational element of UGHE, students will have the core competency and biosocial approaches to solve and plan for the most critical and emerging global health challenges.

| *Joyce Cummings and the mesmeric Dr. Paul Farmer, 2014*

UGHE will train clinician-leaders who will be uniquely qualified to bridge the gap between knowledge and implementation. Its novel approach, however, has required rethinking every aspect of a university, from its curriculum to its research priorities to the location and design of its campus. In a May 2014 email to me, Dr. Farmer wrote, "We're all so excited about the idea of this whole new type of 'foreign aid,' one that focuses on real delivery and on real capacity building. And this 'One Health' notion is going to move all of this forward in Rwanda and beyond."

UGHE will take on great inequities and will attempt to lessen the deepest of them in some of the farthest corners of the world.

While PIH immersed itself in research and the early planning for UGHE in 2014, much of West Africa was devastated by a massive and deadly Ebola epidemic. Dr. Farmer told me that, at one point, he could not return to his family in Rwanda for seven months because he had so frequently been in and out of Ebola-affected regions of Africa. Because of weak and, in some cases, non-existent healthcare delivery systems, the disease spread rapidly from country to country, creating one of the worst public-health catastrophes of our time. This tragedy highlighted the urgent need to train health professionals to build and sustain effective and equitable health systems. Fortunately, with enormous local efforts, Ebola was kept at least somewhat at bay on the African continent.

> THERE ARE NO LIVES THAT ARE NOT WORTH SAVING, yet there are still so many millions of fully preventable deaths each year. In many remote areas of the world, with appalling disparities, even the most basic of medical services will make enormous life-and-death differences.

Aside from its work already in helping to launch UGHE, Bill and Melinda Gates Foundation is achieving magnificent international improvements, and is saving hundreds of thousands of lives, year after year. The graduates of UGHE will soon be offering their services in a worldwide market. Rwandans are busily reconstructing a beautiful and brave nation as they continue to resurrect it from the catastrophe of genocide. BMGF to date has reportedly invested well over $15 billion in Africa alone.

❈ *Entrepreneurs cannot become so enamored with one idea that they miss a greater opportunity. Joyce and I walked into that Kigali meeting with the idea of supporting a dental clinic. Because we really listened to a conversation about Rwanda's broader healthcare needs, we left the meeting with the beginnings of a much larger idea that quickly turned into a major new international university.*

❈ *When a friend or colleague is seriously hurting about some private matter, it may oftentimes be best to mostly just listen to the friend's problem. Hear what may be behind the spoken words and let the friend know you are there to help find a solution.*

❈ *Every business leader must know by now how necessary it is to sometimes criticize others, but always in private. But do they also know the importance of* praising colleagues in public, *whenever practical?*

[19]

Building the Future

Joyce and Bill speak to a delighted crowd of grant winners during a recent Grant Winner Celebration, held in the Atrium Lobby at TradeCenter 128, Woburn. Massachusetts' enormously popular Governor Charlie Baker attended this event in 2018 and 2019.

AS CUMMINGS FOUNDATION'S assets first approached $1 billion, then $2 billion, it was time to greatly expand our grant making through our open application process. This decision is in line with our thinking that a critical interdependence exists between a business and its community: the stronger the community, the stronger the potential success for business. Any successful company has a responsibility to contribute to the strength of its community by helping to care for the people who live there and patronize the business.

Although a company can invigorate a community merely by its presence—by paying its taxes and by contributing financially to the economy of a municipality—Cummings Foundation was initially created to truly enhance the communities where Cummings Properties thrived. We did so first through the two New Horizons residences, plus Cummings School of Veterinary Medicine, and then through grant programs that provide significant support for multitudes of other resources all over northeastern Massachusetts.

A $6 million pilot program in 2012 was so well received by the local nonprofit community that we increased the total to $10 million the following year. Originally named OneWorld Boston, the program evolved over the next several years. It became *$100K for 100*, and then we added a second program, Sustaining Grants, that offered long-term funding to prior winners. Most recently, we streamlined these funding initiatives, merging them into the now annual Cummings $20 Million Local Area Grants Program.

We revisit and slightly modify our eligibility requirements each year, yet two criteria have remained unchanged: geography and size. Our funding primarily supports nonprofits in the Massachusetts counties where Cummings Foundation operates commercial properties and where most staff and clients of the Cummings organization live—Middlesex, Essex, and Suffolk counties. Foundations considering a similar program may not have a compelling reason to limit the geography in this way, yet it is an important factor for us. Other grant makers might wish to serve an entire state or perhaps a country.

As for size, our grants primarily fund small and medium-sized charities, because such groups do not typically enjoy the large donor bases and endowments that support so many larger institutions in the Boston area. "The little guy needs our money," Joyce explained in 2014 to a reporter who asked why national organizations don't typically receive funding from the foundation. "We want our grants to go where they can really make a difference and will be much more than a drop in the bucket."

AS OF 2020, we are awarding one hundred thirty annual grants; the first one hundred are all for $100,000 each, payable mostly over three to five years ($10 million). The other thirty, totaling another $10 million, consist of "sustaining" grants of $200,000 to $500,000 each, all of which are paid over ten years. Spreading the grant over multiple years provides some meaningful stability, allowing organizations time to develop additional funding sources and avoid a "bolus" effect, in which the sharp drop-off after a large front-loaded grant leaves the organization in a difficult position. These much larger grants go to prior winners of $100,000 awards.

More than half of all new awards are determined completely by outside volunteers, and the other grants are identified through an in-house process as "Early Decision" awardees. The current iteration of our grant program is so easily replicable, and we welcome any interested foundation(s) to use all or parts of the process described in some detail below.

Nonprofit organizations learn about the grant process and apply through the foundation's website, www.cummingsfoundation.org. Applicants first submit a one- to two-page Letter of Inquiry (LOI). Since 2012, the number of LOIs has increased each year, from about 200 to 738. Our online software and the foundation's grants manager perform cursory reviews, removing all applicants that either have been identified for Early Decision status or that simply do not meet the eligibility criteria. The remaining applicants then undergo the following evaluation—and winnowing—process, which is conducted completely by volunteers:

LOI Review: During a six-week period, the twelve-member LOI Committee decides which of the applicants will be invited to the full application stage. Volunteers are divided into pairs, with each pair independently evaluating the same set of 100 or so LOIs. To the extent possible, LOIs are grouped by cause (e.g., education, social justice) so volunteers can more easily compare requests. Each pair then meets to share notes and finalize a jointly agreed upon list of nonprofits to invite to submit full applications. (The foundation provides each pair with a specific number of LOIs that may be advanced from their list.)

Application Review: Nonprofits that advance beyond the LOI stage receive an email with a link to the full application and have about two months during December and January to complete this more comprehensive proposal. Thereafter, during February, the eighteen-member Application Review Committee determines which applicants will advance to the Final Grant Selection Committee. Similar to the LOI review process, this completely different cadre of volunteers is divided into pairs, with each pair independently evaluating the same set of final applications, and then meeting to compare notes and finalize a jointly agreed upon list of nonprofits to advance in the process as finalists.

Financial Review: Cummings Foundation wants to help small nonprofits get to the next level. It does not, however, intend to provide "life support" for struggling organizations. To ensure that grant candidates are on solid financial footing, the foundation reviews the Form 990s of all finalists. We are enormously grateful for the assistance we receive in this important task

| *Some of Cummings Properties' in-house staff at 2017 Grant Awards night*

from LGA, formally Litman Gerson Associates, a prominent Woburn, Massachusetts CPA and business advisory firm that just happens to also be one of the foundation's longest-term leasing clients.

Final Selection: Next, during a six-week period in March and April, the forty-member Final Grant Selection Committee determines which (non-Early Decision) applicants will receive grant awards. Volunteers will work in ten teams of four, with each volunteer independently evaluating the same set of fifteen applications and then meeting to compare notes and finalize a jointly agreed upon list of nonprofits to receive grants. Volunteers typically serve on this committee for three years before rotating off and oftentimes then serve on a different committee. One member of each four-member committee is usually a Cummings Properties staff member, serving for one year. Whether plumbers, accountants, or architects, these colleagues seem to greatly appreciate the opportunity to help decide how to allocate the funds that they play such a major role in generating.

Ten-Year Grant Selection: After one hundred thirty winners are selected, foundation staff will review the proposals of the winners that have received previous Cummings grants, selecting a limited number of them to be considered for the larger grants, totaling an additional $10 million, to be paid over ten years. These nonprofits will be invited to meet with a panel of volunteers to make a case for having their grants elevated from $100,000 to the more significant awards. In preparation, volunteers will independently review applications, plus the Site Visit Reports and most recent Impact Report generated in connection with their previous grant(s). These volunteers will determine which grant winners will receive long-term funding from the foundation, as well as finalize grant installments based on a budget provided by Cummings Foundation.

VOLUNTEERS HAVE BECOME *the essence* of Cummings Foundation's grant program. By tapping into the deep expertise and rich diversity of greater Boston's professional community, the foundation is so much better able to understand the issues local communities are facing, identify the most promising and effective nonprofits to fund, and strengthen relationships with beneficiaries. Because the needs presented in LOIs and applications are so compelling, many committee members tell us they had no idea how difficult it would be to give money away. They tell us how challenged they were to make the final decisions, yet they almost all want to continue working year after year as foundation volunteers.

Past and current volunteers include a former White House staffer for First Lady Michelle Obama, a retired justice of the Massachusetts Supreme Judicial Court, former state legislators, CEOs, a noted *Boston Globe* reporter, a renowned cardiologist, and several college presidents, among so many other Boston-area professionals and distinguished citizens.

After sending award letters each year, the foundation is awash with phone calls, emails, social media shout-outs, and letters of gratitude. A word we hear from many grant winners is "transformative," and that is exactly what we want to be. We want to provide the support necessary to help hands-on grassroots organizations make larger impacts on the community. At the same time, many of these smaller organizations have reported that their Cummings grant has greatly helped them in securing significant funding from other foundations.

As of June 2020, the foundation has established meaningful donor relationships with more than seven hundred local organizations in eastern Massachusetts—and has made cumulative grants to them totaling more than $280 million. Improving access to high-quality educational opportunities is an important cause to us, as are initiatives concerning homophobia, poverty, job training, recidivism, bullying, and genocide education. Programs supporting English skills for immigrants and refugees and those promoting better writing and computing skills also rank high in our minds. An extensive list of the highly diverse grant winners is readily available at www.cummingsfoundation.org.

The 2020 Site Visit Committee chairpersons (left to right): Paul Lohnes, Susan Lewis Solomont, Peggy Kemp, Bob Keefe, and Karen Grant

Although the vast majority of charities supported by the foundation were previously unknown to Joyce or me, every so often we personally add a grant recipient that is "close to home" for us. One such grantee is the Royall House and Slave Quarters, which has been diligently unearthing parts of Medford's long-hidden colonial history. It is little known, for instance, that Massachusetts was not only the first American colony to abolish slavery but also the first to pass laws legalizing slavery, in 1641. This historical house, just three miles from our home, reportedly housed one of the largest slave populations in Massachusetts. It has been special to include the Royall House in our grant programs and to support its important social justice work.

MAINTAINING RELATIONSHIPS with the nonprofits we fund is a priority of the foundation. We consider them our partners and have much to learn about—and from—their successes and challenges as they spend the funds granted to them. Neither Joyce nor I nor our small staff has the bandwidth to connect with hundreds of charities each year, so we rely again on our robust volunteer force to conduct site visits.

We plan to visit recipients of ten-year "sustaining" grants each year, whereas recipients of $100,000 grants are typically visited during the final two years of the grant term. About sixty volunteers generously commit to performing at least ten site visits each year and completing a brief report sharing their impressions and insights, as well as any items for follow-up by either foundation staff or future visitors. Because perspectives can vary, two volunteers try to attend every site visit, and each volunteer completes his/her own report. When related couples volunteer in any manner they are often paired with another couple and cast just one vote (or complete just one report) per couple.

Before embarking on these previously scheduled site visits, which typically last between ninety minutes and two hours, volunteers undergo an orientation session. Beyond the details and logistics, we also share our approach to relating to nonprofits. In an effort to make the experience as positive as possible for both parties, we discuss the use of inclusive language and the goal of learning rather than investigating or judging. There often times tends to be some kind of a power dynamic at play when a funder is meeting with a nonprofit that needs funding. We do our best to minimize this dynamic, paving the way for many highly respectful and productive conversations.

Many small projects the foundation has undertaken have grown much larger than expected. Together, those small projects resulted in a huge difference in the quality of life for hundreds of thousands of people. Similarly, Cummings Properties started from a recognition that the unused land of Old Medford Foods should be something more. Meanwhile, we have tended to specialize in small clients that might—and in many cases do—grow and expand. Small is not insignificant. Collectively, the impact from the organic growth of our leasing clients as well as our philanthropic clients has been gigantic.

AFTER FORTY YEARS in commercial real estate, I came to a point where Cummings Foundation was now occupying the majority of my time and attention. Cummings Properties, under Dennis Clarke's capable leadership, meanwhile, is operating quite successfully without anything like my daily involvement. Eric Anderson became our third-ever executive vice president in 2013, and then its fourth president in 2018. Joyce's and my early involvement in Rwanda was central in distancing or removing me from my desk at West Cummings Park—so much so that even when I am in the office now, I can sometimes be there a full day without my desk phone ringing a single time. Continually updating some significant parts of this book has also certainly taken a fair share of my time.

All profits earned by Cummings Properties are for the exclusive benefit of the foundation, as are all earnings from any personal investments. Except for our personal belongings that will go to family members, any and all real estate and remaining financial assets will eventually go to the foundation. Our children and grandchildren have no need for anything more. Joyce and I are pleased and proud that all our children have been totally supportive of our philanthropy.

Rather than being just a place for our extra earnings, or a place where our net worth will go when Joyce and I reach our journey's end, Cummings Foundation gives us many extra reasons—or perhaps excuses—to continue working. I stopped drawing a salary in 2006, but the foundation is my motivation to keep on building, both literally and figuratively. No trustees are paid for their service as trustees, and the total of all administrative expenses paid by the foundation average much less than 1 percent of its annual income, and those expenses include nothing for trustee travel, meals, entertainment, etc.

The most dramatic change from my previous work schedule is that I now routinely average fifty or so hours in the office each week (when I am in town), as opposed to sixty or more. Since 2008, however, I have also managed to take ten to twelve weeks of vacation every year, including time that Joyce and I dedicate to foundation work, which sometimes involves visits to remote places.

Among the most rewarding aspects of our foundation work are the frequent opportunities to help connect like-minded nonprofits that can work synergistically to benefit the communities they serve. We are so delighted about the valuable relationships Partners In Health has created with Cummings School of Veterinary Medicine and with Agahozo-Shalom Youth Village. We find it quite fitting that University of Global Health Equity, at its beginnings, is already partnering with these tremendous organizations, too.

Billions of dollars have been invested by so many benefactors in medical infrastructure throughout Africa, including mega-sized hospitals in many major cities. UGHE, with no billions, but perhaps about $80 million starting out, will teach providers of effective healthcare for some of the most *under*served areas of Africa and the world. Indeed, its greatest emphasis, as already noted, will be on healthcare *delivery*, including to many of the planet's most remote areas.

Joyce and I have both been abundantly blessed with extraordinarily good health. I cannot remember ever taking a day off and hanging around the house not feeling well. With the exception of a couple of hernia repairs a half century ago, plus two outpatient surgeries for cataracts, and a malignant melanoma twenty years ago, I have needed almost no sick days over the past half-century, and I am so grateful for that. This has surely heightened our interest in wanting to help in our own small way to provide and help ensure good healthcare for others.

THE SOURCE OF most of Cummings Foundation's assets has been internal, including the remarkable returns from its equity investments with the guidance of the foundation's *pro bono* CFO, Bill Grant, and David Leland of Merrill Lynch, a chartered Advisor in Philanthropy. Bill and David were extraordinarily effective for decades in handling almost all of the combined Cummings investments. As a director of wealth management and a certified specialist in foundation investing, David operated from a large Merrill Lynch office at Cummings Center in Beverly, which he helped lobby for and develop.

We were shocked and so deeply saddened in January 2017, when David was diagnosed with esophageal cancer. Despite a valiant fight and the best available care, he succumbed to the disease a few short months later, on May 4, 2017.

David was a trusted, beloved, and extraordinarily important part of the Cummings organization. He helped to build and then service the first $1 billion of Cummings' securities, accumulated since the foundation's earliest days. Aside from much smaller investments through Commonfund and Goldman Sachs, Merrill Lynch held the vast majority of Cummings' financial investments. David, and now Brandon Bergstrom, along with their great Merrill team and our Bill Grant, increased the value of our invested funds by several hundred million dollars. We could not have been more pleased, and we fully expect to continue working extensively with the Leland Group in Merrill's Beverly office.

Right up until a few days before his death, this master investor continued his daily supervision of his Merrill Lynch investment practice from his hospital bed. David played such a major role in our lives as he constantly strengthened the foundation. Thanks so much to David, the foundation now has the ability to meaningfully help people in need, all over this world. I was so moved to learn after his death that David was having the last of an early proof of this book read to him at Mass General Hospital.

David Leland and Bill Grant, 2017

Like the passings of Jamie McKeown and Doug Stephens, this was so much more than the loss of a close business colleague, as David and his wife, Karen, and Joyce and I were also close as couples. For decades we played golf and did so many other activities together. David's parents were our friends before we knew David and Karen. We also shared such fond memories of time spent with David and Karen, and with Bill and Kathy Grant, at the iconic Wianno Club in Osterville on Cape Cod, where we were all non-resident members.

This relationship with the Lelands was so much like our relationships with Doug and Carrol and with Jamie and Denise. Because of these unusually close connections, my sense of any business loss has been overshadowed in each case by profound and enduring personal sorrow. The compounded emotional effect from these three deaths, though spread over many years, has sometimes seemed enormously cumulative.

David, Doug, and Jamie were all so totally supportive of everything Joyce and I hoped to do, or were already doing, and once again many of us felt so bereft with yet another untimely death. As we go on establishing partners for sustainable giving, we shall do so in their collective memory. We shall also continue recognizing the wonderful current Cummings staff, in whose honor we shall move the company and the foundation forward. There is so much more we can do, and so much we will do to use these funds wisely.

❇ *Whereas many companies find financial efficiencies by "farming out" various functions, our dedicated in-house staff and hands-on approach have driven our success. This vertically integrated structure underpins our responsiveness and control over the final product. It also affords us exceptional flexibility in decision-making, which has won us many leases in situations where competitors simply did not have the ability to respond promptly to the prospective client's requirements.*

❇ *Surrounding myself with smart outspoken professionals has always served me well. By enlisting assistance from dozens of highly accomplished volunteers, the foundation is further benefiting from the thinking of some of the most qualified members of our local communities. Through at least 2020, volunteers have made the majority of all final grant-winner selections.*

❇ *In most negotiated deals, if the buyer cannot get to the seller's lowest price, the seller will be quietly gloating about the great deal he just pulled off.*

❇ *The most important thing about getting lucky is realizing that you have been, and then taking advantage of it.*

[20]

Setting a Better Pace

Joyce and Bill are shown above during the 4th Annual Oxford Saïd Entrepreneurship Forum on March 1, 2019 at the University of Oxford

AFTER JOYCE and I met in 1965, and then married in August 1966, our early vacations were limited, but they included a dozen great family trips to places throughout the Caribbean, and in Bermuda and South America. We also enjoyed several wonderful multi-week shunpiking trips to Great Britain and the rest of Europe, navigating back roads, usually with only a single night's hotel reservation to start each adventure. In between these many special vacations, however, I was always overly busy with mostly sixty-hour work weeks.

More recently, with our four children all off on their own, of course, we arranged a self-guided trip with seven other mostly Winchester friends to Dubai, United Arab Emirates, and Egypt. In Dubai, we saw unimaginable new growth everywhere. I could not get over the stunningly unique and even fanciful buildings throughout the entire downtown. Anchored by Burj Khalifa, which with one hundred sixty-three stories stands more than a *half mile* tall, these structures represented a staggering variety of designs, and my enthusiasm to see every one of them amused all present. I was like a kid let loose at a carnival.

The Egypt portion of that trip continued with four or five nights on the Nile River, starting just below the two-mile-long Aswan High Dam. We traveled on the river all the way to Cairo, with many cultural visits each day and enormous exposure to the fascinating history of that area at every stop along the way. There appeared to be no end to the wonders we saw of that ancient world, as each stop seemed even more outstanding than the last.

We organized another special journey with a different hometown group to Iceland, where, among other activities, we golfed through the bubbling hot springs outside Reykjavik. This trip also amounted to a Winchester Country Club trip, and even today, we often reminisce at the club about that little adventure.

Joyce and I traveled alone, for a change, to China for three weeks, including four captivating nights on the Yangtze River, in October 1998. When we signed up for an escorted tour, the operators advertised that no more than fifteen travelers would be permitted. Upon our arrival in Beijing, however, we were met by a driver in a Mercedes and a fine English-speaking guide who informed us that we would be the *only* people on the tour for our entire fifteen-day itinerary—and off we went.

An early 2013 trip to Myanmar (formerly Burma)—a country that had been mostly closed to Americans for many years—and Thailand was strictly for tourism. There, one of the highlights was a day trip on the busy Irrawaddy River. The welcome for Americans in this distant land nestled between China and India could not have been more pleasant. The Myanmar trip nicely rounded out our other trans-Pacific trips to Hawaii, Australia, New Zealand, and China.

We did other Tufts Travel-Learn trips to the Greek Islands, Turkey, Scandinavia, and India. Joyce also traveled, without me, to India, with our daughter Patty to South Africa, and with Patty and our daughter Marilyn to Alaska. Joyce and I returned to South America with another Tufts Travel-Learn trip, this time exploring the biodiversity of the mighty upper Amazon River, some two thousand miles inland, sometimes trekking far into the forest. Flying into Iquitos, Peru, from Lima, we boarded our nineteen-passenger ship in what is the world's largest metropolis totally inaccessible by roadways from any direction. This is a major city with boulevards and buses and 180,000 people, but everything, even the buses, came to the city via the river or the city's small airport. We recently counted up our visits in more than eighty foreign nations, to date.

THE MAJOR CHANGE in my work life after age seventy-two or so was a significant alteration in our yearly routine. After purchasing our modest beachfront Reaches Condominium in Singer Island, Florida, in 1988, we finally began to use it regularly after the year 2000, and now we manage about three months there each winter, with lots of additional travel.

Bill preparing for a deep-water wreck dive off Jost Van Dyke, in the British Virgin Islands, with Chat Watts

We have also enjoyed some great ocean-sailing weeks, always with no captain or crew. Our first such trip, in 1995, was a sailing and scuba-diving adventure in the British Virgin Islands with our dear friends and former Winchester neighbors Nancy and Chat Watts. May is a perfect time to sail in the Caribbean, and we enjoyed a delightful week in a bareboat charter from The Moorings. We had a great time island-hopping, scuba-exploring, reef-snorkeling, and fancy island dining, at least for most of our evening meals. Some delightfully mellow local rum helped set the tone for dinners once we were safely anchored each evening.

After the British Virgin Islands, we sailed with another Winchester couple, Laura and Bill Shea, on two bareboat charters. On the last day of our first trip with the Sheas, an unexpected squall quickly engulfed us. Sailing off Guadeloupe near the center of the Leeward Islands, we were suddenly all alone on an angry sea. There were no other boats in sight, and our marine radio was useless behind the nearby mountains off the northeastern coast of Grande Terre. With no radio contact, we had no way of knowing what we were in for.

For almost two hours a vicious windstorm whipped the Caribbean into a frenzy as our sailboat heeled hard on the port gunwale, and the sea rose higher and higher. Off our port side, the surf crashed onto a ten-mile-long stretch of jagged barrier reef. There was no harbor or other refuge anywhere within reach, and we were soaked with repeated explosions of salt spray. There were plenty of reasons to be scared, and we all were.

I had much earlier partially reefed the mainsail, but now it needed to go lower. I clutched whatever I could and inched my way out of the cockpit and brought the sail down to about a third of its usual size. Earlier I had tried to furl the jib, but the line controlling it had somehow jammed into the side of a broken brass pulley that was well beyond my reach. We had no chance of repairing it then, because with one slip, I could be instantly overboard. We had practiced man-overboard drills, but Joyce, Laura, and Bill would have had only the slightest chance of getting to me if I had gone overboard. Under such wild conditions, I would surely have been torn apart on the reef.

Just then, an extra-strong gust grabbed the still-extended jib and instantly rent it in half while our tiny boat continued sliding sideways toward the treacherous reef. Ever closer, the jagged reef appeared ready to devour the whole boat and grind us up with it. Finally, I was able to cut loose half of the jib, which flew away with a giant whoosh, but the other half was still attached at the top of the mast—flying straight out, perpendicular to the horizon, if there was one.

By then, I had already started the engine to try controlling our fate. With most of the jib gone and the smaller piece more or less out of the way, we finally began to make a little headway into the wind, but we were still in truly mortal danger. Only a few hundred yards from the jagged outcroppings, I pushed the diesel engine almost to its limit, and then I shoved the throttle to its absolute maximum output. The RPM gauge was solidly in the red danger zone, but I knew that if our boat had been blown onto the reef, the condition of the engine would have mattered little. With extra engine help and the wind beginning to relax ever so slightly, we gradually inched our way back on course.

At one point Laura, a Canadian by birth, started to sing, "O Canada. Our home and native land. True patriot love, in all thy sons command…" I was reminded of the *Titanic* story about how the ship's band bravely played *Nearer My God to Thee* as the stern lifted high before the ship finally plunged nose first to the bottom of the North Atlantic. For us, however, the wind eventually just stopped as quickly as it had started, and we were soon back in port for our final night, no worse off except for our lost jib sail.

In 2013, we and other friends chartered a fifty-foot bareboat catamaran sailboat with four sleek double-bed cabins for a week. We sailed with Dennis Clarke's parents, Nancy and Dick Clarke; Tufts friends Jane and Dr. Mark

Hirsh, from Boston; and Tufts classmate Dr. Bob Belin and his wife, Jo, from Lexington, Kentucky. They joined us on a trip to and around the French island of St. Martin, including the Dutch half, known as St. Maarten, and neighboring islands for another great but this time generally quiet adventure.

Joyce and I celebrated our fiftieth wedding anniversary in August 2016. For our anniversary trip to Amsterdam, Venice, and the Dalmatian Coast, we broke our self-imposed ban and purchased premium-class airline tickets for the first time ever. Joyce said she deserved special treatment after putting up with me for fifty years. Just before our trip, the entire family gathered at a unique family vacation inn called East Hill Farm, in Troy, New Hampshire, to more properly celebrate our family's first half-century.

We also traveled that summer to Tufts' European campus in Talloires, France, for an intensive session titled What Happens Next?, which addressed questions important at the "older and wiser stage" of attendees' lives. This was a special collaboration between Tufts' Rabbi Summit and Rev. William "Scotty" McLennan, a former chaplain at Tufts and now a retired dean for religious life at Stanford. "What happens next?" is a question that Joyce and I have long tried to help answer in a positive way, for ourselves, our colleagues, and our community.

Our most recent bareboat charter, in September 2017, was something quite different. We chartered a sixty-foot-long, four-bedroom *houseboat* on the Erie Canal. Joining us and sharing the cooking and operations duties were two Winchester couples, Dr. Ric and Judy Bush and Dr. Denis and Joan Byrne—all fairly serious bridge players. It was a four-day weekend of marvelous dining, camaraderie, and bridge games along the Lakes Seneca and Cayuga branch of the Erie Canal. The early morning smell of cooked bacon wafting in from the galley was always so welcome. The people with whom Joyce and I most often sail are our many, many good friends from the last fifty or so years.

ABOUT 60 PERCENT of the real estate Cummings Properties manages is the commercial property Joyce and I donated to Cummings Foundation. The company receives no fees for its management work on behalf of the foundation, yet the Cummings staff who assist, on a *pro bono* basis, in the

Bill with Rabbi Jeffrey Summit of Tufts University

management of the foundation-owned properties have a clear fiduciary responsibility to manage these assets to the best of their ability and solely in the best interests of the foundation. A foundation-owned maintenance firm also directly employs a significant crew that does a great many of the needed repairs and modifications to the foundation-owned properties.

Cummings Properties now has a well-established corporate culture. To help prospective new colleagues better understand this culture and, more importantly, to encourage them to think beforehand about whether it would be a good match for their personal working styles, we created a carefully worded Corporate Philosophy document. If we think employment candidates might have potential with our team, we often give them a copy of the Corporate Philosophy (as well as a copy of this book) and invite them to come back to learn more if they remain interested after considering their contents.

The outline of our corporate environment describes in some detail the sense of urgency with which most of the staff try to stay ahead of our competitors, and also the type of work ethic expected. After outlining what some find to be the more challenging aspects of our work, the sheet describes the work of the foundation. Since 2010, Cummings Foundation has been the sole financial beneficiary of all that the company does. The document goes on to describe some of the special benefits of joining our truly outstanding team of colleagues.

Interestingly, whenever we have asked staff what they like most about working at Cummings Properties, the dominant response for decades has been "the people." Employees genuinely like their colleagues to a remarkable level, and this more than anything else may be why people work here as long as they do. We currently have a dozen members in the company's super special 40-Year Club, while the average tenure of Cummings staff is more than eleven years.

Our ten Executive Committee members have an average company seniority of more than twenty-three years as of mid 2019. It is also interesting that all ten are still married to their first spouses, and have been for an average of twenty-seven years, and have a total of twenty-six children. The family stability and business life stability among the firm's senior management are truly extraordinary, notwithstanding the well above average work ethic of the entire team.

As a privately held, half-century-old firm, we are so fortunate to have so many colleagues who have chosen to have long-term careers here. We also benefit immensely from the continuity of experienced staff who have learned "The Cummings Way." As it becomes better known how much good Cummings Foundation can accomplish, prospective employees who want to benefit more than just themselves and their own families are becoming

increasingly interested in working with Cummings Properties.

New employees often tell me they were attracted to the company because they knew about our charitable purposes. And we have come to realize that the Cummings Community Giving program has become the most universally popular employee fringe benefit we have ever added. I think staff like it even better than "casual Fridays."

Each Thanksgiving since 2012, in addition to receiving a fresh or frozen turkey, all of our four hundred-plus regular full-time colleagues receive either $1,000 or $2,000 to give away on behalf of the firm. Participants are encouraged to think locally, and the recipients include many schools and PTOs, as well as youth sports organizations, Boy and Girl Scout troops, and animal shelters—in other words, nonprofits with which families are directly involved.

The following quote comes from *Quartz*, an online magazine that called Cummings Community Giving "bottom-up giving": "One employee donated her funds to a local social service agency after her teenage daughter was heartbroken to learn that her best friend's family was relying on its soup kitchen to eat." We also especially liked the story about a children's librarian bursting into tears when Eric and Kari Anderson's two young children, Clara and Caden, presented her with their $1,000 check to support their local library. The librarian thought she was receiving a holiday card.

We have heard many more stories about employees talking with their entire families to decide which charity they want to support and then often going as a family to present the check. Not every eligible employee has taken advantage of the program, but we do get more than 90 percent participation. These modest checks have now been gratefully received by thousands of mostly small groups that had no idea anything was coming.

❈ *Using bankruptcy as a so-called "smart" way to repeatedly cheat unsuspecting customers, suppliers, and business partners is a despicable business practice, but one that some highly prominent business people have even bragged about to show how smart they think they are. Just as bad are the apparently successful people who get there by climbing over the backs of trusting suppliers or subcontractors in the construction business by refusing to pay just bills often because of some imagined or trumped up deficiency. After embroiling the plaintiffs in court costs, they then expect to routinely settle these bills for a small fraction of their value.*

- *Becoming a successful entrepreneur often requires much more time and hard work than most people are willing to give. Those who do put in the effort and achieve prosperity, however, should reap some of the rewards. Make time for the pursuits (other than business) that fuel you. For me, they have always been primarily family, travel, community good, and philanthropy.*

- *Regardless of their stage in life or career, entrepreneurs always keep an eye out for the next great opportunity, though perhaps they do so unconsciously at times. Because of this predilection, most will probably never truly retire. Their focuses and roles, however, may change over time—sometimes in unexpected ways, like with our decision to take a public stance on the contentious 2016 election.*

- *Business or facility owners and operators do themselves a great disservice when they fail to always maintain any premises in a clean, neat, and orderly way. Developing habits of cleanliness and care pays great dividends.*

- *A "transformative" gift is of such a magnitude that it will often result in a meaningful change in even the goals and aspirations of the receiving entity.*

- *All successful businesses have a responsibility to fortify their communities by helping to care for people who live there and patronize local firms.*

- *And when an apology is needed, make it real… "What I did was wrong, and I'm sorry I hurt you."*

- *Caution is always wise, but don't always insist on a belt and suspenders.*

[21]

New Directions

Artist rendering of Joyce Cummings Center at new Medford/Tufts University rail station

BECAUSE CUMMINGS PROPERTIES and the foundation are positioned well to survive Joyce and me, it seems important to tell this story for the ultimate benefit of those who will follow. This book does that well, as will the wonderful cadre of colleagues and others who do so much to guide and support both entities through each day. The book has also proven to be extremely beneficial to me in trying to order some details of my life, also for the possible benefit of those who will later lead these organizations.

As I finish this sixth edition in 2020, Joyce is now seventy-seven, while I am four-score and three years. Our five terrific grandchildren are everything we might want to brag about and our fondest hope is that we might live long enough to know them all as young adults, God willing. Sonia and

Nate Morris, in New York, are the oldest, with Sonia, now sixteen. Nate, when he was twelve years old, completed an extremely long *walk*—from New Rochelle, New York to Boston with his mom. Gus Cummings, in Winchester, is now in second grade, while Patricia's preschool daughters are busy learning what life is all about from their two moms, Patty and Jadine, who relocated to New Rochelle in 2018 from San Francisco.

None of our children, or their spouses, has ever expressed much interest in management roles in the company, although there has been considerable thought about the likelihood that Marilyn and/or Patricia may later become more involved in Cummings Foundation. Third-generation family involvement in the company will hopefully develop in time as well.

> THERE IS NO REASON for any of us to change who we are just because we become good (or lucky) at whatever we do in life. Any and all talents we have we are given, and what we do with those talents tells the most about who and what we are. Certainly, our occasional exposure to the Giving Pledge environment has caused Joyce and me to think more about who we want to be. We hope and believe we have been able to comfortably stay almost exactly the same as we always have been.

I have now grown fully complacent about not retiring, although I will someday turn over my office. The notion of Joyce and me taking off and traveling somewhere for about twelve weeks each year is working out well, although that time is at least partially occupied with our joint foundation-related activities. The foundation work, however, is something we do and enjoy together. I have worked my way out of most outside board positions that I greatly enjoyed for many years, but others have since represented the firm well.

Chairman Dennis Clarke has been in volunteer leadership roles with Winchester Hospital and is finishing his tenure on the board of the Massachusetts chapter of NAIOP after having earlier served as its president and chair. Our CFO, Bill Grant, has served effectively on the board of Associated Industries of Massachusetts for a decade.

While spending the vast majority of my career creating things, I also collected so many experiences along the way. I frequently went out of my way to encounter people, things, and events outside of my regular realm. Exploring the innards of the old

| *Dennis A. Clarke*

Charlestown Penitentiary and flying deep into the Pennsylvania coal mine on my belly, plus biking around Damascus during a revolution, and deep-water wreck-diving off Cyprus were all prime. Swimming to the frightening edge of Victoria Falls on the Zambezi River and bungee jumping with Patty in New Zealand were also among the best. And at this later stage in life, Joyce and I are just enormously proud and grateful to still be part of the lives of our four children and five grandchildren.

After we turned Old Medford Foods into a thriving business, we launched Cummings Properties and later our three newspapers. We developed Place Lane Condominium, and we established and built Cummings Foundation to serve and help support the many communities that contributed to Cummings Properties' success. I had help from so many as we rebuilt or erected building after building, starting with our first construction projects on Henshaw Street.

My seeing the opportunity in the oversized Henshaw Street lot was the first step in Cummings Properties' successful history. Each new client, building, employee, and manager has been another block or beam that strengthened and sustained the business. After fifty years now of building, Cummings Properties can point to achievements that are more than outsized for the small local firm we have always been. With such capable staff and future leadership now in place, the firm will be prosperous for many decades to come.

First, we made and saved $1 million, and now the foundation has already given away $280 million, through June 2020. Nothing I have ever done has been massively successful, but I have built successful businesses and have repeatedly run many successful organizations. Collectively, these entities have provided or facilitated thousands of new jobs and greatly aided local economies. Along the way, I have had great fun and fulfillment, and Joyce and I together are now gaining much satisfaction by giving away more and more, and trying to make a success of that, too.

Trying also to make a little more room in my life, I started giving up golf after 2017. Although I was never all that good, I had immeasurable fun playing golf for close to fifty years, as has Joyce, who is still playing. My most memorable golf experiences came from playoff wins in several three-

Bill with Dr. Bob Shirley at Brae Burn Country Club

and four-day member-guest tournaments at Winchester Country Club, all a decade apart. The first two wins were with Jamie McKeown before he became a WCC member himself, and then with Don Lewis. The last was with the late Dr. Bob Shirley of Braeburn Country Club. Bob sank a huge sixty-foot curving birdie putt with an excited green-side crowd of at least one hundred other Winchester members and their guests looking on. Bob's sensational putt across the ninth green turned out to be the last shot of the tournament, giving us the overall walk-off win in one of my (and his) last "serious" golf games. We were told we were the eldest twosome in the tournament.

DURING 2016, Joyce and I spoke together before large Boston-area audiences during four widely differing events. The first of these was in May at the John F. Kennedy Presidential Library and Museum, where we received the Compassion and Justice Award from Catholic Charities of Boston. The following month, we were honored to accept Friends of Israel citations, presented by Robert Lappin, a longtime Massachusetts sponsor of Operation Birthright.

We also addressed four hundred guests during the annual celebration of Cummings Foundation's ***$100K for 100*** program, when we announced the recipients of that year's $10 million in local grants. Finally, Joyce and I also received honorary doctorates from Endicott College in 2016 and delivered our third joint commencement address to several thousand attendees there.

Beginning in 2018 and 2019, our annual grants presentation ceremony became a distribution of $20 million divided among one hundred twenty-five local organizations. These multi-year grants are mostly in the range of $20,000 to $50,000 per year, and the entire sum is distributed each year during an Awards Night Gala in early June. Much larger grants have included many multi-million dollar grants in Massachusetts and Rwanda, but these are privately presented.

Millions of Americans are disillusioned by the actions or inaction of many of the nation's political leaders, of both parties, and there is an enormous faction of disgruntled citizens contesting a deeply entrenched federal bureaucracy. This disaffected portion of our citizenry, in our opinion, was promised anything it wanted to hear by those who railed for or against gun control, immigrants, and all available scapegoats. The Endicott College commencement address that Joyce and I made was prominently referenced in a *Boston Globe* story by Sacha Pfeiffer on June 16, 2016. Joyce and I are not political, but we felt compelled to speak up. This situation for us was a moral imperative in every sense of the word.

Our comments were enthusiastically embraced at all four of these major speaking events, but nowhere more loudly than during the foundation's annual grants presentation. There, we were again recognizing the efforts of one hundred of the most deserving local nonprofits. These were the frontline organizations reaching out to help the neediest among us, so many of them targets in minority communities, singled out for ridicule and scorn.

During our 2016 *$100K for 100* event, one of the award winners scored a rousing audience response. She jumped up on a chair while Joyce was speaking and loudly shouted, "We want Joyce… Joyce for President!" Following is a common element in our several major addresses in 2016:

> "Never forget, my friends…Never forget that when prejudice and intolerance are tolerated, they are as well condoned and encouraged. We urge all of you to continue to be strong leaders, to educate young people, and help counteract divisive rhetoric in our country and the world. Recognize the great danger.
>
> "Let me close by also asking all of *you* to be the force that helps to build bridges, especially for our marginalized neighbors. So much more than bridges over rivers and highways, build bridges of love, bridges of hope, and bridges of understanding.
>
> "Let there be bridges of opportunity, too. Let bridges such as these take us all where we otherwise could not go."

Throughout the summer, we were acutely mindful of these words of Elie Wiesel: "We must take sides. Neutrality helps the oppressor, never the victim. Silence encourages only the tormentor, never the tormented." Joyce and I first met Mr. Wiesel during a Remembrance Day celebration at the United States Holocaust Memorial Museum, where we were especially pleased to introduce him to our late Israeli friend, Elie Ayalon, during an inspiring private meeting there with museum officials.

A powerful recent major exhibit at the United States Holocaust Memorial Museum depicted the enormous role Nazi propaganda played in acclimatizing war-ravaged Germans of the 1920s. Although much lesser known, the International Museum of World War II in Natick, Massachusetts, also has a highly impressive collection of Holocaust propaganda. The foundation has contributed a combined $500,000 to the Holocaust museum, the Museum of World War II, and Yad Vashem.

We also recently fulfilled a matching grant to help fund a new Holocaust Center in Guatemala and other Holocaust education work of Father Patrick Desbois. Jews and the free press were incessantly portrayed as the reason for Germany's devastating losses in the Great War. Then, with the decade of the

Bill and Joyce accepting induction into the Academy of Distinguished Bostonians, 2017

Great Depression, this manufactured anti-Semitism created a catastrophe of unfathomable degree. Many Americans say that exhibits at each of these museums offer powerful signals of things that could be to come if American politics do not become more civil and respectful to all.

Adolf Hitler finished the Great War as a corporal, but he soon became a political force. He developed great oratory skills, quickly learning the issues that would rouse his beleaguered audiences. While imprisoned for his activism in the mid 1920s, Hitler wrote *Mein Kampf* ("My Struggle"), developing the plan and basis for the monstrous Holocaust he would soon unleash. Through the early 1930s, however, most people had no idea of the threat Hitler posed.

Thousands of miles to the south, and six decades later, Hitler's playbook emerged again. The forces behind the 1994 genocide against the Tutsi in Rwanda used many of Hitler's techniques in demonizing the country's population of "Tutsi cockroaches," "conditioning" the citizenry for the horrifying eight hundred thousand murders there in just four months.

IN ADDITION TO ASKING Ralph Nader for the blurb that appears on the back cover of this book, I asked him to comment on all of the recent turmoil roiling America. Ralph did not disappoint: "A daily democracy requires daily citizenship engagement with the public affairs of our times. That starts with family upbringing and our educational civic experiences as youngsters in and

Joyce and Bill Cummings, 2016

outside of schools," he wrote. "If we the people are otherwise indifferent, distracted or fooled, we will get the politics of our times—unworthy of our better selves and trending toward ever more injustices, cruelly damaged lives and a battered, endangered posterity." It is high time right now for Americans to smarten up about their politicians.

With seventy years of real business experience to look back upon now, and a steadily shortening runway ahead, I am much more self-reflective, particularly regarding my career in business. It has been a productive one with a few exceedingly sad experiences to be sure, but with a preponderance of highly satisfying work and accomplishments. When Joyce and I celebrated our fiftieth wedding anniversary in Venice in August of 2016, we both rather optimistically "signed up" for twenty more years together. We are among the oldest people we know now, but we are as determined as ever to preserve our active days until something stops us.

We publicly joined the Giving Pledge organization during its first year, but that membership does not in any way define us. We had long before donated the vast majority of our wealth for charitable purposes, and Joyce and I are still so much the same people we were when we married in 1966.

Someone asked me recently how it felt to have started out as a totally self-funded entrepreneur and to come as far as we have. The question was a little "off," because while I was always self-funded, I have also always had enormous support of other types from colleagues, suppliers, teachers, and sometimes even competitors. Almost all of my "career" now involves the work of Cummings Foundation, but my business mindset remains entrepreneurial. And just as I clearly remember hearing in an industrial psychology class a full sixty years ago, it is so easy for me to get stuck in minutiae.

I continue to spend time working with or on behalf of various Tufts University interests in Medford certainly, as well as on behalf of Cummings School. We have been particularly pleased to develop a close relationship with Tufts' current president and his wife, Drs. Anthony and Zoia Monaco, while working toward the proposed new Joyce Cummings Center. This new

150,000-square-foot Tufts structure is now under construction in conjunction with the soon-to-emerge Tufts College rail station at the corner of College Avenue and Boston Avenue, on the extended Green Line to Boston.

In the meantime, foundation trustee David Harris, the former Provost of Tufts, assumed the presidency of Union College, in Schenectady, New York. With Tufts' President Monaco, there are now three sitting major college presidents among the trustees and *emeritus* trustees of the foundation.

Additionally, as concerns "presidents," we certainly felt a sense of quiet pride when Cummings Foundation's trustee *emeritus* Larry Bacow was inaugurated as the twenty-ninth president of Harvard University in October 2018. Cummings Foundation trustee Dr. Deborah Kochevar moved in 2018 from Dean of the Cummings School of Veterinary Medicine to Provost *ad interim* of Tufts, succeeding Dr. Harris.

In the long run, however, fifty years of running this business in an old-fashioned way has paid off so much more than I could ever have imagined. I never yearned to become a millionaire when that level was beyond my status, and I certainly never thought at all about becoming a billionaire. Finding good ways to accomplish good tasks with our funds now is incredibly rewarding.

MEANWHILE AT CUMMINGS PROPERTIES

we determined to sell off parts of the major Dunham Ridge development we acquired in late 2011. We sold one prominent six-acre parcel near the center of that development to Vitality Assisted Living, of California. We then closed on a second six-acre lot at the top of Dunham Ridge in a sale to HD Systems, Inc. (Harmonic Drive), in August 2018. The first two land-only units there were

Pres. Anthony Monaco
Tufts University

Pres. David Harris
Union College

Pres. Lawrence Bacow
Harvard University

both marketed and sold at $6 million each with no broker involvement. The third new building site, at 44 Dunham Ridge, is being readied for sale.

Derek Russell was appointed vice president of operations at Cummings Properties in May of 2018. An upstate New York native, Derek graduated from Bentley University, and later joined Cummings Properties in 2002 as an account manager. He oversees all sales and relationship management with existing client firms in the company's central divisions. Derek's character-driven leadership illustrates the value the company derives from its practice of promoting from within. Sought after for his sound decision-making, encyclopedic knowledge of Cummings' portfolio, and keen business sense, Derek takes a special interest in mentoring colleagues throughout the company. Derek joined the company's Executive Committee in July 2018. The next most senior officers reporting to Derek are Erica Wright and Kathryn Jendrick.

| *Derek Russell*

In a front-page story, *Boston Globe* reporter Thomas Farragher offered an extremely supportive look at the work Joyce and I are doing at Cummings Foundation. The story resulted in an astounding number of notes, comments, and emails from old and new friends from all over. Prompted by a media release from the Giving Pledge about the latest group of members to join, Tom first talked with us by phone while we happened to be attending a Giving Pledge meeting, and then in person in Woburn. He also included extensive comments from a telephone interview he conducted with our daughter, Marilyn, in New York.

"It's a profound lesson," Farragher concluded, "one passed down from the people who once lived above that Medford liquor store—a mom and dad who taught their kids that generosity has an enduring and priceless dividend all its own."

❦ *Although I managed to make time to serve on many hospital and bank boards and other similar groups, I never personally served much in industry trade associations. I have been delighted, however, to watch colleagues serve in top spots with local organizations. All such roles are appropriate when organizations find they can make the time and there are suitable groups nearby.*

❦ *The essential resource in my career was dedication. I loved what I was doing—opportunistically creating value and jobs—more than any financial return. Would-be entrepreneurs who, instead, launch into something merely for the money may inevitably struggle to muster the requisite commitment.*

[22]

Afterword

Speaking at The University of Alabama, Tuscaloosa on April 8, 2019

BENJAMIN FRANKLIN in his autobiography wrote: "Were it offered to my choice, I should have no objection to a repetition of my same life from its beginning, only asking the advantages that authors have in a second edition to correct some faults of the first." By this now sixth edition of *Starting Small and Making It Big*, I have, hopefully, snared most typos or other errors, and have also made some meaningful changes. It is different enough from the several earlier editions, first introduced in 2017, that it even has an entirely new cover design.

As a first-time author with no experience with anything to do with writing a book, I was greatly buoyed by the reactions of a few early readers who dug enthusiastically into the first copies of *Starting Small*. In a somewhat rare "timid" approach, I purchased only a thousand copies of the book and brought it forth as the "Winchester edition." (Only a month later, James Comey's first

Bill draws a standing-room-only crowd at his first book event, at Book Ends in Winchester.

book burst onto the national scene with *six hundred thousand* copies.)

I was quickly proven at least a little too conservative, and it did not take long before I ordered another two thousand copies, and then three thousand, and then five thousand. I heard that for a new author with no agent and no publisher behind him, selling more than ten thousand copies in total would be highly unlikely, but we reached that goal fairly quickly. I finally placed an order for ten thousand more copies—all at once. That last order is also now all but depleted, prompting this new revised edition. This book has never been in bookstores, except our local Winchester shop, Book Ends, which proved that Joyce and I must have at least a few local friends. This small Winchester shop alone has now sold more than five hundred copies.

Somehow, but primarily with great encouragement from Professor John McArdle at Salem State University, I started a grand book tour that has developed into more than one hundred talks with college and university groups, entrepreneurship conferences, libraries, regional business meetings, philanthropy leaders, etc. After early appearances at a raft of eastern Massachusetts colleges and universities during 2018, I met with all sorts of undergraduates, and other student and alumni groups for a good two years.

Other special sessions included one sponsored by *Forbes* magazine at the United Nations headquarters in New York City, and several talks at Harvard Business School in Boston. Another keynote address, for about 800 attendees at the annual meeting of the Massachusetts Association of Fundraising Professionals, was particularly interesting. Some in the audience had two days earlier read a badly placed story in a national professional magazine. Appearing on the obituary page, the article left many readers prematurely pondering the effects of my demise.

That period led to a much more diverse list of appearances in early 2019 as far away as the grand opening of University of Global Health Equity in Butaro, Rwanda and a surprise one thousand-person flash crowd in Kigali, Rwanda the same weekend.

In March 2019, a month after our third African visit, Joyce and I flew from West Palm Beach to England to participate in a sparkling three days, the highlight of which was speaking during a conference on entrepreneurship at the University of Oxford. Then, after returning to our place at Singer Island, Florida, we later had a big swing home via Joyce's *alma mater*, The University of Alabama in Tuscaloosa. Joyce was treated like a returning rock star for our two days there, and I spoke at an estimated 800-student session.

We have accepted invitations in 2020 to speak at Duke University and to participate in two more commencement ceremonies and at a variety of other interesting venues. I have no plan or desire, however, to go on indefinitely with the speaking tour.

One major reason I wrote this book has been to continue encouraging the heads of corporations—many of whom are making more money and profits than ever before in history—as well as the most fortunate individuals among us—to take the responsibility to give back to the less fortunate. Say "thank you" to a nation that has given so many the opportunity to become as successful as we have been. I urge all those Democrats, Republicans, and Independents

| *Bill speaking at Saïd School of Business at University of Oxford, 2019*

who have been able to benefit the most from that greatness to find many more ways to assist those who need our collective help. Despite any of our country's shortcomings, we are so appreciative and grateful for the blessings of living in the United States of America.

ASIDE FROM CORRECTING ERRATA, as Mr. Franklin reflected, this section is also a convenient place to provide some important late updates. For my work during 2017, we were cutting, blasting, filling, and grading the rugged terrain for almost a year to create the building site and foundation for a 120,000-square-foot 52 Dunham Ridge, Beverly—probably my last total immersion in any new site preparation. When I finally do give up the option to continue weighing in on the current and future direction of the combined operations, however, considerable opportunities for decision-making will certainly still await my successors.

On the foundation side of things, we have been extraordinarily successful in working out an engaging new type of philanthropic decision-making. Our new program of heavy volunteer involvement has so easily attracted a wide range of mostly retired professional men and women volunteers who are all far too vital to sit at home, and who do so much more than most casual part-time jobs require or even allow.

Another obvious update regards the story of Cummings Properties, which continues to provide the vast majority of all outside funding for Cummings Foundation. The foundation now has its own endowment consisting of commercial real estate and financial investments. The great real estate bust following the Enron debacle and the financial collapse of 2001 have mostly passed us by, and the business of building and leasing space has picked up greatly in Boston and in most of the U.S., at least into 2020.

MOST RECENTLY, our management team has also been busy working with Harvard Business School as it introduced a brand new Harvard case study on Cummings written by senior lecturers Christina Wing and Robert White. The case was taught two times in October 2019, and is expected to have a multi-decade run. It highlights some of the challenges students will likely see for our successors in operating both our highly profitable commercial real estate and Cummings Foundation, long after my departure.

Harvard officials told us they believe this case has substantial potential to influence and teach students of business at Harvard and at other prominent business institutions to which Harvard cases are routinely circulated, all over the world. The case scrutinizes the highly unusual organizational structure at Cummings, which diverts all earnings from the brick and mortar assets of Cummings Properties to the ongoing operations of Cummings Foundation, offering so many options for further study and decision making. *Starting Small* was used as assigned reading to accompany the case study.

It was special treat to return again to the Business School campus, located on the Boston side of the Charles River, in January 2020. Our new case study was then used as part of a special course for a large international group of business leaders. We have learned that "Bill Cummings: The Cummings Way" is also planned for regular presentation starting in April 2020 for the entire first-year student body.

The large majority of Cummings Properties' one hundred plus commercial buildings display interior graphics informing visitors that "This Building Powers Charities." Other communications inform our clients that 100 percent of all net rent paid by some two thousand-plus client firms goes either directly or ultimately to support our rapidly developing charitable initiatives. Cummings Foundation is one of the three largest private foundations in New England, and certainly one of the most unique.

In round numbers, the endowment of Cummings Foundation consists of about $1 billion of mostly domestic stocks and other securities, either currently owned by the foundation or pledged to it, plus another $1 billion invested in a wide variety of debt-free commercial real estate. These real properties primarily consist of more than 10 million gross square feet of office and research buildings in northeastern Massachusetts, most of which are actually owned by Cummings Foundation.

All of this real property is still carefully managed, serviced, and maintained by about three hundred sixty full-time employees of our wholly owned Cummings management organization. We are most proud that, as of January 1, 2019, our *seventy-five* longest-tenured Cummings Properties colleagues have an average seniority of twenty-five years, with our *eight* longest-serving colleagues now averaging forty years' seniority. For all of this collective loyalty, I shall be eternally proud and highly appreciative.

Although the foundation never solicits contributions, even from its trustees, it depends heavily on the rental income derived from its many leased commercial properties in eleven northern suburbs of Boston to fulfill its work. It uses these funds judiciously in cash grants to mostly small, low-profile charities primarily in Essex, Middlesex, and Suffolk counties of Massachusetts each year.

The foundation occasionally receives bequests, and until recently its largest contribution was a gift of $300,000. It was notified in 2019, however, that another recently closed local charity that benefited Woburn seniors had petitioned the Massachusetts attorney general for approval to transfer in excess of $1 million specifically to be managed and used for the benefit of our mostly Woburn seniors at New Horizons at Choate.

The foundation is especially proud to have close working relationships with Boston-based Partners In Health, and with Bill and Melinda Gates Foundation in the construction and development of the brand-new University of Global Health Equity, in Butaro, Rwanda. During the opening of the University's new campus in January 2019, Joyce and I made a surprise $10 million challenge grant from Cummings Foundation which directly led to a total of $21 million in unplanned additional receipts during the next thirty days.

MORE THAN A DOZEN years ago, Cummings Properties and I agitated for the United States government to abolish the comically useless U.S. penny. This had already been bothering your writer for decades. "Retire the Penny," we softly pleaded, but then we got away from that. Well, now it is back on our public service radar for the consummate benefit, we think, of all Americans, except perhaps for those who mine and process zinc and copper.

The fact that the U.S. penny is still in circulation does not mean it is in any way useful. Inflation has eaten away at the value of the penny to such a degree that it no longer facilitates commerce. The penny cannot buy anything!

Several years later, Walgreens and the National Association of Convenience Stores estimated that handling pennies adds an average of two seconds to each cash transaction. Given the 107 billion cash transactions per year in 2012 (U.S. Federal Reserve Payments Study), using pennies therefore wastes 120 million hours of time per year for just the counting time of both the customer and the store employee. At the U.S. median income/hour of $17 at that time, that wasted time alone costs the economy $2 billion every year.

Retiring the U.S. penny seemed like a fine goal in the late 90s, when I had a little spare time to devote. Then, when we were not one bit successful in finding someone to spearhead this personal gripe of mine, we lost track of it. As much as anything, it appeared that there might be too many political leaders who depend on the largesse of the zinc and copper industries to block any attempts to dislodge this long-useless coin. With all of the big money factors stoking the fires of public opinion, what chance would there be to finally dislodge these ancient coins for which there is simply no longer any reasonable use? Please write to me via www.cummings.com if any reader would like to reinvigorate the cause to retire this venerable money waster.

Today I could envision President Trump waving his magic pen and instantly decreeing an end to this silly and preposterously expensive coin. The President thrives on news coverage, and his taking decisive action on this issue would gain him enormous highly positive coverage. I would hope even the most left-leaning newspapers and commentators would have to treat him to what, for them, would be rare kudos. Mr. Trump makes negative headlines work, but it would be so nice to witness what he could do with a real positive lead like this.

REFERRALS OF PROSPECTIVE LESSEES from various sources are the lifeblood from which we are able to continue to grow our support to benefit so many worthy charities. In the end, 100 percent of all rental profits are dedicated to Cummings Foundation, Inc., or they are directly donated by Cummings Properties to charitable causes in many cases. Absolutely nothing benefits any Cummings family member.

By 2020, the foundation's regular annual grants program is distributing many millions of dollars each year, while Joyce and I still have sufficient resources outside the firm to live more than comfortably. Our four children and their families have fully supported our philanthropic endeavors from the beginning and have all been a source of great personal comfort and pride for us.

The foundation, in the meantime, has enjoyed the benefits of an outstanding board of trustees for several decades, and now we are formalizing a remarkably strong group of prominent community volunteers. More than one hundred such community leaders help support about eight hundred local grant recipients. Indeed, for many years now, more than half of all local-area grants have been determined strictly through our several volunteer groups. Teams of two volunteers are typically visiting each current grant recipient for at least one on-site meeting each year.

Our philanthropy continues to evolve, although we still award grants to many hundreds of local-area nonprofits and many others every year. In total, more than a cumulative quarter *billion* dollars has been given locally through January 2020.

Everyone needs a strong sense of values, even though we may regularly fall short of practicing them in our daily lives. Joyce and I are both extraordinarily appreciative for our family, love, faith, and good health. Gifts of friends and trust are ever more meaningful as we begin to witness how many good friends and peers have ended their earthly journeys with so much left undone.

Although this book necessarily concludes below, we expect that this grants program and the steadily growing larger capabilities of the foundation will continue to evolve to help meet local area needs for generations to come.

AUTHOR BILL NOVAK, who read an early draft of this book as a friend, offered some great insight just before we published the first edition. His most critical concern was that I had not adequately portrayed Jamie McKeown's enormous role in the business, in the foundation, and in my life. Readers deserve to hear more about that, he insisted.

Mr. Novak's advice led to many story tweaks, and also to the two-page letter that Jamie's wife, Denise, was so kind to write for Chapter 12, containing her many personal insights about Jamie. His advice also prompts me now to add this latest 2020 update to close out this new sixth edition.

Following Jamie's tragic death in 1996, Denise, of course, spent years raising their girls, and then she worked many more years with the firm in a variety of ways at our TradeCenter 128 in Woburn. Most notably, she was a senior member of our Beacon Grille management team and then at our Executive Office Suites for several years as well. Denise and Jamie's daughters, Kelly and Molly, have since matured beautifully and graduated from Merrimack College and University of New Hampshire, respectively. Kelly is now an elementary school teacher in Wilmington, Massachusetts.

Molly married a Boston College MBA graduate and football standout, Robert Vardaro, and their first son, James Robert Vardaro, was born March 11, 2019. Denise then decided it was time for her to resign from Cummings to begin a new career babysitting for her and Jamie's first grandchild.

A perfect ending for *Starting Small and Making It Big* presented itself when our charming, statuesque Molly joined Cummings Properties' management team in September 2019, forty years after her dad first joined me in 1979!

| *Molly McKeown*

COVID-19

As I prepared this sixth edition of *Starting Small* for publication, the world was struck by COVID-19, a virus whose unrelenting global spread has been unlike anything Joyce or I have seen in our lifetimes. The so-called novel coronavirus pandemic continues to devastate the physical and professional wellness of so many individuals and businesses the world over. The economic ramifications are especially striking also for the local nonprofits everywhere serving those most affected by the sickness, as well as by layoffs and school closures.

During this time of widespread fear and hardship, Cummings Properties and Cummings Foundation must continue to operate to the fullest extent possible while ensuring the safety of employees, client firms, and volunteers. It has been important for us to maintain business continuity at a time when many so-called non-essential businesses have been forced to take a break. Cummings Properties manages space for a multitude of healthcare providers and medical and biotech firms, many of which are on the front lines combating this crisis.

It is impossible to predict how long this rapidly evolving public health disaster will last or what toll it will ultimately exact, but we are confident we will rise above the tough times ahead.

A Special Remembrance

James "Jamie" McKeown   Douglas Stephens   David Leland

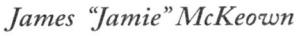

During the writing of this book, these truly special people were always on my mind. They were three of my closest colleagues and best friends with whom I worked with such admiration for a combined total of ninety years. All three died so prematurely as they approached the apexes of their professional careers. Jamie, Doug, and David were so integral to the ultimate success of Cummings Properties and Cummings Foundation. Our total organization would not be anything like what it is today without their wisdom, dedication, and guidance. Sorely missed every day, all three were wonderful human beings who left us far too soon.

Acknowledgments

The single most important acknowledgment and thanks is to my family, for all of their many sacrifices, during so many times that various issues kept me away from them. During the months before we were married, in 1966, Joyce and I spoke extensively about that probability, and Joyce graciously accepted those times as they developed.

Although we now take extended annual vacations, I know that Joyce was expecting more time together in retirement and that surely would not have included a serious writing project during my eighties. Yet, she has been immensely helpful with this book, especially in fact-checking, answering my endless questions, and all of our marketing efforts.

One hundred percent of all proceeds from the sale of this book will directly benefit the strictly charitable work of Cummings Foundation and, in turn, many hundreds of grant recipients.

Instead of being a guide for entrepreneurs on the wave of brilliant revolutionary technologies, this book pays more attention to helping to teach some of the much more basic bedrock needs so necessary in any business: integrity, hard work, innovation, service, persistence, guts, and the other commonsense elements of building and running commercial ventures.

This book is a substantially edited edition of five-plus earlier editions of *Starting Small and Making it Big*, which I self-published in 2018, and sold primarily through college and university book sales and through other speaking engagements.

Special thanks to: Joyce Vyriotes; Abby Johnson; Michael Lamothe; Jim Trudeau; Lisa VanStry; Cindy Canavan; and so many others who have assisted me along the way, including Deirdre Sartorelli, director of Endicott College's Angle Center for Entrepreneurship, who created and shared a teaching guide for *Starting Small*. Special appreciation also to Gerry Sobkowitz and Alison Harding for their superb "last-look" reads.

Index

Abate, Dr. Joseph, 170
Adams, Dennis, 126, 130
Adventure Capital of the World, 128
Advest, 139
Aegis Trust, 196
Africa, 43, 187, 196, 198–99, 211, 214–15, 217, 219, 227, 231
AFROTC, 18–19, 42
Agahozo-Shalom Youth Village, 182, 195, 197, 227
Agresti, Ernie, 164, 167–68
Ahearn, Greg, 159, 168
Alperin, Thomas, 130
Amazon River, 231
American Museum of Tort Law, 32
Amuguni, Dr. Hellen, 217
Anderson, Eric and Kari, 164, 183, 185, 201, 226, 236
Anderson, Mark, 20
Archdiocese of Boston, 22
Architecture critic, 156
Armenia, 196–97
Associated Industries of Mass., 239
Aswan High Dam, 231
Atari, 201
Australia, 127–28, 231
Ayalon, Elie, 181, 242

Bacow, President Lawrence, 181, 185–86, 245
Bacow, Adele Fleet, 187
Ballou, Richard, 54
Barger, J.P. and Mary, 124
Bar Harbor, 88
Bass River, 138, 207, 210
Beacon Grille, 173–74, 194
Beijing, 231
Belin, Dr. Bob and Jo, 234
Bergstrom, Brandon, 228
Berkinshaw, Deborah, 138
Berkshire Hathaway, 193
Beverly Athletic Club, 208
Beverly Conservation Commission, 127, 133, 203
Beverly Historical Society, 135
Beverly Hospital, 153, 158
Bill and Melinda Gates Foundation, 190, 216, 219, 252

Binagwaho, Dr. Agnes, 213, 217
Black & Decker Corp., 122, 125–27, 129–31
Blacksmith Shop Restaurant, 13
Bloomberg, Hon. Michael, 193
Blue Water Seafoods, 39–41
Bohnen, Atty. Michael, 187
Bonhoeffer, Dietrich, 150
Boston Architectural College, 158
Boston Army Base, 31
Boston Globe, i–ii, 71, 108, 110, 115, 142, 184, 241, 246
Boston Herald, 132
Boston Innovation District, 31
Boston Marathon, 125, 145
Boston's North Shore, 119, 131
Botsford, Hon. Margot, 183
Botswana, 213
Boulder Dam, 121
Boys & Girls Club, 103, 148, 161, 171–72
Boy Scouts, 9
Brand, Atty. Susan, 177
Brandeis, Hon. Louis, 119
Brigham's, 10–11, 13, 200
British Virgin Islands, 232
Brown, Douglas and June, 92
Brown University, 115
Buffett, Warren, i, iv, 28, 189–92, 200
Bungee jumping, 213
Bunker Hill Community College, 173
Burera District, 199
Bush, Dr. and Mrs. Ric, 234
Butaro Ambulatory Cancer Center, 213
Butaro Hospital, 199, 216
Byrne, Darin, 101
Byrne, Dr. Denis and Joan, 234

Cabot, Cabot & Forbes, 162
Cahill, Hon. Michael, 129
Cairo, 231
California, 32–33, 52, 59, 148
Campbell, Patricia, 213–14
Cape Ann, 13
Cape Cod, 13, 88, 91, 229
CARE, 33
Carlson Real Estate Company, 113
Cassidy, Tina, 129
Catholic Charities, 241

Cedars of Lebanon, 43
Chanin Building, 27–28
Charlestown State Prison, 47
Children's Hospital of Philadelphia, 105
China visit, 231
Choate Medical Center, 100
Choate Memorial Hospital, 99
Christmas trees, 20
Chronicle of Philanthropy, 182
Clarke, Dennis and Alicia, 110, 117, 127, 146, 151, 163, 183, 201, 226, 239
Clarke, Dick and Nancy, 68, 110, 114, 233
Cleveland, 39–40, 103
Cohen Auditorium, 22
Colby College, 105, 164, 185, 201
Columbia University Medical Center, 105
Commodore Hotel, 27
Commonfund, 228
Community Newspaper Co. (CNC), 114–15, 117
Compassion and Justice Award, 241
Contamination, 122, 131
Continuum, 74, 139
Cotton, Prof. Philip, 215
Courthouse construction, 167
Cousens Gym, 19
COVID-19, 175, 255
Cronin, Robert, 125, 130
Crowley, Joe, 75, 113
Cummings, i–ii, iv, 2–3, 6–7, 11, 30, 32, 34–36, 41, 45, 47, 51, 55–56, 59, 61, 66–80, 82, 85–89, 95–99, 101–5, 107–8, 110–15, 117, 119–20, 122, 124, 127, 130, 132–35, 138–41, 146, 150, 152–64, 166–67, 169, 171–74, 176–79, 181–96, 199, 201–2, 204–10, 213, 215–17, 219–20, 224, 226–29, 232–36, 239–41, 244–46, 250–53
  Augustus, 2
  Daniel, 58, 67, 80, 104–5, 155
  Dorothy, 2
  Dorothy Purington, 2
  Isaac, 3, 138
  Joyce, i–ii, 6, 55–59, 62, 64, 67–69, 80, 88–91, 97–101, 103, 105, 107–8, 112, 124, 127, 129, 132, 142–43, 149–50, 158, 162, 172, 179, 181–82, 184–85, 187–90, 192–94, 198–200, 211–15, 219–21, 226–31, 233–34, 238–42, 244, 246, 257
  Kevin, 58, 67, 80, 104–5, 152, 173
  Marilyn Morris, 58, 67, 80, 105, 149, 158, 194

  Patricia, 67, 80, 104–5, 127, 133, 184, 213–14, 239
Cummings Center, 133–35, 138–40, 152–60, 162, 164, 167, 206–10, 228, 244
Cummings Executive Committee, 122
Cummings Family Chair of Entrepreneurship, 185
Cummings Foundation, i–ii, 59, 71, 97–98, 112, 124, 146, 150, 161, 164, 172, 176–77, 182–89, 196, 204–6, 215, 226–27, 234–35, 239–41, 244–46, 250–51, 253, 257
Cummings/Hillel Program, 181
Cummings School of Veterinary Medicine, 186, 217, 221, 227, 245
Curtis, Grant, 182
Cuyahoga River, 42
Cyprus, 240

Dahl, Ophelia, 195, 198, 216
Daily Times Chronicle, 93, 106, 110
Dalmatian Coast, 58, 234
Damascus, 43, 240
Daniel, 67, 104, 155
Dartmouth College, 105
Davis Square, 2, 8, 12
Desbois, Fr. Patrick, 242
Devil's Pool, 211–12
Donovan, Carol, 184
Dripcut Starline Corp., 52
Drobac, Dr. Peter, 199, 213–14
Drohosky, Stephen, 159
Drug testing routine, 96
Dubai, 231
Dunham Ridge, 204, 206, 208

Eastern Bank, 55, 202
Eastland Savings Bank, 120
Egypt, 43, 231
Eighty percent rule, 87, 130
Elements of Style, 96
Elfers, Bill, 114
Elliott Landing, 138, 206–10
Endicott College, 115, 241
England, Fred and Valerie, 55
Entrepreneurs, iv, 35, 48–49, 57, 79, 126, 165, 177, 219
Erie Canal, 234
Europe, 42–43, 80, 179, 230
Extreme sports, 129

Faneuil Hall Market, 21
Farmer, Dr. Paul, 192, 195, 198, 213–15
Farnsworth, Llewellyn, 45–46, 48
Farragher, Tom, 246
Feeney, Chuck, i
Fernway, 145, 179
Fidelity, 114, 127, 151
Flaherty, Greg, 169
Florida, 105, 142, 194, 232
Fort Dix, 31–32
Fortin (Commonwealth) Real Estate, 179
France, 80, 193, 234
Friend's Grist Mill, 140, 209
Friends of Israel, 241
Frohn, Stephen, 75, 82
Frommer, Arthur, 43
Fuller, Dr. Arlan and Alice, 199, 214, 216

Gabriel, Laurie, 183–84
Galilee, 180
Galvin, Hon. Scott, 81, 130
Gardner, Charles, 77–78, 98
Gardner, Kevin, 78
Gary and Mary West Foundation, 206
Gates, Bill and Melinda, i, 189–94, 216, 219, 252
General Mills, 37, 202
Gillette, Jim, 106
Giving Pledge, i–ii, 187, 189–90, 192–95, 200, 239, 244, 246
Globe Magazine, 115
Gloucester, 13, 36, 38–39, 44
Goff, John, 210
Goffstown, 2
Golden Gloves Boxing, 110
Goldman Sachs, 228
Gorton's of Gloucester, 36–37, 39–41, 44, 103
Grand Canyon, 34
Grant, Bill and Kathy, 162, 228–29, 239
Grant Winners, 220, 224
Great American Smokeout, 95
Great Barrier Reef, 128
Great Northeast Blackout, 50
Great War, 242–43
Greek Islands, 231
Greensboro, 23
Green Textile Assoc., 64
Guadeloupe, 232

Haggerty family, 110
Haines Square, 9

Haley & Aldrich, 122
Halifax, 19
Hancock, John, 12
Hanscom Field, 18, 104
Harkness Commons, 53
Harkovitz, Pauline, 53
Harris, Dr. David R., 184
Harriss, David G., 184
Harvard, 250
Harvard Business School, 28, 54, 191, 250
Harvard Law School, 31, 47, 53
Harvard University, 15, 214, 245
Harvey, David, 109
Herlihy, Mark, 115
Heyman, Anne, 197
Higgins, Hon. Thomas, 103, 109
Hirsh, Dr. Mark, 233–34
History of Modern Israel, 180
Hitler, Adolf, 243
Holland, George, 77
Holocaust, 181–82, 196–97
Hood Milk Company, 47
Horn Pond, 109, 124
Hurricane Carol, 16
Huxtable, Ada Louise, 155–58

In-house design group, 71, 132, 155, 167, 170, 176, 205
In-house legal department, 138, 176–77
Ipswich, 3, 138
Iraq, 164
Ironman Triathlon, 145
Isaac Cummings Family Association, 3
Israel, 43, 179–81, 241

Jackson, David, 20
Jacobs, Paul, 37
James L. McKeown School, 161
Jendrick, Kathryn, 246
Jerusalem, 180–81
Johns Hopkins University, 21
Jordan River, 180
Jorgenson, Peter, 108
Jost, Van Dyke, 232

Kagame, Pres. Paul, 213–14
Kelly, 142, 144
Kerouac, Jack, 27
Kevin, 58, 67, 80, 104–5, 152, 173
Kidder, Tracy, 199, 214

Kigali, 192, 195–96, 198, 213–14, 217, 219
Kigali Genocide Memorial, 196
Kim, Dr. Jim Yong, 198
King, Lawrence J., 54–55, 186
Kinney, Robert E., 37
Kirshnit, Herb and Charlotte, 56–57
Knox, Don, 18, 20, 36, 76
Kochevar, Dean Deborah, 183–84, 187, 245
Kosch, Dr. Philip C., 187

Lamb, Atty. Jonathan "Bo", 203
Lamothe, Michael, 66, 162, 175, 252
Lappin, Robert, 241
Laudano, Debbie, 141
Lavian, Hon. Harold, 99
Leeward Islands, 232
Leland, David and Karen, 101, 139, 162, 228
Lewis, Don, 55, 103, 241
Livingston Island, 212
Lower Shoe Pond, 127, 138

MacEachern, Don, 61
Madonna Hall School for Girls, 112
Manley, Prof. Lou, 26
Marlborough, 100, 105, 112–13
Martin, Sue Ellen, 78
Massachusetts Appeals Court, 178, 203
Massachusetts Capital Assets Mgmt., 167
Massachusetts Eye and Ear, 56
Massachusetts General Hospital, 56
Massachusetts Institute of Technology, 15, 47, 51
Massachusetts Restaurant Association, 13
Massachusetts Supreme Judicial Court, 177–78
Mauriello, Prof. Chris, 182
Mayer, Pres. Jean, 64
McAndrews, Prof. Robert, 182
McCauley, Fred, 54, 61–62
McClay, Dennis, 76, 112, 121
McDonald's, 39–40
McElhinney, Leo, 82
McKeown, Denise, 89–90, 141–42, 179, 254
McKeown, Jamie, 78, 82, 89–91, 93–95, 98, 102–5, 108–11, 119–22, 125–27, 130, 134–35, 139, 141–52, 158, 160–61, 163, 166, 172–73, 228–29, 241
McKeown, Kelly, 142, 144, 146, 254
McKeown, Leonard and Connie, 102, 142
McKeown, Molly, 142, 144, 146, 254

McKeown Boys and Girls Club, 161, 171
McKeown Elementary School, 161
McKeown Scholars Program, 161
Medford, 5–10, 12, 15, 18, 20–21, 28, 45–48, 50–67, 75, 79, 85, 87–88, 111, 124, 162, 186, 193, 226, 244, 246
Medford Public Library, 7
Medford Savings Bank, 5
Medicine, 188
Melbourne, 128
Menlo Park, 59
Mer-made Fish Emulsion, 37
Merrill Lynch, 139, 159, 162, 228
Microsoft, 132
Middlesex County Probate Court, 168
Middlesex County Superior Court, 167–68, 176, 178
Monaco, Pres. Anthony, 184, 187, 244–45
Monash University, 127
Monopoly, 7, 201–2
Montenegro, 58
Montessori School, 176
Morgan, Dr. John, 214
Mountain gorillas, 195
Mountains Beyond Mountains, 199
Mount Holyoke College, 185
Moynihan, David, 129, 138
Mulligan, Hon. Robert, 168
Museum of World War II, 242
Myanmar, 231
Myopia Hill, 179
Mystic River, 12

Nader, Atty. Ralph, 31, 108, 243
NAIOP, 239
National Newman Club Federation, 21
National University of Rwanda, 214
Native Americans, 197
Naval Reserve Officers Training Corps, 18
New England Institute of Art, 105
New England Patriots, 178
New Horizons, 99–101, 104–5, 111–13
New York Life Insurance Company, 122
New York Times, 156
New Zealand, 127–29, 213, 240
Nichols, Corie, 124
Nile River, 231
North Africa, 43
North Carolina, 23

Northeastern University, 163
Northeast Trade Center, 134, 166
North Shore Medical Center, 158
North Suburban Chamber of Commerce, 104
North Suburban YMCA, 145
Nutter, McClennen & Fish, 120, 187

Obama, Pres. Barack, 190
Ockerbloom, Richard, 184
Old Medford Foods, 46–47, 50–61, 63–67, 75, 79, 85, 88, 162, 186, 226
Old Medford Rum, 46
O'Malley, Cardinal Sean, 185
Omidyar, Pierre and Pam, 187, 193
Operation Birthright, 241
Oral Health stakeholders meeting, 214
Oveson, Bruce, 154
Oxford University, 200

Palestine, 180
Parker Brothers, 201–2
Partners In Health (PIH), 192, 195, 198–99, 213, 215–16, 218, 227, 252
Pascavage, Mike, 112, 142, 151, 154, 163, 170
Peru, 199, 231
Peters, Tom, 87
Pfeiffer, Sacha, 241
Phi Beta Kappa, 105
Phi Mu, 58
Phinney, Fred, 108
Phi Sigma Kappa, 36, 61
Place Lane Condominium, 92–95, 98, 100–101, 172, 240
Planters Landing, 138
Princeton, 31
Program in genocide education, 181–82, 196–98, 213–14, 219, 243
Pulitzer Prize, 155–56
Purington, John and Mary (Clarke), 2–3, 214

Quartz, 236
Queenstown, 128–29, 213

Residuum, 138
Resnek, Josh, 108–9
Reykjavik, 231
Rhode Island, 138
Riverside Yacht Club, 12
RMS Queen Mary, 42
Rockport, 13

Rocky Mountains, 34, 90
Rubona, Rwanda, 197
Ruderman's, 10
Russell, Derek, 246
Rwanda, 182, 187–88, 191–92, 195–99, 211, 213–15, 217–19, 226, 243, 252
Rwandan genocide, 196
Rwinkwavu Hospital, 199
Ryan, Atty. Jack, 94

The Salem News, 160
Salem State University, 78, 182
San Francisco Orthodox Hebrew Academy, 105
Saugus, 9, 55
Saugus Bank and Trust Company, 55
Sembagare, Samuel, 213
Sexeny, George, 32
Shea, Dr. Bill and Laura, 232
Shepley Bulfinch Architects, 216
Shindler, Colin, 180
Shirley, Dr. Bob and Althea, 241
The Shoe, 119, 121–22, 125–26, 130, 132–33, 139, 156–59, 165–67, 202
Shoe Pond, 127, 133, 138, 160
Simonson Company, 45–47, 50, 75
Sisters of the Good Shepherd, 112
Skanska, 171
Smith, Prof. Newlin, 17
Solar panels, 159
South America, 2, 230–31
Stanford University, 234
Starting Small and Making It Big, ii, 254
Stephens, Doug and Carrol, 61, 65, 73, 75–77, 89, 109, 111, 142, 162, 164, 172, 228
St. Eulalia Church, 124, 143
St. Martin and St. Maarten, 234
Stoneham Sun, 112
Strega Prime, 175–76
Strength in What Remains, 214
Strunk and White, 96
Summit, Rabbi Jeffrey, 182, 234
Swets, Joel, 184–85
Swidey, Neil, 115
Sylvania Electric, 166
Symmes Hospital, 99
Syria, 43

Talloires, France, 193, 234
Tanners National Bank, 55, 81
Tanzania, 214

Tapela, Dr. Neo, 200, 213
Tax Increment Financing Agreement, 129
Thompson, Sandy, 68
Tide Mill Institute, 210
Tower Office Park, 75
TradeCenter 128, 78, 134, 166–67, 169–71, 173–76, 178–79, 194, 220
Trudeau, Jim, 106, 108–9
Trump, Pres. Donald, 253
Tufts Cummings/Hillel Program for Holocaust and Genocide Education, 181
Tufts Department of Economics, 26
Tufts University, 18, 20–22, 59, 102, 115, 149, 155, 182, 186, 188, 193, 215, 217, 233–34, 244–45
Tufts University School of Dentistry, 214
Tutsi, 196, 243

Uganda, 195
Union College, 245
United Shoe Machinery Corp., 131, 135
United States Holocaust Mem. Museum, 182, 242
United States Marine Corps, 164
University of Alabama, 56–58, 99, 249
University of Global Health Equity, 187, 216, 227, 252
University of Oxford, 200, 217, 230, 249
University of Pennsylvania, 163
U.S. Agency for Intl. Development (USAID), 187
U.S. Army Cook School, 31–32
USI Insurance, 55

Vacuum, 82
van der Rohe, Mies, 121, 158
Varano, Nick, 174–75
Vick Chemical, 23, 25, 27–28, 34, 44
Victoria Falls, 211–13, 240
Video recording, 178
Virunga Mountains, 195
Vitality Senior Living, 206

VNA Hospice Care, 98
Volcanoes National Park, 195
Vyriotes, Joyce, 184–85

Walker Memorial, MIT, 52
The Wall Street Journal, 155–56, 165
Warren House, 111
Watts, Chat, 232
WBZ-TV, 95
Weld, Gov. William, 119, 127
White, Thomas J., 198
Whiting's Milk, 47
Wianno Club, 229
Wiesel, Elie, 242
Wilbur, Fred, 76, 121, 154
Wilde, Oscar, 48
Winchester Country Club (WCC), 81, 89, 98, 101, 124, 144, 241
Winchester High School, 68, 110
Winchester Hospital, 58, 68, 81, 141–42, 148, 163, 239
Winchester Star, 108, 142
Winchester Town Crier, 112
Woburn Advocate, 75, 107–9, 112–14, 117, 151
Woburn Boys & Girls Club, 77–78, 81–82, 92, 98, 102–3, 148, 161, 184
Woburn Business Association (WBA), 104
Woburn City Council, 92, 99
Woburn Industrial Development Auth., 103
Woburn Memorial High School, 161
Woburn Police Department, 143
World War I, 50
World War II, 2, 5, 139, 242
Wright, Erica, 246

Yad Vashem, 181, 242
Yangtze River, 231
YMCA Teen Center, 145, 165

Zambezi River, 211–12
Ziady, Atty. Craig, 176

About the Author

This book is not a Horatio Alger story, or maybe it is a little bit. Born during the Great Depression, I grew up poor, but first tried my hand at being an entrepreneur at six or seven years old. A decade later, I talked my way into Tufts University and was able to pay all of my tuition and expenses by always working and by being forever frugal. The book is a treasure chest filled with a lifetime of business and (mostly) success stories.

I became a serial entrepreneur in earnest after first working all over the country with two national consumer products firms. Then, in 1964, it was time to spend $4,000 to purchase my first real business, a hundred-year-old manufacturer of concentrated fruit-juice-beverage bases. I quickly expanded this business by providing refrigerated dispensers and drinks to several hundred mostly east coast colleges and universities.

With the proceeds from the sale of that once tiny firm in 1970, I founded a suburban-Boston commercial real estate firm. Cummings Properties quickly grew from one small building to a debt-free portfolio of more than 10 million square feet today. Along the way, we accumulated uncommon wealth, which my wife Joyce and I have begun actively disbursing through Cummings Foundation, which we established together in 1986.

Joyce and I were the first Massachusetts couple to join the Giving Pledge, an international philanthropic organization founded by Bill and Melinda Gates and Warren Buffett in 2010. We have since been honored to receive dozens of community accolades, from organizations as varied as the Irish International Immigrant Center, Friends of Israel, the Archdiocese of Boston, and NAIOP, the association for the commercial real estate development industry. We have both received several honorary doctoral degrees and have several times also served together as joint college commencement speakers.

In 2012, *The Boston Globe* named us runners-up as Greater Bostonians of the Year. More recently, the Greater Boston Chamber of Commerce named Joyce and me to its Academy of Distinguished Bostonians. We have lived happily together in Winchester, Massachusetts, for fifty-one years.

Bill Cummings